CiTY·SMaKi™

GUIDEBOOK

Indianapolis

Second Edition

Helen Wernle O'Guinn
and
Betsy Sheldon

John Muir Publications
Santa Fe, New Mexico

Acknowledgments

The authors would like to thank the following people for their contributions to this book: Laurie Borman, Benjy Ekhaus, Tom Harton, Julie Pratt McQuiston, Les Morris, Dave O'Guinn, Deborah Simon, Debbie Blackwell Smith, Ken Turchi, Abby Workman, and all those friends and family who recommended restaurants, leisure spots, nightlife, shopping sites, parks, entertainment places, and other best-kept secrets, making this a one-of-a-kind, *bona-fide* guide to Indianapolis.

We'd like to dedicate this book to Aaron, Ben, Davy, Robby, and Torie. Wherever you go in life, may you always discover the best that each destination has to offer.

John Muir Publications, P.O. Box 613, Santa Fe, New Mexico 87504

Printed in the United States of America.
Second edition. First printing August 1999.

ISBN: 1-56261-447-9
ISSN: 1092-5929

Editors: Marybeth Griffin, Elizabeth Cate
Graphics Editor: Heather Pool
Production: Janine Lehmann
Design: Janine Lehmann
Cover Design: Suzanne Rush
Typesetter: Kathleen Sparkes, White Hart Design
Maps: Julie Felton
Printer: Publishers Press
Front Cover: Lisa Tyner ©1998—The Canal Walk
Back Cover: © Peter Guttman—Union Station

Distributed to the book trade by
Publishers Group West
Berkeley, California

CONTENTS

MAP CONTENTS

See Indianapolis the CiTY·SMaRT™ Way

The Guide for Indianapolis Natives, New Residents, and Visitors

In *City•Smart Guidebook: Indianapolis,* local authors Helen Wernle O'Guinn and Betsy Sheldon tell it like it is. Residents will learn things they never knew about their city, new residents will get an insider's view of their new hometown, and visitors will be guided to the very best Indianapolis has to offer—whether they're on a weekend getaway or staying a week or more.

Opinionated Recommendations Save You Time and Money

From shopping to nightlife to museums, the authors are opinionated about what they like and dislike. You'll learn the great and the not-so-great things about Indianapolis's sights, restaurants, and accommodations. So you can decide what's worth your time and what's not; which hotel is worth the splurge and which is the best choice for budget travelers.

Easy-to-Use Format Makes Planning Your Trip a Cinch

City•Smart Guidebook: Indianapolis is user-friendly—you'll quickly find exactly what you're looking for. Chapters are organized by travelers' interests or needs, from Where to Stay and Where to Eat, to Sights and Attractions, Kids' Stuff, Sports and Recreation, and even Day Trips from Indianapolis.

Includes Maps and Quick Location-Finding Features

Every listing in this book is accompanied by a geographic zone designation (see the following pages for zone details) that helps you immediately find each location. Staying in the downtown area and wondering about nearby sights and restaurants? Look for the Downtown Indianapolis label in the listings and you'll know that statue or café is not far away. Or maybe you're looking for the Indianapolis Museum of Art. Along with its address, you'll see a "North" label, so you'll know just where to find it.

All That and Fun to Read, Too!

Every City•Smart chapter includes fun-to-read (and fun-to-use) tips, trivia, and sidebars to help you get more out of Indianapolis. And well-known local residents provide their personal "Top Ten" lists, guiding readers to the city's best nightlife, lodging, restaurants, and more.

Hotels, restaurants, museums, concert venues, and other sights noted with a ♿ are wheelchair accessible.

INDIANAPOLIS ZONES

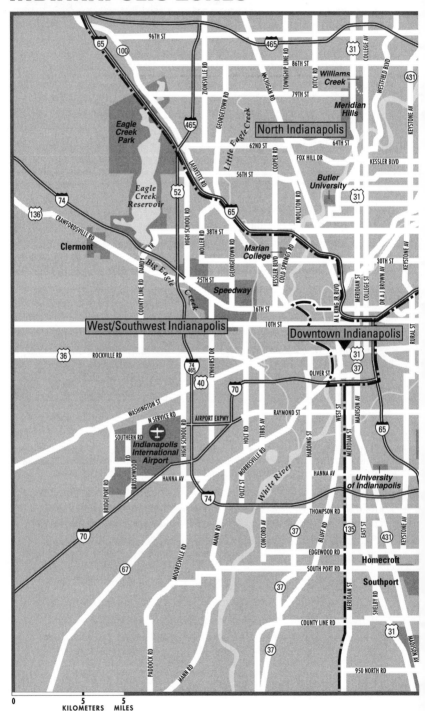

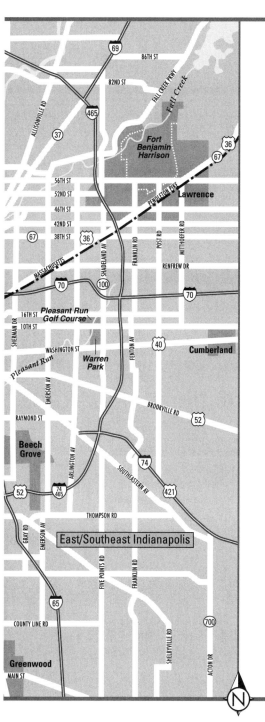

INDIANAPOLIS ZONES

Downtown Indianapolis (D)
Bounded by I-70 on the south, I-70 on the east, I-65 on the north, and the west bank of White River on the west.

North Indianapolis (N)
Bounded by I-65 on the south and southwest and covers the area north of Massachusetts Avenue/Pendleton Pike on the southeast. Includes Zionsville, Carmel, and Geist Reservoir.

West/Southwest Indianapolis (W/SW)
Covers the area west of I-65 and the White River, circles downtown, extends west of Meridian Street on the south side of the city. Includes the Speedway and the Indianapolis International Airport.

East/Southeast Indianapolis (E/SE)
Extends south and east of Massachusetts Avenue/Pendleton Pike, circles downtown east of the inner loop, and covers the area east of Meridian Street on the south side. Includes Greenwood and Southport.

1

WELCOME TO INDIANAPOLIS

They used to call it "India-no-place." They bypassed the city on their jet-set jaunts from one coast to another, stopping instead to refuel on culture, fashion, fine dining, and sports in Chicago. One Hoosier expatriate recalls his father's reaction when the family flew into Indianapolis for the first time in 1964. When they spotted the nearly nonexistent downtown skyline, Dad observed, "Take a look, Son, four farms had to be sacrificed for all this." India-no-place.

But that was 1964; the city has changed since then. In 35 years sleepy Indianapolis has been transformed into a city that pulses with energy, yet remains comfortably livable. The downtown area, once as silent as a ghost town, is bustling around the clock with workers, shoppers, diners, theatergoers, and out-of-town visitors in for conventions and sporting events. Where there was once decaying neighborhoods and boarded-up buildings, there are now lovingly restored homes, romantic promenades and parks, and a state-of-the-art sports complex. Parks that children were warned to stay away from are today magnets for family activity, packed with playground equipment and trails and offering a variety of sports programs.

The accolades we've earned are more than self-serving pats on our own backs. Here's what *they're* saying about us: We're included in *50 Fabulous Places to Raise a Family* (1997). *Employment Review* (1998) lists Indianapolis as the second-best place in the country to live and work. *Fortune* (1997) ranked Indy as the seventh-most-improved city for business in the United States. In 1996 *Entrepreneur* rated the city as the fifth-best site in the country for small businesses.

New residents are coming from the East and West Coasts for job

Hoosier Time

Indiana is one of only a few states that doesn't observe Daylight Savings Time. That means that when the rest of the nation is moving clocks up or back, most Hoosiers leave theirs alone. Indianapolis is on Eastern Standard Time year-round, but the northwestern corner of the state is in sync with Chicago, while the southeastern corner observes Cincinnati time, and the section by Louisville is in time with Kentucky. For sanity's sake, take off your watch.

opportunities and affordable housing. One transplant from New York claims she encouraged her husband to transfer to Indianapolis after she learned they could buy two homes there for the price of one in New York. And they're not scared away by any perceived lack of culture—the critics are applauding our theaters, music venues, and museums. What's more, we've got world-class shopping, with the upscale Fashion Mall on the north side and the new Circle Centre mall, which houses stores such as Nordstrom and Parisian, downtown. The chichi West Coast in-laws of one native paid the city the highest compliment when they observed, "Wow, you don't have to buy your wardrobe out of state anymore!"

Getting to Know Indianapolis

As the plane to Indianapolis dips below the clouds, passengers begin to discern the city's landmarks: Three pyramid-shaped office buildings loom to the north, industrial complexes sprawl across the southwest quadrant, and vast reservoirs reflect the sky east, west, and north. The tight circle of skyline marks the heart of the city. On a clear day, you can perhaps see the Indianapolis Museum of Art or the oval outline of the Indianapolis Motor Speedway from an airplane.

Once on the ground, you will find Indy's attractions scattered throughout the 400-plus-square-mile city. But since the most populated sections—and hence, the highest concentrations of shopping, nightlife, restaurants, and whatever else you might be looking for—are downtown and in areas north of Washington Street, it's fairly easy to see many of the city's interesting sights without spending too much time driving around. Historic neighborhoods such as Chatham Arch, the Old Northside, Lockerbie, and Meridian Kessler shelter tour-worthy homes and notable landmarks. Circle Centre mall, Castleton, Clearwater, and Keystone at the Crossing lure caravans of shoppers on weekends and during holiday season. Nightspots such as Massachusetts Avenue and Broad Ripple offer endless evening-entertainment options.

That's not to say that there aren't plenty of reasons to explore the west, east, and south sides of the city. The west side is the home of the Indy 500 and other racing traditions, not to mention Eagle Creek Park and unique treasures such as the quirky Indiana Medical History Museum. On the east side you will find the new Fort Harrison State Park and the only horse trail-riding outfit in the city, as well as colorful neighborhoods such as Irvington. And south of downtown are historic

Over 16,000 runners compete in the Indianapolis 500-Fest mini-marathon.

parks (Garfield is the city's oldest and one of the most charming) and delightful neighborhoods, such as Fountain Square, with nightspots that feature rockabilly and swing bands and activities such as duckpin bowling.

Because of the population distribution and idiosyncrasies of the Indianapolis community, the zones designated in this book, while not being balanced in a graphic sense will come to make a great deal of sense to the reader as he or she becomes more familiar with the city.

A Brief History of Indianapolis

The Nineteenth Century

The capital of the territory of Indiana was Corydon, which was chosen because of its proximity to the Ohio River, Indiana's southern border. But after Indiana became a state, in 1816, early legislators agreed that the capital should be built on a site near the confluence of the White River and Fall Creek in the center of the state. Back then, settlers envisioned a city connected by water to the Wabash River, but the White River proved willful, flooding regularly and persistently stymieing efforts to harness it. Indianapolis remains the largest city in the country not located on a navigable body of water.

Alexander Ralston, who had helped map Washington, D.C., began the plan for Indianapolis—a neat grid of streets with a center and radiating spokes—in 1821. Pragmatic (or, perhaps, uninspired) legislators tacked "polis," the Greek word for "city," onto the state's name to create a name for the capital. A cluster of cabins, with a population of fewer than 1,000, was the first settlement.

In 1836, to create an alternative to river transportation, the general assembly passed the Mammoth Internal Improvements Bill, which authorized spending for roads, railways, and a canal. The canal flopped, but railroads rolled into the city, earning Indianapolis the nickname of "Railroad City" by the mid- to late-1800s. In fact, Indianapolis had the first Union Station—a station where many private rail lines converged for the convenience of passengers and shippers.

During the Civil War, the Union Army built an arsenal (the land is the site of today's Arsenal Technical High School), a large prisoner-of-war camp, and a training campsite in Indianapolis. After the war, the city's industrial base grew. In 1876 Colonel Eli Lilly, a Civil War veteran, created Eli Lilly and Company—Indianapolis's best-known corporate citizen— which makes insulin, penicillin and other antibiotics, and Prozac.

The end of the nineteenth century brought patriotic fervor. Indianan Benjamin Harrison was elected president (1889–1893). Civil War veterans and others pushed for building the Soldiers and Sailors Monument on the Circle, a circular street in the heart of downtown.

The Twentieth Century

By the turn of the century, Indianapolis was a major player in the new automobile industry, nipping at the tires of Detroit. In 1903 Nordyke and Marmon turned its flour mill into an automobile factory. Cole, Allison, and Prest-O-Lite all started here, and the Indianapolis Motor Speedway was built. Over the years, 64 makes of cars and five types of motorcycles have been manufactured here, including the Stutz Bearcat and Duesenberg Model J. Ultimately, though, the city became best known for parts manufacturing.

The Roaring Twenties were marked by political corruption and the rise of the Ku Klux Klan. Between 25 and 40 percent of the city's white adult males joined the Klan. When Grand Dragon D. C. Stephenson was tossed in prison on second-degree murder charges in 1925, the Klan's popularity diminished.

Through the Depression and World War II, Indianapolis continued as a railroad hub and industrial city. After the war, as railroads declined in importance, Indianapolis lost ground as a transportation hub. The completion of I-465 in 1970 and the convergence of I-70, I-74, I-69, and I-65 have restored the city to its hub status, now augmented by a FedEx facility at the airport.

In 1970, under the leadership of then-mayor Richard Lugar (now the state's senior U.S. senator), the city began implementing a pioneering plan to make government more efficient. Unigov, as the plan is called, stretched the city limits to the edges of Marion County and consolidated many government functions, expanding the city's tax base and streamlining operations. The bold plan became a model for large cities nationwide.

The past 20 years have been a boom time for downtown, with more than $3 billion invested in projects such as green spaces, historic preservation, sports facilities, and cultural institutions. Locals are delighted that their city is finally becoming known for treasures such as its art museum, parks, and amateur sports.

The People of Indianapolis

If you flip through an Indianapolis phone book, you will quickly see that the city isn't exactly what you'd call a melting-pot community. Surnames of German, English, and Irish origin predominate, reflecting the fact that the city was, for the most part, settled by northern European immigrants. Today their descendants make up more than 75 percent of the city's 817,525 citizens.

It may be true that Indianapolis is not as ethnically diverse as many major metropolitan areas. Yet, the city's minority communities are active

TRIVIA

Henry Ward Beecher, famous pastor and orator, delivered his first antislavery sermon on May 28, 1843, to the congregation of Indianapolis's Second Presbyterian Church, where he was pastor from 1839 until 1847.

INDIANAPOLIS TIMELINE

1820   Indianapolis is chosen to replace Corydon as the site for the state capital.

1821   The city's first church (Methodist) is established, and the city gets a school.

1839   The first nine miles of the Central Canal are completed, and the state runs out of money.

1847   Indianapolis becomes a chartered city, and its residents elect their first mayor, Samuel Henderson. The steam railroad arrives in the city.

1862   Camp Morton becomes a prisoner-of-war camp for Confederate soldiers.

1865   Abraham Lincoln's funeral train stops for the day on April 30, and citizens pay their last respects.

1877   Robert B. Bagby becomes the first African American to serve on the Indianapolis City-County Council.

1878   Colonel Eli Lilly founds his drug company.

1880   Chinese immigrants come to Indianapolis.

1888   Denizen Benjamin Harrison is elected president.

1894   The first basketball game is played in Indianapolis.

1903   The *Indianapolis Star* debuts.

1904   The city's first municipal golf course opens.

1909   The Indianapolis Motor Speedway is built.

1910   Madame C. J. Walker builds a factory (hair-care and makeup products for African American women) in Indianapolis.

1911   The first Indianapolis 500 is held.

1919   The new American Legion announces its intent to build its headquarters in Indianapolis, and Booth Tarkington receives the Pulitzer Prize for *The Magnificent Ambersons*.

1924   Broad Ripple Park hosts the Olympic swimming tryouts. Johnny Weissmuller, who later starred in *Tarzan* movies, was a participant.

1926   The Children's Museum, now the largest of its kind in the world, opens its doors.

1929   Indianapolis buys land for an airport—the site is still used today.

1939   Indianapolis is the world's largest hog shipper.

1943   Geist Reservoir is created to supply water to the city.

1953   The city's high schools are integrated.

INDIANAPOLIS TIMELINE (continued)

Mayor (now Senator) Richard Lugar creates Unigov, a consolidation of city and county governments, which serves as a nationwide model for big-city administration.	1969
The first Black Expo, now the largest event of its kind in the country, is held.	1971
Jacqueline Means becomes the first female priest ordained by the Episcopal Church of the United States.	1977
Radio stars Bob Kevoian and Tom Griswold debut their radio show, known today as the *Bob and Tom Show*, on WFBQ.	1983
The Baltimore Colts become the Indianapolis Colts.	1984
Ryan White, young AIDS activist, dies at Riley Hospital for Children. The tallest building in the state, 52-story Bank One Tower, opens.	1990
Stephen Goldsmith becomes mayor.	1992
Circle Centre mall opens.	1995
Construction begins on Conseco Fieldhouse, a new stadium for the IBA's Indiana Pacers.	1998

and thriving. The African American community is the largest minority group in Indianapolis. It is the sixteenth-largest African American population in the country and the sixth-largest in the Midwest. Indiana Avenue and surrounding neighborhoods are rich in historical landmarks and still-standing institutions, including the Bethel African Methodist Episcopal Church, founded in 1836, the Madame Walker Theatre Center, and Crispus Attucks Middle School. The Indiana Black Expo and the Circle City Classic are just two events spotlighting and sponsored by African Americans.

The Hispanic population, just 1.1 percent of the metro population, is also active, and it shares its culture with all citizens during the Fiesta celebration in September. Other small but vibrant communities include Koreans, Chinese, Filipinos, Indians, and Russians. They are represented and supported by numerous associations and community groups.

Oktoberfests and St. Patrick's Day parades continue to dominate the calendar, while other events, such as the Italian Festival at Holy Rosary Church in June, the Greek Festival at Holy Trinity Greek Orthodox Church in September, and the Asian Festival at Broadway United Methodist Church in October, offer visitors and residents a chance to learn about the city's minority communities. Celebrations such as the International Festival in October and the Children's Folk Dance Festival in April offer a wide variety of cultural displays and activities.

Indianapolis Weather

	Average Temperature	Average Precipitation	Sunshine
January	26.0°F	2.65"	41%
February	29.9°F	2.46"	49%
March	40.0°F	3.61"	50%
April	52.4°F	3.68"	54%
May	62.5°F	3.66"	61%
June	71.6°F	3.99"	66%
July	75.1°F	4.32"	66%
August	73.2°F	3.46"	69%
September	66.6°F	2.74"	66%
October	54.8°F	2.51"	61%
November	41.8°F	3.04"	42%
December	31.5°F	3.00"	39%

Source: National Climatic Data Center, Asheville, North Carolina

Weather

Anyone who moves to the South or the West and misses the changing seasons can get a full dose of them in Indianapolis, including blizzards, tornadoes, rain, hail, and 100-percent humidity. But there are also days when the sky is blue, the winds are warm and gentle, and the air is refreshing.

Every season can be mercurial. Winter can be cold and damp, with snow, ice, and rain. Sometimes there's a string of gray days. Just when the gloom seems relentless, the sun breaks through. There are at least a handful of days when children and parents grab sleds and saucers and head for Butler Hill. When the weather begins to warm in February, crocuses poke their heads up through the sodden, dingy grass. It sometimes snows in March, and even April, but the profusion of blossoms persists, leaving yards awash in color.

Summer comes quickly and lasts long. Humidity slows down people and seems to slow down time as well. Sunsets are late and glorious.

Many consider autumn the best season. The days are warm and clear and the foliage turns red, orange, gold, and yellow. Burning bushes turn scarlet. Even late in fall, Indiana is apt to have an Indian summer, when temperatures rise and residents are reminded how quickly the city's weather can change.

Dressing in Indianapolis

There are no ironclad fashion rules in Indianapolis, although extreme fashions and the very latest looks from the coasts are sure to draw second glances. Downtown on weekdays, most workers are in classic business attire: suits, pantsuits, sport coats, or dresses. On weekends, people dress in khakis, golf shirts, jeans, sweaters, and casual dresses. No matter where you travel, you're sure to see jeans. Although cocktail dresses are donned for evenings at the symphony, sequins and tuxes are usually left at home. Few restaurants require a tie.

Calendar of Events

January
Indianapolis Home Show, Indiana State Fairgrounds

February
Kids' Fest, Indiana Convention Center and RCA Dome

The Indianapolis Art Center sponsors exhibits, lectures, and classes, p. 121.

Indianapolis Art Center

Who's Who in Hoosierdom

The following is a list of some of the famous people who were born or have lived in or around Indianapolis.

Abraham Benrubi, ER *star*

Babyface (Kenneth Edmonds), musician and songwriter

Larry Bird, basketball legend and Pacer coach

John Dillinger, notorious bank robber

Pete Dye, golf course architect

Vivica A. Fox, actress

Michael Graves, internationally known architect

John Gruelle, creator of Raggedy Ann

Benjamin Harrison, 23rd president

John Hiatt, musician and performer

Neil LaBute, film director

Dave Letterman, entertainer

Dave's Mom

Eli Lilly, founder of the city's famous drug company

Richard Lugar, former mayor and current U.S. senator

George McGinnis, basketball player

Steve McQueen, actor

Reggie Miller, Pacer star

Wes Montgomery, jazz great

Nancy Noel, artist

Jane Pauley, newscaster

Dan Quayle, vice president under George Bush

James Whitcomb Riley, poet and author

Oscar Robertson, basketball star

Wilma Rudolph, U.S. Olympic athlete

Booth Tarkington, Pulitzer Prize–winning author

Kurt Vonnegut, author

Dan Wakefield, author

Madame C. J. Walker, America's first black female millionaire

The Why Store, rock group

David Wolf, astronaut

March

IHSAA Boys' Basketball Finals, Indiana Convention Center and RCA Dome

IHSAA Girls' Basketball Finals, Conseco Fieldhouse (in 1999, Market Square Arena)

NCAA Final Four Division I Men's Basketball Championships (in 2000), RCA Dome

NCAA Men's and Women's Division I Indoor Track and Field Championships, RCA Dome

St. Patrick's Day Parade

April

Children's Folk Dance Festival, Indiana Convention Center

Decorators' Show House, locations vary

Earth Day, various locations

Hoosier Horse Fair and Expo, Indiana State Fairgrounds

May

Broad Ripple Art Fair, Indianapolis Art Center

Carburetion Day, Indianapolis Motor Speedway

Children's Folk Dance Festival, Indiana Convention Center

Delco Electronics 500 Festival Parade, downtown

Indianapolis Life 500 Festival Mini-Marathon, downtown

Indianapolis 500-Mile Race, Indianapolis Motor Speedway

IPALCO 500 Festival Parade, downtown

Qualifications for the 500 Mile Race, Indianapolis Motor Speedway

June

Indian Market, Eiteljorg Museum of American Indians and Western Art

Italian Festival, Holy Rosary Church

Middle Eastern Festival, St. George Orthodox Christian Church

Midsummer Fest, Monument Circle

Strawberry Festival, Christ Church Cathedral

Talbot Street Art Fair, Talbott Street between 16th and 19th Streets

In what must be a historical oddity worldwide, former Confederate prisoners of war, held at Camp Morton in Indianapolis, commissioned a bronze bust of camp commandant Richard Owen as a tribute to his "courtesy and kindness."

July
A Glorious Fourth, Conner Prairie Farm
Fourth Fest, World War Memorial Plaza
Hoosier State Games, locations vary
Indiana Black Expo, Indiana Convention Center and RCA Dome
Kroger Circlefest, Monument Circle

August
Brickyard 400, Indianapolis Motor Speedway
Indiana Jazz Festival, Madame Walker Theatre Center
Indiana State Fair, Indiana State Fairgrounds
National Hot Rod Association U.S. Nationals, Indianapolis Raceway Park
Peace in the Park, Military Park
RCA Championships, Indianapolis Tennis Center
WENS Skyconcert (fireworks), banks of White River

September
Comfort Classic at the Brickyard (golf), Indianapolis Motor Speedway
Fiesta (celebrates Hispanic culture), American Legion Mall
Greek Festival, Holy Trinity Greek Orthodox Church
Hoosier Storytelling Festival, Indianapolis Art Center
International Violin Competition of Indianapolis (biennial), various locations
National Hot Rod Association U.S. Nationals, Indianapolis Raceway Park
Oktoberfest, German Park; Penrod Arts Fair, Indianapolis Museum of Art
Western Fest, Eiteljorg Museum of American Indians and Western Art

October
AfricaFest, Indianapolis Museum of Art
AIDS Walk and Festival, Military Park
Asian Festival, Broadway United Methodist Church
Coca-Cola Circle City Classic (football and festivities), RCA Dome and
    downtown locations
Haunted House, Children's Museum
International Festival, Indiana State Fairgrounds
OctoBearfest, Eagle Creek Park
Oktoberfest, Athenaeum

November
Heartland Film Festival, locations vary

December
Celebration of Lights, Monument Circle
Toy Soldiers Playground and Breakfast with Santa, Indiana State Museum

Business and Economy

Pork-packing firms, flour mills, and rolling mills were major industries in nineteenth-century Indianapolis. Following World War II, the city became too dependent upon durable-goods manufacturing; during the recession of 1979 to 1982, Chrysler, Western Electric, and other manufacturers closed their doors in the city, with a net job loss of around 30,000. Since then, the city has worked to again diversify and sweeten the climate for starting businesses. The efforts have succeeded under the dynamic leadership of former mayor William Hudnut and current mayor Stephen Goldsmith.

In 1997 *Fortune* named Indianapolis one of the top 10 most improved cities for business in the United States. Employers were paying attention: Anthem Inc., a health-insurance company, recently broke ground on a $60 million complex just south of downtown, Emmis Broadcasting built a seven-story building on Monument Circle, and Intech Park, an office park for high-tech companies, is being developed on the north side.

Once a railroad hub, Indianapolis is now an airline hub with a large FedEx facility, a United Airlines maintenance center (a nearly $1 billion investment), and the U.S. Postal Service's express mail hub. Indianapolis

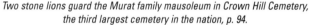
Two stone lions guard the Murat family mausoleum in Crown Hill Cemetery, the third largest cemetery in the nation, p. 94.

Steven P. Stine

Top Ten Employers

(By number of jobs, excluding city, state, and federal governments)

1. **Clarian Health** (hospitals and health care)—10,000 jobs
2. **Eli Lilly & Company** (pharmaceutical research, development, and manufacturing)—10,000 jobs
3. **Marsh Supermarkets/Village Pantry Markets**—7,000 jobs
4. **St. Vincent Hospital and Heath Care Center**—6,000 jobs
5. **Kroger Company** (grocers)—5,400 jobs
6. **Community Hospitals**—5,000 jobs
7. **Allison Transmission** (medium- and heavy-duty automatic transmissions)—5,000 jobs
8. **Allison Engine Company** (gas turbine engines)—4,300 jobs
9. **Bank One Indianapolis**—3,810 jobs
10. **PSI Energy** (electric utility)—3,366 jobs

Source: Indianapolis Chamber of Commerce, 1998

International Airport is the first major U.S. airport to be managed by a private company, BAA, which manages London's Heathrow and Gatwick Airports.

Tourism has also become important since Indianapolis has been discovered as an inexpensive, welcoming, and interesting city for hosting conventions, with its cohesive downtown and spectacular Circle Centre mall. And the city is headquarters for American Trans Air, the eleventh largest airline in the country; for its sister company, Ambassadair, a large travel club; and for RCI, the world's largest time-share–exchange company and a major travel provider worldwide.

In its earliest days, Indianapolis's medical facilities and health-care services were appalling, and the city had the dubious distinction of having one of the highest death rates of any city in the country. Today, Indianapolis is a world-renowned center for medical research. In 1998 *U.S. News & World Report* named Indiana University Medical Center one of America's best hospitals—for the sixth year in a row.

Sporting events generate a great deal of revenue (over $1 billion to

TRIVIA

Thomas Edison was once a Western Union telegraph operator at Union Station in Indianapolis.

The Circle Theatre in downtown sees performances by the Indianapolis Symphony Orchestra, p. 173.

date) for the city and its residents, in addition to hosting the Indy 500 and the Brickyard 400, Indianapolis has hosted hundreds of amateur-athletic events, including the NCAA basketball championships, pre-Olympic competitions, the PGA Championship, and the World Gymnastics Championships. The city has persuaded many national sports organizations to move their headquarters and governing bodies to the city: U.S. Diving, Inc., the U.S. Rowing Association, U.S. Synchronized Swimming, USA Track and Field, and the NCAA are all based in Indianapolis.

Low utility costs, affordable office space, and low taxes lure companies to the city. With continuing diversity and a strong government–private enterprise partnership, Indianapolis's economy promises steady growth.

For all that it has to offer, Indy is a very affordable city. According to the ACCRA Cost of Living Index (second quarter 1998), the city's overall cost of living is 96.7 percent of the national average. Housing and transportation are the best values, but all categories that ACCRA tracks fall below the national average. Here are the specifics:

Groceries	104.1%	Miscellaneous	96.3%
Health Care	93.7%	Transportation	95.8%
Housing	93.4%	Utilities	97.7%

So how does all this translate in terms of day-to-day living? Take a look at some of these average costs:

Five-mile taxi ride: $9.90 (rides from the airport to downtown range between $15 and $20)

Average restaurant dinner: $20 to $25 (with drink, dessert, and tip)

Daily newspaper: 50¢ (or 30¢ per day for a weekly subscription); Sunday $1.50

Month's rent for a two-bedroom, two-bathroom apartment: $592

Movie admission: $7

A liter of seltzer water: 59¢

And the tax? Sales tax is 5 percent, although prescription drugs and some food products (groceries) are exempt. There's an extra 1 percent tacked on to restaurant food and beverages.

Currently, property tax rates range from 8.157 percent to 10.8205 percent, assessed at one-third the value of the property. For example, taxes on a $100,000 home might be approximately $1,500, but rates vary widely throughout the city. State income tax is 3.4 percent of income after exemptions. Federal income taxes are not deductible.

Housing

Many a transplant from the East or West Coast faces reverse sticker shock when confronted with the cost of a home in the Indy area. The ACCRA Cost of Living Index (second quarter 1998) indicates that housing prices are nearly seven percent below the national average. The Indiana Association of Realtors reports that the median home price (first quarter 1998) is $102,100 and the average price is $117,238.

Indy offers a variety of home styles, neighborhoods, and price ranges. In just about any corner of the city, you can find starter homes in the $60,000 range and spanking-new show homes for $500,000 or more. Although most new construction has occurred on the north side of the city, other areas are now experiencing growth spurts, including Perry Township on the south side, Lawrence Township on the east side, and Hendricks County.

In addition, plenty of older communities within the metro area offer established neighborhoods with a range of housing. In the downtown area, you can find charming historic homes—from fixer-uppers for as little as $50,000 to restored mansions for $500,000.

Schools

Education of the city's youth continues to generate concern and controversy among Indy residents, as issues such as budget cuts and efforts to increase scholastic scores command the attention of the citizenry. IPS is the state's largest school district, serving the neighborhoods of Center Township. The county's other 10 districts include Washington, Pike, Perry, Lawrence, Franklin, Decatur, Speedway, Warren, Wayne, and Beech Grove.

Despite concerns about low graduation rates and test scores within the IPS system, the districts schools are improving. IPS magnet programs (such as Broad Ripple High School's performing arts program) and some excellent elementary programs offer promise. There are several award-winning schools in the city's other districts. In addition to the public schools, there is a well-established and affordable Catholic school system, as well as a selection of other parochial and private schools at both primary and secondary levels.

The city's higher education institutions are outstanding. Indianapolis is home to Indiana University-Purdue University at Indianapolis (IUPUI), with nearly 30,000 students. IUPUI offers more than 170 degree programs, including several doctorate programs, and includes a highly regarded medical school, the country's largest nursing school, the state's largest law school, and the John Herron School of Art. Other colleges in the metro area include Butler University, the University of Indianapolis, Marian College, Martin University, Ivy Tech State College, and the Christian Theological Seminary. There are a number of business and technical schools, as well as Bible colleges. Within an hour's drive are Purdue University in Lafayette, Indiana University in Bloomington, and Ball State University in Muncie.

2

GETTING AROUND INDIANAPOLIS

Although Alexander Ralston was commissioned in 1821 to draw up a plan for a four-mile-square city, he didn't believe that the new capital would ever be so large, so he drew it only one mile square (the area of downtown that was the original mile square is called, appropriately, the Mile Square). Indianapolis now covers 408 miles square. The city's boundaries extend to the Marion County lines, but citizens rarely think about them. Homes on 96th Street are in the same vicinity as those on 106th, even though they're in different counties. And shopping at Greenwood Park Mall seems like shopping in Indianapolis, even though it's technically in Johnson County.

Indianapolis Layout

Streets

Ralston's original Mile Square plan, which has survived the years fairly well intact, provided for a harmonious and tidy city layout. Bounded by North, South, East, and West Streets, the downtown is divided into a grid with Monument Circle at the center. Most major downtown streets are named after states, with the exception of Market and Meridian, which are the only two streets that intersect the Circle, and Capitol and Senate, which run on either side of the capitol. Four spokes radiate from the hub: Virginia, Massachusetts, Indiana, and Kentucky. Washington Street divides the north-south addresses and Meridian the east-west.

Outside the Mile Square, most streets follow a grid pattern, although there are many new residential areas, and a few old ones such as Irvington,

Yes, there *is* a dark side to Indianapolis

Lest we leave you with the impression, by highlighting the best of Indianapolis here, that we live in a sugar-coated paradise, let us be the first to admit that the city has its share of dark spots. Whether grisly crimes, horrific catastrophes, or notorious characters, Indy has witnessed some events that have devastated its citizens and caught the nation's attention. We open the closet to reveal some of our skeletons.

1924   About 40 percent of the city's white males are estimated to belong to the Ku Klux Klan, and many politicians, including the governor and the mayor, are linked to the organization.

1925   KKK Grand Dragon D.C. Stephenson is imprisoned for the rape of a young woman, which leads to her suicide. The upside: This event is the beginning of the decline of the KKK in Indiana.

1934   The city buries one of its most notorious sons, John Dillinger, the FBI's Public Enemy No. 1.

1963   During an ice-skating performance at the State Fairgrounds, a propane tank explodes, killing 74 and injuring about 400.

1954   James Jones founds his first congregation, later known as the People's Temple, which eventually directs his 900-plus followers to commit suicide by drinking a cyanide-laced fruit drink in Jonestown, Guyana.

1987   An air force jet crashes into a Ramada Inn at the airport, killing nine.

1992   Mike Tyson is tried and convicted of the rape of a young beauty contestant.

1996   Police discover the remains of seven bodies buried on the Baumeister family estate. Herb Baumeister flees and commits suicide.

where streets are serpentine. Heading north, streets are numbered beginning with Ninth, just beyond the Mile Square. The numbering system, which continues all the way to Westfield, makes it easier to find one's way around. Names on the south side offer no directional help.

The city can be confusing to navigate in certain areas. For example, if you follow the traffic flow of what seems to be Meridian Street south from downtown, you'll soon find yourself on Madison Street and eventually East Street—all three comprise U.S. 31 South. On the north side, 86th Street turns into 82nd on the east side of the White River.

It's wise to rent a car in order to see Indianapolis.

Highways
Four of the nation's interstates—I-70, I-65, I-74, and I-69—converge upon the city, which is belted by a three-lane interstate, I-465. Of the interstates, only I-70 and I-65 cut across I-465 and snake into the downtown, where they form what is referred to as the "inner loop," although it has no western leg. (The inner loop forms three of the four downtown boundaries defined in this book; the White River, roughly, forms the western boundary.) The northeastern and southeastern corners of the inner loop and the stretch between them are the most heavily traveled and treacherous segments. On the west side, the Airport Expressway veers off I-70 and heads straight for the airport. U.S. 31 is the major north-south highway.

Public Transportation

Need to get around easily and quickly in Indy? One word of advice: getacar. Bus routes are often limited to a few times a day, stops may not be convenient, and waits can be long. The city has no commuter train or subway, and while a cab is just a phone call away, you won't find them buzzing the streets waiting for you to wave them down as you will in other major metro areas. Here's what is available to those who must rely on public transportation:

City Buses
IndyGo, the metro bus system, offers nearly 50 routes. Bus fare is $1 anywhere in the city, transfers are free, and exact change is required. The

TRIVIA

Prior to 1976, Indy's airport was known as Weir Cook Airport. It was named for World War II fighter ace, H. Weir Cook, a Hoosier who died in a plane crash in 1943.

monthly MAC Pass, which offers unlimited rides, is available for $38. Half-price fares are available for seniors and passengers with disabilities. Customers can call the IndyGo Transit Store at 317/635-3344 for details about specific routes.

Taxis and Shuttles

Stand at the curb, stick your hand in the air, and while you'll attract some curious stares, it's unlikely you'll succeed in hailing a cab in most Indianapolis neighborhoods. Drivers don't usually cruise for fares but rely instead on phone-ins for business. The good news is that within 10 minutes to a half-hour of your call, you'll almost always have a cab at your door waiting to take you to the airport, downtown, or wherever else you need to go. There are more than a dozen cab companies listed in the phone book; some work only in certain parts of town, cater to airport business, or require advance reservations. The following are some of the cab services that cover the entire city and do both reservation and call-in business:

**Airline Taxi
& Packaging Delivery**
317/631-7521, 800/359-7521

Barrington Cabs
317/786-7994

Hoosier Cab Company
317/243-8800, 800/243-8802

Indy Airport Taxi
317/381-1111

Yellow Cab
317/487-7777

Some hotels provide free shuttle service. Some even offer transportation to and from downtown and other shopping or business areas. Others advertise relationships with limousine companies that shuttle guests to and from the hotel for a fee.

While Indy's limo and shuttle services typically feature special-event usage, some companies offer a very affordable shared-ride service to and from the airport. Indy Connection, 317/241-6700 or 317/241-2522, for example, charges only $8 per passenger plus driver tip for a ride from downtown to the airport, and from $12 to $16 from north side hotels. Other limo

A Travel Writer's 24-Hour Twister

If you've got only a day to tour, taste, and take in all the best of Indy, try out this whirlwind tour, suggested by Laurie Borman, author of The Smart Woman's Guide to Business Travel *and editor-in-chief of* Endless Vacation, *an international travel magazine published by Indianapolis-based timeshare–exchange company RCI. All sites, restaurants, and accommodations are listed with addresses and phone numbers in the appropriate chapters in this book.*

In the morning:

From the airport, head downtown and fuel up with a hearty serving of eggs and hash browns at **Shapiro's Delicatessen Cafeteria***, 317/872-7255.*

Then visit the **Eiteljorg Museum***, 317/636-9378, which is filled with contemporary Native American and Western art, including Remington bronzes.*

Next door, check out the **IMAX** *3-D theater, 317/233-4626, where 3-D images come alive on a screen 10 times the size of a regular movie screen.*

Stroll the **Indianapolis Canal Walk** *and continue on to the* **Indianapolis Zoo***, 317/630-2001, where you'll enjoy the antics of the polar bears, the free-roaming creatures in the Desert biome, and the whale and dolphin show.*

In the afternoon:

For lunch, pick one or more of the 52 toppings for your pizza at **Bazbeaux's Pizza***, 317/636-7662, or relax at* **Ruthellen's***, 317/631-7884, both downtown.*

See the antique medical instruments, preserved specimens, and autopsy room at **Indiana Medical History Museum***, 317/635-7329.*

Ride around the track and imagine hitting the straightaway at more than 200 MPH at the **Indianapolis 500 Motor Speedway**, 317/481-8500. **The Hall of Fame Museum**, 317/484-6747, displays winning cars.

The Children's Museum, 317/924-5431, the largest children's museum in the world, has an IWERKS CineDome theater, a planetarium, and hands-on exhibits.

President Benjamin Harrison and John Dillinger are the two famous men buried in the 555-acre **Crown Hill Cemetery**—Check out the view from James Whitcomb Riley's tomb.

In the evening:
Visit **Conner Prairie** settlement, 317/776-6000, a living-history recreation of 1836 Indiana where docents in period costume engage in daily activities. Check to see if dinner is being served at **Governor Noble's Eating Place**, 317/776-6008.

Tumble into bed in a former-farmhouse-turned-bed-and-breakfast at **Frederick-Talbott Inn**, 317/578-3600.

or

Dine at **Arturo's**, 317/257-4806, a white-tablecloth restaurant. Call ahead and ask for a table in the kitchen, where the chef will let you sample the various dishes he's preparing.

Work off dinner with a spin around the ice rink at the downtown **Pan Am Plaza**, 317/237-5555, a swim at the **I.U. Natatorium**, 317/274-3518, or a few games at **Action Duckpin Bowl**, 317/686-6010, a restored 1928 duckpin bowling alley.

Take in a **Pacer**, **Colts**, **Indians**, or **Ice** game, depending on the season.

Finish the evening at the **Slippery Noodle Inn**, 317/631-6978, Indiana's oldest tavern, for soul-stirring blues.

Tuck in at the **Canterbury Hotel**, 317/634-3000, a European-style hotel.

You may turn right on red unless a sign says otherwise.

companies charge a flat fee. Aristocrat Limousine Service, 317/923-5351, charges $40 for a ride from downtown to the airport—which is very reasonable if the expense is divided among several individuals. Most services require some advance notice (24 hours, typically). Also, because the limo or van may be making several other stops, you should allow for more travel time. For further details on taxis, shuttles, shared-ride services, and private limo services, contact the Visitors Information Center at 317/487-7243. Or rent a car:

Alamo	800/327-9633	**Hertz**	800/654-3131
Avis	800/831-2847	**National**	800/227-7368
Budget	800/527-0700	**Thrifty**	800/367-2277

Driving in Indianapolis

Once, an interurban train connected Indianapolis with major towns within 120 miles, and streetcars connected points within the city. But city residents now have an unabashed love affair with their cars. Indianapolites used to boast about their many and unclogged highways. Rush-hour news copters were rare, and reports of slowdowns were equally rare.

Locals now groan about traffic, but the city is considered to be one of the least-congested large cities in the country. Morning rush hour, between about 6:30 and 8:30, is worse than evening rush hour, between 4:30 and 6:30. The nastiest slowdowns are at interstate exit ramps by rapidly developing areas, such as Greenwood and Fishers, and the most hair-raising maneuvers take place on the portion of the inner loop known as the "Spaghetti Bowl," where I-70 and I-65 come together, merge, and split. The biggest surface-street headaches are northeast around Castleton and Fishers, northwest by the Pyramids (the city's famous office buildings at 86th Street and Michigan Road), and in Greenwood and Oaklandon.

If, in the winter, the driver ahead of you swerves suddenly, he's apt to be avoiding a pothole. With regular freezing and thawing, pavement buckles early and often. The city doesn't get enough snow to make drivers proficient at driving in the white stuff, so on snowy days you'll find some people crawling while others are zipping along. In fall, wet leaves create a surprisingly slick hazard.

Indianapolis International Airport

Air Travel

The Indianapolis International Airport, with its 31 gates and 17 commercial carriers, serves more than seven million passengers per year—quite an increase from the 1970s, when a mere two million travelers passed through its portals. A lot has changed since then. In 1976 a new international arrivals and departures building with full customs service was added. In the late 1980s, the airport experienced a dramatic expansion and facelift to better serve visitors coming in for the Pan Am Games and other events the city planned to host. The airport is currently undergoing another expansion.

The 6,000-acre facility, off 1-465 and I-70 exits on the southwest side, is a user-friendly terminal efficiently run by BAA, the same private British firm that operates London's Heathrow and Gatwick Airports. Travelers find the terminal's logical layout provides quick access to departures and equally speedy getaways from the airport. A parking garage and surface lot provide convenient short-term parking just a few steps from the terminal, and a remote lot offers lower rates for long-term parking.

A retail corridor makes last-minute souvenir shopping a dream—buy jars of homemade apple butter and those cute country suncatchers you passed up in Nashville, or pick up a leather briefcase before you take off for an important business meeting. If your plane is delayed, you can play an arcade game, eat a Big Mac, or have your shoes shined.

For passenger services, paging, and visitor information, call the airport at 317/487-7243. For airline ticketing and reservation information, call

the specific airline. Major airlines serving Indianapolis International Airport include:

American	800/433-7300	**Southwest**	800/435-9792
American Trans Air	800/225-2995	**TWA**	800/221-2000
Continental	800/523-3273	**United**	800/241-6522
Delta	800/221-1212	**US Airways**	800/428-4322
Northwest	800/225-2525		

Train Service

Amtrak service has been severely curtailed, but you can still get to Chicago
six days a week—if you don't mind traveling at inconvenient times. Leave
Indy at the ungodly hour of 5:05 a.m. Tuesday through Sunday and arrive
in the Windy City by 10:15 a.m. The train leaves Chicago at 7:40 p.m. and
returns to Indianapolis at 12:25 a.m. The Cardinal (the Chicago-Washington,
D.C., route) also provides service to Cincinnati, leaving Chicago Indy on
Wednesday, Friday, and Sunday at 12:55 a.m. and returning Monday, Thursday, and Saturday at 4:35 a.m. Trains still arrive at and depart from Union
Station. Amtrak also runs a daily bus service to Chicago. Reservations are
required for both train and bus services; call 800/872-7245.

Bus Service

Bus service has been reduced over the past few years. But you can still
hop on a bus any day of the week and get to just about anywhere in the
United States—eventually. The downtown Greyhound terminal, 350 South
Illinois Street, 317/267-3076, serves several lines in addition to Greyhound,
including Southeastern Trailways and Illini Swallow Lines. For departure
times and destinations, call Greyhound's toll-free number, 800/231-2222.
They'll, of course, quote Greyhound routes first, but will offer information
about other lines.

Canterbury Hotel

3

WHERE TO STAY

As recently as the seventies, accommodations in Indianapolis were limited to a few hotels downtown, out at the airport, and near the Speedway. With the astounding growth of the city in the past 20 years, lodgings, too, have sprung up. Today, 130-plus accommodations offer nearly 18,000 rooms for travelers. And two new hotels slated for development near the convention center will add nearly 1,000 additional rooms to the downtown area by the year 2000. From traditional motel rooms with an ice machine down the hall, to homey bed-and-breakfasts, to full-service facilities with everything from four-star restaurants to business services, Indianapolis offers accommodations to suit almost everyone's needs.

Factors that determine room rate include location, amenities, and timing. The same room that cost you $69 a night in February may spike up to $400 for a three-day package over race weekend. Special events notwithstanding, room rates in Indy don't seem to be based on any consistent model. Some hotels have higher rates during the week, others charge more for weekends.

Accommodations in Indy tend to be clustered in the heart of downtown or concentrated along I-465, where virtually every major hotel chain is represented at every exit. In addition, only-in-Indy lodgings exist, offering out-of-towners unique experiences not to mention providing romantic getaways or restful retreats for residents.

Price rating symbols:
$ $50 and under
$$ $51 to $75
$$$ $76 to $125
$$$$ $126 and up

Note: Prices reflect a general range and may fluctuate depending on season and availability.

DOWNTOWN INDIANAPOLIS

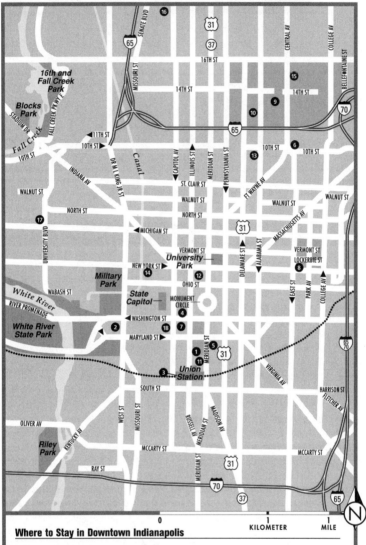

Where to Stay in Downtown Indianapolis

1 Canterbury Hotel
2 Courtyard by Marriott Downtown
3 Crowne Plaza Union Station
4 Embassy Suites Downtown
5 Hampton Inn Downtown
6 The Hoffman House
7 Hyatt Regency Indianapolis
8 Lockerbie Inn
9 The Looking Glass Inn
10 The Old Northside Bed-and-Breakfast
11 Omni Severin Hotel
12 Radisson Hotel City Centre

13 Renaissance Tower Historic Inn
14 Residence Inn on the Canal
15 Stone Soup Inn
16 The Tranquil Cherub
17 University Place Conference Center
   and Hotel
18 The Westin Hotel

DOWNTOWN

Hotels and Motels

CANTERBURY HOTEL
123 S. Illinois St.
317/634-3000 or 800/538-8186
$$$$
Accommodations more elegant and pampering are not to be found. Rooms have Chippendale four-poster beds, marble vanities, gold-plated fixtures—and a phone and TV in the bathroom. Services include twice-a-day housekeeping as well as business services. It's no wonder that celebrities like Mick Jagger and Elton John have stayed here. A member of Preferred Hotels and Resorts Worldwide, Canterbury Hotel is also listed in the National Register of Historic Places. The hotel features 99 impeccably appointed rooms, including suites and duplex penthouses with whirlpool tubs, wet bars, and adjoining sitting rooms. Practicalities for the business traveler include voice mail and data ports. All guests at the Canterbury receive a complimentary continental breakfast. From the hotel you can walk to any downtown site—the Circle Centre mall is connected by a private entrance on the second floor; the Convention Center and RCA Dome are just a block away. & (Downtown)

COURTYARD BY MARRIOTT DOWNTOWN
501 W. Washington St.
317/635-4443 or 800/321-2211
$$$
The Courtyard is convenient to the zoo, the IMAX Theater, the Eiteljorg Museum, the Indiana State Museum, and all that White River State Park has to offer. Its 233 standard hotel rooms offer comforts for families as well as business travelers—coffee makers, hair dryers, data ports, cable, and pay-per-view. On the property are an outdoor heated pool, exercise facilities, a playground, and a TGI Friday's restaurant. The hotel offers special weekend packages, customized for families or couples. & (Downtown)

CROWNE PLAZA UNION STATION
123 Louisiana St.
317/631-2221 or 800/227-6963
$$$–$$$$
The fate of Union Station remains unknown at press time (the historic building is still on the market), but this full-service hotel will continue to offer guests easy access to the Indiana Convention Center, RCA Dome, Circle Centre mall, and downtown dining and nightlife. Of the 276 rooms, 26 are within original Pullman train cars. An indoor pool, whirlpool, and exercise room are among the amenities. & (Downtown)

EMBASSY SUITES DOWNTOWN
110 W. Washington St.
317/236-1800 or 800/362-2779
$$$$
This all-suite hotel in the heart of downtown connects by skywalk to Circle Centre mall. Its 360 suites offer two bedrooms, two TVs, a microwave, a refrigerator, and a coffee maker. In addition, there are 12 penthouse suites for $400 and up. Room rates include a full breakfast and an evening reception, including complimentary cocktails and hors d'oeuvres. Catering to the business traveler, the hotel offers services such as faxing, copying, and shipping. For fitness buffs, the hotel offers an indoor pool and exercise room. & (Downtown)

HAMPTON INN DOWNTOWN
105 S. Meridian St.

317/261-1200 or 800/426-7866
$$$–$$$$

This 180-room hotel makes its home in the historic Chesapeake Building, across the street from Circle Centre mall. The hotel's rooms and suites offer a number of conveniences, including whirlpool tubs, coffee makers, irons and ironing boards, and fax/computer hookups. The traditional decor features rich cherry furnishings and dark floral prints. The hotel is connected to a popular eatery, BW3, which offers delivery and carryout for hotel guests. Be sure to ask about the hotel's getaway packages. ♿ (Downtown)

HYATT REGENCY INDIANAPOLIS
1 S. Capitol Ave.
317/632-1234 or 800/233-1234
$$$–$$$$

This 500-room, full-service hotel offers a range of extra services. You can buy aspirin, have your hair done, work out, or withdraw cash without leaving the hotel. At the top of the Hyatt's 20-story atrium is the Eagle's Nest, a revolving rooftop restaurant. A convenient skywalk allows guests to get to the Convention Center and Circle Centre mall in any weather. The hotel also provides free airport shuttle service and full business services. ♿ (Downtown)

LOCKERBIE INN
345 N. East St.
317/636-7527
$$–$$$

The three suites in this Queen Anne–style house were designed to provide convenience and comfort for long-term guests. (Most guests stay at least a week.) Each offers a bedroom, sitting room, private bath, and fully equipped kitchen. A washer-dryer unit on the second floor is available for guest use. Smoking is not allowed. (Downtown)

OMNI SEVERIN HOTEL
40 W. Jackson Pl.
317/634-6664 or 800/843-6664
$$$$

The Convention Center, the RCA Dome, shopping, Union Station, the Pan Am Plaza, and other popular downtown attractions are all an easy walk away from the Omni. This Triple-A, Four Diamond–rated hotel offers plenty of pluses for business people, including three business-class floors with computer and fax access in the rooms. The Omni has 423 guest rooms and 38 suites and features an indoor pool, fitness facilities, a restaurant, a café, and a martini bar. The hotel is connected by skywalk to the Circle Centre mall. ♿ (Downtown)

TRIVIA

The Bates House, built in 1853, was once considered the finest hotel in the Midwest. Abraham Lincoln made one of his earliest speeches promoting the preservation of the Union from the balcony of his room there. In 1901 the hotel was torn down to make way for the Claypool Hotel. Two young women were murdered there—one in 1943 and the other in 1954. The Claypool closed in 1967. Today, the Embassy Suites Downtown stands in its place.

Hotels on the National Register of Historic Places

Three downtown hotels are listed on the National Register of Historic Places. The Renaissance Tower Historic Inn, near the Murat and the nightlife of Massachusetts Avenue, has served as an extended-stay hotel since 1985, but it began its existence as an apartment building in 1922. The Canterbury Hotel first opened in 1928 as the Lockerbie Hotel and served travelers from the then-bustling Union Station. On Monument Circle, the Columbia Club, a members-only facility, makes 90 overnight rooms available to members and their guests in this grand structure. It was founded by the Harrison Marching Society, supporters of Hoosier presidential candidate Benjamin Harrison, in 1888. The current structure was built in 1925. One of the highlights of the grand lobby is a large marble-top table, which was in Harrison's White House.

RADISSON HOTEL CITY CENTRE
31 W. Ohio St.
317/635-2000 or 800/333-3333
$$$–$$$$
Monument Circle is just a stone's throw from the accommodations at the Radisson. The hotel features 374 rooms and suites, English's Café restaurant, a lounge, a fitness center, a gift shop, and an outdoor pool. Both suites and rooms have coffee makers, hair dryers, and irons and ironing boards; the suites have small refrigerators. Business travelers can take advantage of fax/modem access in the rooms, meeting facilities, and a variety of other business services. Current renovations to the guest rooms, meeting rooms, lobby, and exterior will be completed by late 1999. ♿ (Downtown)

RENAISSANCE TOWER
HISTORIC INN
230 E. 9th St.
317/261-1652 or 800/676-7786
$$$
Listed on the National Register of Historic Places and included in *The Official Guide to American Historic Inns* (by Deborah Edwards Sakach, published by American Historic Inns Society), this 1922 apartment house-turned-hotel has 80 fully furnished studio suites. Rooms are appointed with Victorian furnishings, such as solid cherry four-poster beds. All suites feature a well-supplied kitchen with full-sized appliances. Maid service is included. Modern conveniences include cable TV, free local calls, personalized voice mail, and free parking. ♿ (Downtown)

Best One-of-a-Kind Sites for Meetings

Business meetings may be a necessary evil, but there's no reason why they have to be held in charmless settings. The Convention Center and other meeting sites downtown offer outstanding facilities for large conferences and events —and a world of diversions for free time. But there are plenty of smaller facilities outside of downtown that offer only-in-Indy ambience and unique activities for smaller groups. Consider this sampling from DeLoris Gregory-Durm, president of Plan-It, a meeting- and event-planning service.

Frederick-Talbott Inn*—This northside bed-and-breakfast, located at 13805 Allisonville Rd., 317/578-3600, is popular for weddings and romantic getaways, but the inn offers meeting facilities, too. French doors and generous windows welcome in the rural flavor. Meeting attendees love to wander the historic home and grounds during breaks. (North)*

Tuckaway*—World-renowned palm reader Nellie Meier served as hostess here in the 1920s and 1930s. Her guests included such celebrities as Walt Disney and Joan Crawford. The house, on the National Register of Historic Places, 3128 N. Pennsylvania St., 317/926-*

RESIDENCE INN ON THE CANAL
350 W. New York St.
317/822-0840 or 800/331-3131
$$$$
This new all-suite hotel can boast that it is the only Indy lodging to be located on the Indianapolis Water Company Canal. Half the rooms face the canal for a lovely view of fountains, bridges, and walkways. Pull yourself away, however, to take advantage of an evening social hour, indoor pool, hot tub, exercise room, and pool table. Other services include a daily continental breakfast, same-day grocery delivery, and same-day dry-cleaning. Rooms include hair dryers, irons and ironing boards, and data ports. Business services are available. & (Downtown)

UNIVERSITY PLACE CONFERENCE CENTER AND HOTEL
850 W. Michigan St.
317/269-9000 or 800/627-2700
$$$$
An ideal base for those in town to see the RCA Championships, this Triple-A, Four Diamond hotel on the IUPUI campus is connected by covered skywalk to the university's sports complex. The hotel is also connected by skywalk to several major medical facilities at the Indiana University Medical Center. The

0251, appeals to those seeking a creative environment. But take warning: You may be joined by an uninvited guest —Meier's spirit is reported to wander the premises still. (North)

***Jewish Community Center**—Swim, play tennis, walk on the treadmill, take a sauna, or schedule a massage between sessions. The JCC, located at 6701 Hoover Rd., 317/251-9467, is the only kosher-catered meeting site in the city. (North)*

***Allison Mansion Conference Center**—Located at 3200 Cold Spring Rd., 317/955-6120, this magnificent mansion, built in 1911, features lavishly decorated rooms (check out the Tiffany stained-glass ceiling). (West/Southwest)*

***Schnull-Rauch House**—This historic home (3050 North Meridian St., 317/925-4800) offers small, cozy parlors and grand ballrooms for meetings. The house is located next door to the Children's Museum, which offers some great breaktime activities. (North)*

***Indianapolis Museum of Art**—Both large and small groups can view the museum's collections during meeting breaks. Take in an exhibit —or wander outside among the gardens and sculpture. The museum is located at 1200 W. 38th St., 317/923-1331. (North)*

rooms, which are designed to serve business travelers, feature large desks, good lighting, comfortable chairs, computer hookups, and voice mail. Suites with kitchenettes are available for extended stays. The hotel also features conference facilities, restaurants, a lounge, a gift shop, and a museum dedicated to sports in fine art. A free shuttle takes guests to several downtown attractions. ♿ (Downtown)

THE WESTIN HOTEL
50 S. Capitol Ave.
317/262-8100 or 800/228-3000
$$$$
Many of the Westin's deluxe rooms

and suites afford breathtaking views of downtown. The Triple-A, Four Diamond–rated hotel is a year-round warm walk to shopping and entertainment —it is connected by skywalk to Circle Centre mall, the Convention Center, and the RCA Dome. A fitness facility, an indoor pool, and a whirlpool offer guests opportunities for winding down or working out. ♿ (Downtown)

Bed-and-Breakfasts

THE HOFFMAN HOUSE
545 E. 11th St.
317/635-1701

On the northwest quadrant of Monument Circle once stood the English Hotel, where a number of theater greats, including Sarah Bernhardt, the Barrymores, and Laurence Olivier, stayed and performed at the nearby Opera House. The hotel and opera house were demolished in 1948 and replaced by a JC Penney store.

www2.inetdirect.net/~laa4tag
$$

This bed-and-breakfast, in the Chatham Arch Historic District, is within walking distance of art galleries, boutiques, theaters, and nightlife, as well as Lockerbie Square and James Whitcomb Riley's home. The American Foursquare–style home was built in 1903. The three guest rooms share a bathroom (clawfoot tub and modern plumbing), and the double beds are adorned with handmade quilts. A full breakfast—often featuring edible flowers—is included. A plus for business travelers, the Hoffman House makes a fax, copier, and computer available. This is a great find for nonsmoking animal-lovers (two cats and a dog in residence). (Downtown)

THE LOOKING GLASS INN
1319 N. New Jersey St.
317/635-8832
$$$

The owners of Stone Soup Inn recently opened their new bed-and-breakfast. The new property features seven guest rooms, three rooms with Jacuzzi tubs. A large suite with a kitchen takes up the entire third floor of the historic home. The decor is a mix of Empire and Victorian. A first-floor room will appeal to guests who are unable to climb the stairs. (Downtown)

THE OLD NORTHSIDE
BED-AND-BREAKFAST
1340 N. Alabama St.
317/635-9123 or 800/635-9127
www.hofmeister.com/bbb/bbb.htm
$$–$$$

Choose among the poster-covered Theatre Room, the romantic Bridal Room (with large whirlpool tub), and three other themed rooms (all with private baths) in this brick, Romanesque revival–style home. Within walking distance of President Benjamin Harrison's home and not far from downtown, this house features the original wood floors, hand-carved cherry woodwork, and murals on the ceilings and walls. Guests can enjoy a hearty breakfast in the dining room or coffee in their own rooms. (Downtown)

STONE SOUP INN
1304 N. Central Ave.
317/639-9550
www.stonesoupinn.com
$$$

This bed-and-breakfast features six guest rooms in a lovely colonial revival home built in 1901. Four rooms have private baths (one with a steam room/shower; two with a two-person whirlpool tub), and two have a shared bath. Each room is unique — some have tiled fireplaces, one has a bay window, and another is furnished in Mission-style antiques. Two rooms —the Victorian Room and the Craftsman Room —share a bathroom with a stained-glass window and an antique slipper tub. Guests can read or relax in the library, the living room, and the sitting room, which has a balcony. A continental breakfast is served during the week, a full breakfast on weekends. A refreshment area, the "butler's pantry," provides midnight snacks for night owls. (Downtown)

THE TRANQUIL CHERUB
2164 N. Capitol Ave.
317/923-9036
$$–$$$
Even other bed-and-breakfast owners ooh and aah over this grand yellow Greek revival home just minutes from the Children's Museum. Four oversized guest rooms are filled with antiques; each has its own bath. Cherished antiques are used in whimsical ways: a hand-operated clothes washer is used as an end table, a cradle serves as a coffee table, and a cream separator holds the TV. Guests can savor a gourmet breakfast by the fireplace in winter, or on the deck overlooking a lily pond in summer. On the first floor is a parlor with a player piano. The second floor features a sitting room with a TV and a snack-filled refrigerator. The bed-and-breakfast offers shuttle service to the airport and downtown. Special rates are available for guests visiting family at nearby Methodist Hospital. (Downtown)

NORTH

Hotels and Motels

AMERISUITES
9104 Keystone Crossing
317/843-0064 or 800/833-1516
$$$
This hotel's two-bedroom suites provide wet bars, refrigerators, microwaves, coffee makers, and sitting rooms. Guests receive a complimentary buffet breakfast and a free daily newspaper. The hotel offers a fitness facility and an outdoor pool. The Keystone Fashion Mall is within walking distance. Area restaurants deliver to Amerisuites. ᕕ (North)

The indoor pool at Crowne Plaza Union Station, p. 29

The Indianapolis Project

WHERE TO STAY **35**

DOUBLETREE GUEST SUITES
11355 N. Meridian St.
Carmel
317/844-7994 or 800/222-TREE
$$$

This all-suite, full-service hotel features comfortable rooms with a refrigerator, two TVs, two telephones, a coffee maker, and a hair dryer. On-site amenities include a restaurant and a lounge, indoor and outdoor pools, an exercise room, and a guest laundry. Some room rates include a full buffet breakfast. ♿ (North)

EMBASSY SUITES HOTEL
3912 Vincennes Rd.
317/872-7700 or 800/362-2779
$$$–$$$$

This full-service, all-suite hotel near the Pyramids and I-465 offers easy access to business and entertainment areas on the city's north side. The Mediterranean-style building features an indoor pool, restaurants, a gift shop, and a lounge, as well as meeting facilities. Rooms offer conveniences such as coffee makers, microwaves, and small refrigerators. The hotel runs a free shuttle to area restaurants, malls, and movie theaters. ♿ (North)

HAWTHORN SUITES LTD.
3871 W. 92nd St.
317/879-1700

$$

This hotel offers two-room suites with amenities such as microwaves, refrigerators, TVs, and VCRs. A complimentary deluxe continental breakfast is served daily, and a manager's reception, featuring complimentary snacks, is held each Wednesday. Rooms are equipped for the business traveler, with computer hookups and voice mail. A three-room executive suite is ideal for small business meetings. The hotel is close to I-465 and northside business areas such as the Pyramids. ♿ (North)

HOMEWOOD SUITES
AT THE CROSSING
2501 E. 86th St.
317/253-1919
$$$

Homewood caters to extended-stay guests. The suites include a living area and a kitchen area with a full refrigerator, a microwave, a toaster oven, and a two-burner stove. Some rooms have a fireplace. A complimentary continental breakfast is served daily. Guests can mingle at evening cocktail parties Monday through Thursday. Homewood also offers its guests an outdoor pool, a fitness center, and a study with a computer. A shuttle takes guests to nearby shopping and dining areas. ♿ (North)

TRIVIA

The Slippery Noodle Inn, 317/ 631-6978, Indy's popular downtown blues venue, was originally a roadhouse. Built in 1850 as the Tremont House, it is the oldest commercial building in the metro area. While other historic hotels are noted for their elegant lodgings or genteel atmosphere, the Noodle is proud of its past incarnations as a brothel, an alcohol producer during Prohibition, and a hangout for the Dillinger gang.

Best Easy-Access Hotels

Sheraton Indianapolis North Hotel and *Westin Suites Indianapolis North* connect to the Fashion Mall at Keystone Crossing, featuring upscale shops including Aveda, Ann Taylor, and Banana Republic. *(North)*

Embassy Suites Downtown, *Canterbury Hotel*, and *Omni Severin Hotel* are all connected by skywalks to Circle Centre mall. *(Downtown)*

The *Westin Hotel* is connected to three major downtown attractions: Circle Centre mall, the Convention Center, and the RCA Dome. *(Downtown)*

A skywalk offers easy access from the *University Place Conference Center and Hotel* at IUPUI to the IUPUI sports complex, which includes the tennis center, the natatorium, and the NIFS fitness facility. *(Downtown)*

KNIGHTS INN NORTH
9402 Haver Way
317/848-2423 or 800/843-5644
$
Knights Inn offers 110 first-floor rooms, some with kitchenettes. Within walking distance of restaurants and entertainment (a nonsmoking bowling alley is nearby), the motel also features an outdoor pool. This already-affordable inn offers a number of discounts. ♿ (North)

OMNI INDIANAPOLIS NORTH HOTEL
8181 N. Shadeland Ave.
317/849-6668 or 800/843-6664
$$$
This comfortable, full-service hotel near Castleton offers standard hotel rooms and two-bedroom suites. The Omni makes conference and meeting rooms available and contains a restaurant, a lounge, a fitness center, and an indoor pool. A free shuttle delivers guests to shopping, entertainment, and business destinations within a five-mile radius. ♿ (North)

PICKWICK FARMS SHORT-TERM FURNISHED APARTMENTS
9300 N. Ditch Rd.
317/872-6506 or 800/869-7368
$$
Pickwick Farms offers one- and two-bedroom units with full kitchens. The minimum stay is three days. (Studios are also available for 15-night minimum stays.) Rates for long-term stays include utilities and phone. On-site is a fitness center with racquetball, volleyball, and even a bowling alley. Guests can also use the facility's outdoor pool and tennis courts. A laundry

GREATER INDIANAPOLIS

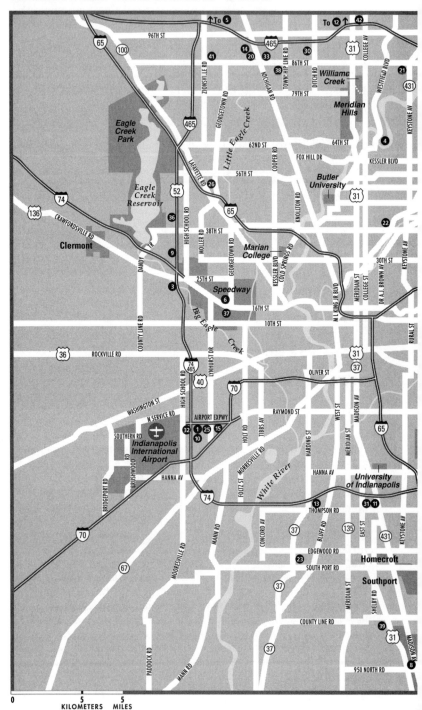

0 5 5
KILOMETERS MILES

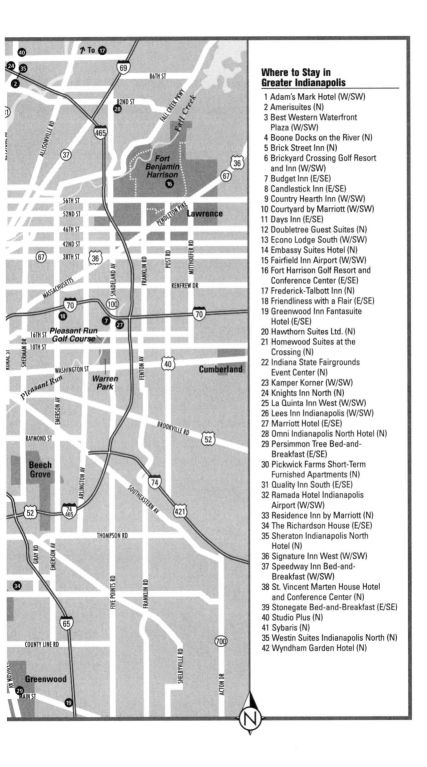

Where to Stay in Greater Indianapolis

1 Adam's Mark Hotel (W/SW)
2 Amerisuites (N)
3 Best Western Waterfront Plaza (W/SW)
4 Boone Docks on the River (N)
5 Brick Street Inn (N)
6 Brickyard Crossing Golf Resort and Inn (W/SW)
7 Budget Inn (E/SE)
8 Candlestick Inn (E/SE)
9 Country Hearth Inn (W/SW)
10 Courtyard by Marriott (W/SW)
11 Days Inn (E/SE)
12 Doubletree Guest Suites (N)
13 Econo Lodge South (W/SW)
14 Embassy Suites Hotel (N)
15 Fairfield Inn Airport (W/SW)
16 Fort Harrison Golf Resort and Conference Center (E/SE)
17 Frederick-Talbott Inn (N)
18 Friendliness with a Flair (E/SE)
19 Greenwood Inn Fantasuite Hotel (E/SE)
20 Hawthorn Suites Ltd. (N)
21 Homewood Suites at the Crossing (N)
22 Indiana State Fairgrounds Event Center (N)
23 Kamper Korner (W/SW)
24 Knights Inn North (N)
25 La Quinta Inn West (W/SW)
26 Lees Inn Indianapolis (W/SW)
27 Marriott Hotel (E/SE)
28 Omni Indianapolis North Hotel (N)
29 Persimmon Tree Bed-and-Breakfast (E/SE)
30 Pickwick Farms Short-Term Furnished Apartments (N)
31 Quality Inn South (E/SE)
32 Ramada Hotel Indianapolis Airport (W/SW)
33 Residence Inn by Marriott (N)
34 The Richardson House (E/SE)
35 Sheraton Indianapolis North Hotel (N)
36 Signature Inn West (W/SW)
37 Speedway Inn Bed-and-Breakfast (W/SW)
38 St. Vincent Marten House Hotel and Conference Center (N)
39 Stonegate Bed-and-Breakfast (E/SE)
40 Studio Plus (N)
41 Sybaris (N)
35 Westin Suites Indianapolis North (N)
42 Wyndham Garden Hotel (N)

room, with plenty of washers and dryers, is convenient to all units. Ground-floor units are wheelchair accessible. (North)

RESIDENCE INN BY MARRIOTT
3553 Founders Rd.
317/872-0462 or 800/331-3131
$$$
This all-suite, extended-stay facility offers 88 rooms (including studios and two-bedroom penthouses) with full kitchens. The Pyramids and other business parks are nearby, and the hotel is close to I-465 for quick access to other areas of town. A daily continental breakfast is served, and guests can also enjoy a hospitality hour Monday through Thursday. Fitness enthusiasts can enjoy free visits to a choice of two nearby health clubs. A length-of-stay discount is available. ♿ (North)

SHERATON INDIANAPOLIS NORTH HOTEL
WESTIN SUITES INDIANAPOLIS NORTH

Great Packages

Frederick-Talbott Inn—The Historic Getaway Package includes accommodations and breakfast for two, tickets to Conner Prairie, lunch, and a voucher for dinner at a local restaurant. The Golf Package includes a one-night stay with two rounds of golf, or a two-night stay with three rounds. (North)

Days Inn Downtown—The Family Fun Package includes 10 percent off meals at Tommy's restaurant, complimentary continental breakfast, surprise fun packs for the kids, and four tickets to the Indianapolis Zoo or the Children's Museum. (Downtown)

Adam's Mark Hotel—This airport hotel also offers a Family Package, which includes four tickets to the Children's Museum or the Indianapolis Zoo. (West/Southwest)

Omni Severin Hotel—A large bath basket filled with loofah, sponges, soaps, and lotions, and a therapeutic massage or facial at a salon in Circle Centre mall are part of the All-Natural Spa Package. (Downtown)

Fort Harrison Golf Resort and Conference Center—The Play and Stay Golf Packages include greens fees, cart, continental breakfast, and lodging at the historic Harrison House. You can buy an overnight or a several-day package. (East/Southeast)

Stone Soup Inn, p. 34

8787 Keystone Crossing
317/846-2700 or 800/325-3535
$$$
These two hotels share a lobby, a reception desk, a lounge, and restaurants. For serious shoppers, this is the place to stay on the north side. A skywalk connects the hotel to the Fashion Mall. Guests have free access to Bally's fitness club next door. Recent renovations have resulted in new comforts for business travelers, including spacious, oversized desks, voice mail, and data ports. The hotel also offers a conference facility. ♿ (North)

ST. VINCENT MARTEN
HOUSE HOTEL AND
CONFERENCE CENTER
1801 W. 86th St.
317/872-4111 or 800/736-5634
$$$
This 161-room hotel is across the street from St. Vincent Hospital and a short drive to the Pyramids and several shopping and dining areas. There are a restaurant, an indoor pool, and a fitness club on the premises. Park-

ing is free and a shuttle takes guests to the hospital. All rooms are standard; executive rooms include coffee makers. ♿ (North)

STUDIO PLUS
9750 E. Lakeshore Dr.
317/843-1181
$$
As the name implies, all 71 rooms in this hotel are studios with fully equipped kitchens. Studio Plus offers a number of other pluses, including an outdoor pool, a sauna, a health club, and a laundry and dry-cleaning delivery service. Rooms have data ports for modems and fax machines. Located at 96th and Keystone, the hotel is surrounded by shops and restaurants. ♿ (North)

SYBARIS
5466 W. 86th St.
317/337-9000
$$$$
Not your typical roadside stop for the night (although conveniently located off I-465 at 86th Street), Sybaris promotes itself as a romantic getaway

for couples. The emphasis is on privacy (each of the 16 rooms is windowless and phoneless) and personal pampering. These love bungalows offer gas fireplaces, in-room pools or whirlpool tubs, and steam rooms. The Chalet Suite even features a water slide. Creature comforts include stereos, TVs and VCRs, microwaves, refrigerators, complimentary toiletries, and plush bathrobes. Sybaris operates as a private club, but you can become a member ($30 annually) when you reserve a room. For those starry-eyed couples who can't get away for a night, there are afternoon rates as well. (North)

WYNDHAM GARDEN HOTEL
251 E. Pennsylvania Pkwy.
317/574-4600 or 800/996-3426
$$$
Catering to the business traveler, this hotel is convenient to northside business areas and offers meeting facilities, a restaurant, a lounge, a fitness center, and an indoor pool. All rooms and suites have data ports in addition to coffee makers and coffee, hair dryers, cable TV, irons and ironing boards, and newspaper delivery. A washer/dryer and laundry service are also available. & (North)

Bed-and-Breakfasts

BOONE DOCKS ON THE RIVER
7159 Edgewater Pl.
317/257-3671
$$
Located just north of Broad Ripple, this 1920s English Tudor –style home overlooks White River. A private entrance leads to the River Room Suite, decorated in white wicker and shades of blue. The suite includes a private bath, cable TV, and queen-size bed. A full, hot breakfast is served on the

screened-in porch or in the sunroom. Guests can wander down to the deck overlooking the river. & (North)

BRICK STREET INN
175 S. Main St.
Zionsville
317/873-9177
$$$–$$$$
Warm, welcoming, and old-fashioned best describe the five cozy rooms at Brick Street Inn. All rooms are decorated with antiques, oil lamps, down comforters and fine linens, and three have private baths. The inn, built in 1865, is situated in the heart of historic Zionsville. It features a common room with a fireplace and a wonderful front-patio terrace. The full breakfast is served outside or in. Step out the door and you're surrounded by quaint shops and restaurants. TDY services are available for the hearing impaired. (North)

FREDERICK-TALBOTT INN
13805 Allisonville Rd.
Fishers
317/578-3600 or 800/566-2337
$$$–$$$$
Featured in *Country Living* magazine (February 1997), this inn, with 10 guest rooms, is a favorite among antique lovers and Hoosier history buffs. The inn is comprised of two farmhouses, and its sitting rooms, entryways, porches, and even closets and corners are filled with finds from Indy institutions. The dining room furniture comes from the old L. S. Ayres tearoom; the gilt mirrors were acquired at the Atkinson Hotel auction. The rooms offer all the conveniences of the late twentieth century, including remote-control TVs and well-appointed private baths. (The plumbing is not antique—hot water is in abundant supply!) A full

breakfast buffet features dishes such as stuffed French toast and homemade coffeecakes. Meeting facilities are also available. Conner Prairie is across the street. ᕕ (North)

Camping

INDIANA STATE FAIRGROUNDS EVENT CENTER
1202 E. 38th St.
317/927-7510
$

The fairgrounds offer a central location to road-weary RVers and others who prefer to sleep in a tent rather than a hotel. Rates are extremely low, especially if utility hookup is not required. Indoor showers and bathrooms are available and security is good. No reservations are taken. The fairgrounds are filled during the state fair, which is held in August. (North)

WEST/SOUTHWEST

Hotels and Motels

ADAM'S MARK HOTEL
2544 Executive Dr.
317/248-2481 or 800/444-2326
$$$

For businesspeople and other travelers who want easy access to the airport and all the comforts of a full-service hotel, the Adam's Mark is the ideal choice. The hotel has meeting facilities as well as a business center with copying, mailing, shipping, and fax services. Guests can choose between the hotel's two restaurants; a nightclub and lounge offer evening diversions. There's also a fitness center, an outdoor pool, free parking, and free shuttle service to the airport. Adam's Mark offers a va-

riety of package deals. ᕕ (West/Southwest)

BEST WESTERN WATERFRONT PLAZA
2930 Waterfront Pkwy. W. Dr.
317/299-8400 or 800/528-1234
$$

This lakeside complex offers recently redecorated guest rooms and more than 17,500 square feet of meeting space. The full-service Waterfront Cafe restaurant and Excalibur II lounge cater to guests and locals. An attractive atrium area features an indoor pool and a whirlpool. Rooms have cable TV, hair dryers, coffee makers, and computer data ports. Business services are available at the front desk, and a complimentary shuttle goes to the airport. ᕕ (West/Southwest)

BRICKYARD CROSSING GOLF RESORT AND INN
4400 W. 16th St.
317/241-2500
$$

There's no lodging more conveniently located to race activity than the Brickyard. Unfortunately, your odds of getting a room during the Indianapolis 500 in May or the Brickyard golf tournament in September are not even slim—they're none. But this 108-room hotel on the grounds of the Indianapolis Motor Speedway offers a great westside location for any other time of the year. On the premises are a challenging 18-hole golf course, a restaurant, a lounge, and an outdoor heated pool. Some rooms offer a refrigerator, a coffee maker, and a view of the golf course. A dry-cleaning delivery service and complimentary airport shuttle are also available. The Indianapolis Motor Speedway Hall of Fame

Museum is a short walk away. ♿
(West/Southwest)

COUNTRY HEARTH INN
3851 Shore Dr.
317/297-1848 or 888/443-2784
$$

Offering convenient access to I-465
and 38th Street shopping, dining, and
entertainment, this inn has 83 stan-
dard hotel rooms with free daily pa-
pers, cable TV, and coffee makers. A
daily complimentary breakfast and a
wine-and-cheese reception Tuesday
through Thursday evenings are pro-
vided. A fax/copy service is available
at the business center. An outdoor
pool and access to a nearby fitness
center are additional amenities. ♿
(West/Southwest)

COURTYARD BY MARRIOTT
5525 Fortune Circle East
317/248-0300 or 800/321-2211
$$–$$$

Located just off I-465, this hotel is not
far from any city destination and is
just a free shuttle ride away from the
airport. The hotel offers both standard

rooms and suites; all accommoda-
tions include amenities such as hair
dryers, coffee, data ports, and irons
and ironing boards. The suites also
have refrigerators. The indoor pool,
fitness room, and hot tub give guests
a chance to wind down or work out.
In the morning the breakfast buffet
gets guests going, and in the evening
guests can order a light dinner. Busi-
ness travelers can send faxes and
ship packages from the hotel. ♿
(West/Southwest)

ECONO LODGE SOUTH
4505 S. Harding St.
317/788-9361 or 800/424-6423
$$

This hotel is only a few minutes' drive
by I-465 from downtown and the airport. Econo Lodge offers the basics
in its 150 standard rooms—free local
calls and limited cable—and there's
a restaurant, lounge, meeting rooms,
and outdoor pool on the premises. A
free shuttle service provides rides
to and from the airport. ♿ (West
Southwest)

FAIRFIELD INN AIRPORT
5220 W. Southern Ave.
317/244-1600 or 800/228-2800
$$–$$$

Because this hotel is so convenient
to the airport, it is popular among
business travelers. The 86 rooms are
comfortable, and they offer extras
such as data ports —six rooms have
Jacuzzis. Guests can take advantage of the faxing, copying, and ship-
ping services at the front desk. Hair
dryers, irons and ironing boards, and
TV video games are also available at
the front desk. Other pluses include
a guest laundry, same-day dry
cleaning, complimentary continental
breakfast daily, a fitness room, and
an indoor pool. A free shuttle makes

Omni Severin Hotel, p. 30

Omni Severin Hotel

airport access a snap. & (West/Southwest)

LA QUINTA INN WEST
5316 W. Southern Ave.
317/247-4281 or 800/531-5900
$$$
All 122 standard rooms (bathrooms included) in this hotel have been recently renovated: everything from the bedspreads to the carpeting to the countertops is new. The rooms are ideal for the business traveler — they are well lit and have data ports. Business services are available at the front desk. Local calls, satellite TV, and video games are part of the room price. Guests can relax in the outdoor heated pool and eat at the JoJo's restaurant in the hotel. The

Indy's Best Romantic Getaways

Canterbury Hotel—*Weekend packages include romantic touches such as horse-drawn carriage rides, champagne, and strawberries and cream. (Downtown)*

Frederick-Talbott Inn—*The Bridal Suite offers a romantic refuge. The Honeymoon Package includes a silver champagne bucket and extra touches. (North)*

Old Northside Bed-and-Breakfast—*The Bridal Room includes a large Jacuzzi and shower—not to mention a fireplace—for a warm ambience. (North)*

The Radisson Hotel—*This hotel pampers the cozy couple with champagne, chocolates, a carriage ride, breakfast, and late checkout. (Downtown)*

Greenwood Inn FantaSuite Hotel—*You're sure to find your favorite expression of romance in one of 20 different theme rooms, from Jungle Safari to Arabian Nights. One package includes body oil, a picnic basket, and chocolates. (East/Southeast)*

Omni Severin Hotel—*The Romantic Escape includes champagne, Godiva chocolates, and a long-stemmed rose delivered to the room, as well as a full dinner for two at the hotel's Hot Tuna restaurant. (Downtown)*

Adam's Mark Hotel—*A bottle of champagne, strawberries, a red rose, and credit toward food and beverages at the hotel are part of this hotel's romantic package. (West/Southwest)*

hotel provides a free, 24-hour shuttle to the airport. ♿ (West/Southwest)

LEES INN INDIANAPOLIS
5011 N. Lafayette Rd.
317/297-8880 or 800/733-5337
$$
Situated close to both I-65 and I-465, this hotel is convenient to the airport and downtown and offers both suites and standard hotel rooms. All rooms include free cable TV and free local calls; the suites feature complimentary continental breakfast and whirlpool tubs. Meeting rooms and business services are also available for business travelers. ♿ (West/Southwest)

RAMADA HOTEL INDIANAPOLIS AIRPORT
2500 S. High School Rd.
317/244-3361 or 800/272-6232
$$$
Just a three-minute walk from the airport, this large hotel couldn't be better situated for business travelers.

But don't worry, you don't have to lug your luggage even that far —a 24-hour shuttle drops guests off at their terminals. The 288 rooms include coffee makers, hair dryers, irons and ironing boards, and hookups for computers. The hotel's restaurant starts serving breakfast at 6 a.m. and its lounge provides a place for guests to relax until the wee hours. ♿ (West/Southwest)

SIGNATURE INN WEST
3850 Eagle View Dr.
317/299-6165 or 800/822-5252
$$–$$$
Guests at the Signature Inn are close to the airport and conveniently near shopping, dining, and Eagle Creek Park. The 101 rooms feature roomy desks, speaker phones, and computer data ports. (If you're planning to work in a little R and R, ask for one of the two rooms with a two-person whirlpool spa.) Most rooms have a microwave and a refrigerator,

Visiting in May? Book Early — And Plan to Spend!

Every resident and Indy-500 regular knows that during the month of May, there's no room at the inn—or hotel, motel, campground, or bed-and-breakfast, for that matter. Lodgings fill up well before the time of the race. Some hotels are booked up years in advance. And if you are lucky enough to find a place to stay, you will likely be charged a room rate that is as much as three times higher than normal. Most hotels require guests to buy a three-day package over race weekend. The Indy 500 isn't the only event that fills rooms, so plan early if you're going to be in town during the Brickyard 400, RCA Championships, or Coca-Cola Classic.

Speedway Inn Bed-and-Breakfast

and all rooms have a coffee maker, a second phone, and an iron and ironing board. An outdoor pool is convenient for warm-weather swimming. A continental breakfast is served daily, and a free shuttle takes guests to and from the airport. ♿ (West/Southwest)

Bed-and-Breakfasts

SPEEDWAY INN BED-AND-BREAKFAST
1829 Cunningham Rd.
Speedway
317/487-6531 or 800/975-3412
$$–$$$
Five guest rooms are available in this home in the heart of Speedway. Four have private baths and one a shared bath. A full breakfast is served throughout the year. This Southern-style plantation home features a shady porch and a view of beautiful flower gardens. The neighborhood is restful and quiet—except during May, when racing activity generates hustle and bustle. Not surprisingly,

race memorabilia can be found throughout the house and rooms. What's more, famous drivers stay at the Speedway Inn during race events. (West/Southwest)

Camping

KAMPER KORNER
1951 W. Edgewood Ave.
317/788-1488
$
Both RV and tent campers will find this facility convenient to downtown (it's just off I-465 and State Road 37). Sites with or without hookups are available. Kamper Korner has bathrooms, showers, a laundry, and a sundries store. Restaurants and shops are nearby. (West/Southwest)

EAST/SOUTHEAST

Hotels and Motels

BUDGET INN
6850 E. 21st St.

317/353-9781
$–$$

Located just off I-70 and Shadeland Avenue, the Budget Inn offers standard hotel rooms with the basics. Coffee, hot chocolate, and donuts are served in the morning. Nearby restaurants are within walking distance. &
(East/Southeast)

DAYS INN
602 E. Thompson Rd.
317/788-0331
$$

All 100 rooms of this hotel were recently completely refurbished. In addition to the standard rooms, this hotel offers two suites with Jacuzzis and a corporate apartment with a refrigerator and a stove. Guests enjoy a continental breakfast daily. The Days Inn is conveniently located near I-465 and Highway 31. Restaurants are nearby and downtown is just minutes away. & (East/Southeast)

FORT HARRISON GOLF RESORT AND CONFERENCE CENTER
6002 N. Post Rd.
317/543-9592
$$–$$$$

This resort is situated on the edge of a 1,700-acre state park, on the site that served as Fort Benjamin Harrison from 1903 to 1995, and on an 18-acre golf course. The lodgings consist of a main house and three houses that formerly served as officers' homes. The main house features seven guest suites: the one- and two-room suites include desks and refrigerators; the VIP King, which once served as quarters for visiting generals, has a huge walk-in closet, a kitchenette, and a sitting room. Common areas include the kitchen, the front room (which has a fireplace), and the sunroom. Each of the three officers' houses has three

bedrooms, two and a half baths, a full kitchen, a dining room, a breakfast nook, and living areas. A continental breakfast is served in the lobby of the Garrison restaurant, which is within walking distance. (East/Southeast)

GREENWOOD INN FANTASUITE HOTEL
1117 E. Main St.
Greenwood
317/882-2211 or 800/444-7829
$$–$$$$

Feel like a romantic weekend in an Arabian tent, a wild night on a jungle safari, or a rendezvous in the depths of a cave? Live out your wildest fantasy in one of 20 theme rooms at this unique hotel. Choose from the Wild West, Caesar's Court, Pink Cadillac, or even Space Odyssey, among others. All theme rooms feature a hot tub. Special packages may include chocolates, flowers, body oils, and food baskets. Standard hotel rooms are available, too. & (East/Southeast)

MARRIOTT HOTEL
7202 E. 21st St.
317/352-1231 or 800/228-9290
$$$–$$$$

This 252-room, Four Diamond-rated hotel offers full-service comfort and convenience. It is located near I-70 and Shadeland Avenue, and offers amenities such as an indoor and an outdoor pool, a restaurant, a lounge, and a fitness center. The rooms have cable TV, hair dryers, irons, and ironing boards. The hotel's Concierge Level, two keyed-off floors featuring a private lounge with an attendant, offers rooms with amenities such as ergonomic chairs and larger desks for business travelers. Guests at the Marriott enjoy a free continental breakfast and hors d'oeuvres. &
(East/Southeast)

QUALITY INN SOUTH
520 E. Thompson Rd.
317/787-8341 or 800/228-5151
$$$

The 184 standard rooms in this hotel were renovated two years ago, and conveniences such as coffee makers and irons and ironing boards were added. The hotel's spacious atrium features an indoor/outdoor pool, a whirlpool, an exercise room, and a game area. Business services are available at the front desk. Guests can take the complimentary shuttle to the airport or to downtown locations. & (East/Southeast)

THE RICHARDSON HOUSE
2422 E. Southport Rd.
317/781-1119
$

Guests at the Richardson House, a stately Queen Anne–style home built in 1899, are required to stay at least one week; monthly rentals are also available. Rates include housekeeping, linens, coffee, condiments, and all paper products. The inn's two fully furnished efficiencies have full kitchens, private entrances, and private phone lines. The decor is fitting with the style of the home, yet pleasingly understated. (East/Southeast)

Bed-and-Breakfasts

CANDLESTICK INN
402 Euclid Ave.
Greenwood
317/888-3905
$$

Always overflowing with fresh flowers, candles, or holiday decorations, this bed-and-breakfast offers guests a romantic retreat in historic Greenwood. One room has a private bath and is decorated in what owner Elise Lawrence describes as "old

English doll motif." The second room features a Cape Cod motif and has a shared bath. Full breakfasts are served in the formal dining room. No credit cards are accepted. (East/Southeast)

FRIENDLINESS WITH A FLAIR
5214 E. 20th Pl.
317/356-3149
$$

This bed-and-breakfast offers all the modern comforts in a charming older home. The two rooms are cheerful, and the house is close to downtown. Each room has access to a shared bath, and a complete breakfast is served in a sunny dining room. No smoking or drinking is allowed in the house; no credit cards accepted. (East/Southeast)

PERSIMMON TREE
BED-AND-BREAKFAST
1 N. Madison Ave.
Greenwood
317/889-0849
$$–$$$

This rambling home in the heart of

Boone Docks on the River, p. 42

Boone Docks on the River

historic Greenwood is a Victorian gem. The six guest units are decorated in antiques and reproductions; three have private baths (with claw-foot tubs). The full breakfast features fresh breads and fruits. Guests can enjoy the common TV room or watch the world go by from the veranda. (East/Southeast)

STONEGATE
BED-AND-BREAKFAST
8955A Stonegate Rd.
317/887-9614
$$$

The Stonegate is not, perhaps, a typical bed-and-breakfast (it's in a luxury condo), but it's nonetheless elegant and comfortable. The guest bedroom includes a fireplace and a Jacuzzi. The condominium complex is convenient to downtown and Greenwood Park Mall. Guests have access to the living room and kitchen. Female guests will enjoy guest-pass privileges to a ladies-only gym; everyone may take advantage of massage therapy by appointment. Breakfast is made to order and served in a dining room overlooking a tiny pond. No credit cards are accepted. (East/Southeast)

Dan Francis for St. Elmo Steak House

4

WHERE TO EAT

Indianapolis is not the place to find the country's most innovative cuisine. Hoosiers still love home cookin': fried chicken, mashed potatoes, corn on the cob, and pie are perennial favorites. But that's not to say that the city is a complete culinary backwater. Like people in many other cities around the country, Indianapolites are having a love affair with pasta, Caesar salad, gourmet pizza, cappuccino, and cooking with wood. Vegetarian dishes (notably portabello mushroom sandwiches) are nudging their way into mainstream dining. And many different types of international cuisine—not just Mexican, Italian, and Chinese—are represented in Indianapolis. So while Indianapolis is no San Francisco or New York when it comes to offering the latest in food trends, visitors can still get a fine meal here. (Visitors should be warned, however, that Indy's restaurants suffer from a chronic shortage of help, due in part to the restaurant explosion of the last decade.)

In choosing the restaurants listed in this chapter—a selection of the city's best—we've included places that offer visitors flavors or features that are distinctly Hoosier. Nationwide chains and even some regional ones aren't generally included, despite the fact that they may be popular and offer delicious food. Chains listed are small ones that don't plan to expand far and new ones that are using Indianapolis as a kick-off city.

This chapter begins with a list of restaurants organized by type of food. For details about each restaurant, consult the geographical listings that follow. Most restaurants are closed on major holidays, and weekend reservations are usually advisable.

Price rating symbols:
$ $10 and under
$$ $11 to $20
$$$ $21 and up

American/Contemporary

Blue Heron (N), p.62
California Café Bar and Grill (D),
  p. 55
Daddy Jack's (N), p. 65
Dodd's Townhouse (N), p. 66
Illusions (N), p. 67
Loon Lake Lodge (N), p. 68
Lulu's Restaurant
  and Cocktails (N), p. 68
Palomino Euro Bistro (D), p. 57
Peter's Restaurant and Bar (N), p. 69
Restaurant 210 (N), p. 69
Rick's Café Boatyard (W/SW), p. 73
Shaffers' (N), p. 70

Asian

Cheng Du (N), p. 65
Daruma (N), p. 65
Forbidden City (N, W/SW), p. 66, 73
Ginza (W/SW), p. 73
India Palace (W/SW), p. 73
Kabul (N), p. 68
Sakura Japanese Restaurant (N),
  p. 70
Thai Café (N), p. 71

Breakfast

Brother Juniper's (D), p. 55
Café Patachou (N), p. 63
Deli Jack's (N), p. 66
Illinois Street Food Emporium (N),
  p. 67
Indiana Bread Co. (D), p. 57
Shapiro's Deli (N, W/SW), p. 70, 76
Sunrise Café (N), p. 71
Three Sisters Café (N), p. 71

Brewpubs/Pubs

Alcatraz Brewing Co. (D), p. 53
Broad Ripple Brewpub (N), p. 62
Elbow Room (D), p. 55
Major Tooley's Public House
  (W/SW), p. 73
Oaken Barrel (E/SE), p. 79
Union Jack Pub (N, W/SW), p. 72, 76

Continental/Fine Dining

Café Nora (N), p. 63

Chanteclair (W/SW), p. 72
Chef Rolf's European Café (N),
  p. 64
Chez Jean Restaurant Français
  (W/SW), p. 72
The Colonnade Room (E/SE), p. 76
Corner Wine Bar (N), p. 65
Hot Tuna (D), p. 56
Midtown Grill (N), p. 69
Peter's Restaurant and Bar (N),
  p. 69
Restaurant at the Canterbury (D),
  p. 59

Delis/Sandwiches/Tearooms

Arni's (N), p. 59
Bay Window (E/SE), p. 76
Brother Juniper's (D), p. 55
Café Patachou (N), p. 63
Delafield's (E/SE), p. 77
Deli Jack's (N), p. 66
The Gathering (E/SE), p. 77
Glass Gazebo (E/SE), p. 78
Illinois Street Food Emporium (N),
  p. 67
Indiana Bread Co. (D), p. 57
Lady Victoria's (E/SE), p. 78
Shapiro's Deli (N, W/SW), p. 70, 76

German

Chef Rolf's European Café (N), p. 64
Deeter's & Gabe's (N), p. 65
German American Klub (W/SW),
  p. 73
Rathskeller (D), p. 58

Hoosier Home Cooking

Dutch Oven (E/SE), p. 77
G.T. South's Rib House (N), p. 66
Hollyhock Hill (N), p. 66
Iron Skillet (W/SW), p. 73

Italian/Pizza

Amalfi (N), p. 59
Ambrosia (N), p. 59
Amici's (D), p. 53
Arni's, (N), p. 59
Arturo's Ristorante (N), p. 62

Bazbeaux (D, N), p. 55, 62
Bertolini's (D), p. 55
Bravo! (N), p. 62
Dunaway's (D), p. 55
Iaria's (D), p. 56
Il Gargano (N), p. 67
Mama Carolla's Old
   Italian Restaurant (N), p. 68
Mezzaluna (N), p. 69
Ruthellen's (D), p. 59
Sangiovese (N), p. 70
Some Guys (N), p. 70
Vito Provolone Italian Restaurant
   (E/SE), p. 79

Kid-Friendly
Acropolis (E/SE), p. 76
Arni's (N), p. 59
Blue Heron (N), p. 62
Café Patachou (N), p. 63
Dutch Oven (E/SE), p. 77
Illusions (N), p. 67
Loon Lake Lodge (N), p. 68

Mediterranean
Acropolis (E/SE), p. 76
Aesop's Tables (D), p. 53
Mediterrano Café (N), p. 69
Palomino Euro Bistro (D), p. 57

Mexican
Café Santa Fe (N), p. 64
Cancun (N), p. 64
El Sol de Tala (E/SE), p. 77
Maria's Restaurant (E/SE), p. 78

Other International
Queen of Sheba (D), p. 58
Russia House (N), p. 70

Seafood/Steaks
Bobby Joe's Beef and Brew
   (E/SE), p. 76
Bynum's Steakhouse (W/SW), p. 72
Daddy Jack's (N), p. 65
Fireside South Restaurant (W/SW),
   p. 77
George's Place (N), p. 66

Hot Tuna (D), p. 56
Johnson County Line (E/SE), p. 78
Keystone Grill (N), p. 68
Majestic Restaurant (D), p. 57
St. Elmo Steak House (D), p. 59
Sullivan's (N), p. 71

Vegetarian
Three Sisters Café (N), p. 71

DOWNTOWN

AESOP'S TABLES
600 Massachusetts Ave.
317/631-0055
$$

Aesop's specializes in the cuisines of various Mediterranean countries, including Spain and Greece. The menu includes many vegetarian selections. Closed Sunday. Lunch, dinner. &
(Downtown)

ALCATRAZ BREWING CO.
Circle Centre, 49 W. Maryland St.
317/488-1230
$$

This brewpub has a festive atmosphere and is popular with folks of all ages. Pizzas baked in the wood-burning oven and hearty sandwiches are favorites. Lunch, dinner. &
(Downtown)

AMICI'S
601 E. New York St.
317/634-0440
$$

The best choice in town for southern Italian–influenced cuisine, Amici's is markedly different from the typical upscale northern Italian restaurant. Popular dishes include mushroom paté and sautéed cod. The flavors are intense, the bread is delicious, and the portions are hearty. Closed Monday. Dinner. & (Downtown)

DOWNTOWN INDIANAPOLIS

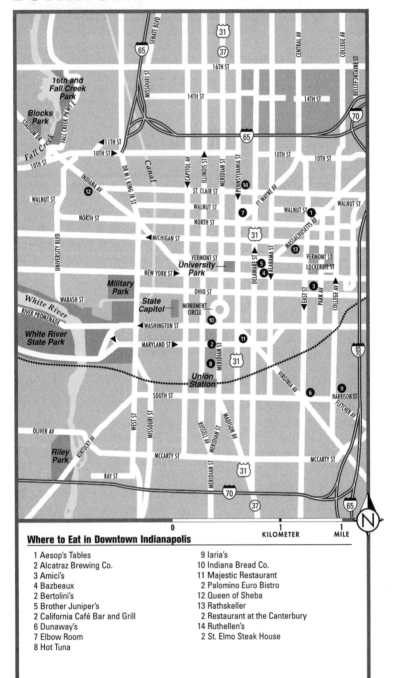

Where to Eat in Downtown Indianapolis

1 Aesop's Tables
2 Alcatraz Brewing Co.
3 Amici's
4 Bazbeaux
2 Bertolini's
5 Brother Juniper's
2 California Café Bar and Grill
6 Dunaway's
7 Elbow Room
8 Hot Tuna

9 Iaria's
10 Indiana Bread Co.
11 Majestic Restaurant
2 Palomino Euro Bistro
12 Queen of Sheba
13 Rathskeller
2 Restaurant at the Canterbury
14 Ruthellen's
2 St. Elmo Steak House

BAZBEAUX
334 Massachusetts Ave.
317/636-7662
$$

Bazbeaux started the gourmet pizza craze. The Bazbeaux Special, with goat cheese and sun-dried tomatoes, is unbeatable. The sandwiches here, often overlooked, are tasty and creative. Lunch Mon–Sat, dinner daily. ᕒ (Downtown)

BERTOLINI'S
Circle Centre,
49 W. Maryland St.
317/638-1800
www.morton.com
$$

Bertolini's, a 12-restaurant chain, serves fine Italian food, including pastas with zesty sauces and risotto. If you skip the appetizers, start the meal with a Caesar or *mista* salad. The restaurant is noisy but has an attractive nineties look. Lunch, dinner. ᕒ (Downtown)

BROTHER JUNIPER'S
339 N. Massachusetts Ave.
317/636-3115
$

Head to Brother J's for a hearty, inexpensive, simply prepared, and tasty breakfast. For lunch, try the Friar Tuck sandwich, with tuna, bacon, Swiss cheese, avocado, and sprouts. Half a sandwich and a cup of soup make an ample meal at this eatery. Credit cards and reservations are not accepted. Closed Sunday. Breakfast Mon–Fri, lunch daily. ᕒ (Downtown)

CALIFORNIA CAFÉ
BAR AND GRILL
Circle Centre, 49 W. Maryland St.
317/488-8686
$$$

This restaurant prides itself on serving fresh foods without additives and preservatives. It is also a smoke-free establishment. The presentation is elegant, and specialties include entrée-sized salads, designer pizzas, and savory pastas. Lunch, dinner, Sunday brunch. ᕒ (Downtown)

DUNAWAY'S
351 S. East St.
317/638-7663
$$$

One of the most elegant and popular new spots in downtown, this restaurant is in the historic Indiana Oxygen Building, which, when it was moved a few years ago, was the heaviest building ever moved in North America. In keeping with the original 1930s look, the restaurant is Art Deco. The extensive menu is a blend of southern Italian and chop house, with a large wine selection. Because the restaurant isn't walking distance from the heart of downtown, the management provides complimentary limousine pick-up from any downtown location and pick-up for a slight charge from locations beyond the downtown. For example, pick up from the airport is $10. In warm weather, there is rooftop dining. Lunch Mon–Fri; dinner daily. Reservations strongly recommended. ᕒ (Downtown)

ELBOW ROOM
605 N. Pennsylvania St.
317/635-3354
$$

The Elbow Room is known for consistently good pizzas, sandwiches, and other pub fare. The lunch hour is particularly busy, so arrive early or late to avoid a wait. Reservations are not accepted. Lunch Mon–Sat, dinner daily. ᕒ (Downtown)

Sweet Treats

Atkins Desserts, 15510 Stony Creek Way, Noblesville, 317/773-7739, and Clearwater Village, 4705 East 82nd St., 317/570-1850, sell celebrated cheesecakes by the cake or the slice, in addition to many other desserts. (both North)

Broad Ripple Pie Company, 5406 North College Ave., 317/259-4743, features caramel apple, cherry almond, sour-cream blueberry crunch, and Kentucky bourbon pies by the pie or slice. (North)

DeBrand Fine Chocolates and Dessert Café, 8487 Union Chapel Rd., 317/466-1100, is a tony spot that will please chocolate lovers. (North)

Delafield's, Vista Village, 50 Airport Parkway, 317/882-5282, sells sumptuous angel-food cake topped with berries. The restaurant offers a good selection of coffee plus a lunch and dinner menu. (East/Southeast)

Heidelberg Café, 7625 Pendleton Pike, 317/547-1230, is a neighborhood German café known for Bavarian cake and brownie balls with bourbon. Sandwiches and other items are also available; nutcrackers, steins, and more are for sale. (East/Southeast)

HOT TUNA
Omni Severin Hotel
40 W. Jackson Pl.
317/687-5190
$$–$$$
Whatever it is that makes most hotel food taste the same has been banished from the kitchen at this restaurant in the Omni Severin. This elegant dining spot has gained citywide recognition for its succulent seafood and other innovative dishes. Breakfast, lunch, dinner daily. ⚲ (Downtown)

IARIA'S
317 S. College Ave.
317/638-7706
$$
Informal and inexpensive, this restaurant serves traditional Italian food—sweet red sauces are a specialty. The minestrone is a meal in itself. Ask for a table in the front room, with its glass-block bar and photos of the restaurant during the heyday of the Italian community. No reservations are accepted on weekends. Lunch Tue–Fri, dinner Tue–Sat. ⚲ (Downtown)

INDIANA BREAD CO.
6 W. Washington St.
317/972-1215
$

For breakfast or lunch, you can't go wrong here. Soups, such as French onion and chicken chili, are popular. Sourdough is the signature bread. The atmosphere is casual, and patrons can dine outside in warm weather. Reservations are not accepted. Closed Sunday; Saturday in January and February. Breakfast, lunch. ♿ (Downtown)

MAJESTIC RESTAURANT
47 S. Pennsylvania St.
317/636-5418
$$$

Housed in the city's first skyscraper (which was built in 1896), the Majestic retains original elegant features, including Romanesque portals and Corinthian columns. The dining room has oriental rugs, intricately tiled floors, and a gleaming grand piano. The restaurant is renowned for its shellfish specialties. Luncheon salads and soups are exceptional. Closed Sunday. Lunch Mon–Fri, dinner daily. ♿ (Downtown)

PALOMINO EURO BISTRO
49 W. Maryland St.
317/974-0400
$$$

Palomino is an upscale restaurant that has been hot since it opened in 1996. The cooking is influenced by Mediterranean cuisine. Patrons are coddled by the upbeat staff. (It's not a good choice for those who like unobtrusive service.) Bartenders know how to mix good drinks. Everything that is cooked in the wood-fired oven and on the wood grill and spit rotisserie is superb, as is the tiramisu. The atmosphere is festive. Reservations are essential on weekends. Lunch Mon–Sat, dinner daily. ♿ (Downtown)

QUEEN OF SHEBA
936 Indiana Ave.
317/638-8426
$$

Check out the margaritas at Café Santa Fe, p. 64

Café Santa Fe

"The people who eat from the same tray will never betray one another" goes an Ethiopian saying. Appropriately, then, patrons at the Ethiopian restaurant Queen of Sheba eat with their fingers from shared trays (of course, the trays are shared among people at the same table). Diners scoop up the food with *injera*, a spongy flat bread. Meat stews and lentil dishes are staples, and there are plenty of vegetable selections, including collard greens. Queen of Sheba is a dining adventure and lots of fun. Closed Sunday and Monday (however, parties of 10 or more can reserve the restaurant on these days). Lunch Tue–Fri, dinner. & (Downtown)

RATHSKELLER
401 E. Michigan St.
317/636-0396
$$$
Built in the late 1800s and a reminder of the city's German heritage, the Rathskeller is grandly decorated with beer steins, wrought-iron fixtures, and a fabulously carved fireplace. Robust fare includes schnitzel, steaks, and chicken. In the Kellerbar, added around the turn of the century, moose and deer heads gaze at guests. Reservations are recommended on

---

Abe's Picks

Abraham Benrubi, widely known as Jerry on the hit television show E.R., gets back to his hometown, Indianapolis, and his stompin' grounds, Broad Ripple, a couple of times a year. When he's here, this is where he hangs out.

Comic Carnival, *6265 Carrollton Ave., 317/253-8882*

My mom's house in Broad Ripple and her store, **Scribble's**, *808 Broad Ripple Ave., 317/251-2331*

Stout's Shoe, *which carries size 17 EEE, my shoe size, 318 Massachusetts Ave., 317/632-7818*

Northside News, *which is owned by some of my high school buddies, 5408 North College Ave., 317/254-1288*

Some Guys Pizza, *6235 Allisonville Rd., 317/257-1364*

The Broad Ripple Brewpub, *840 East 65th St., 317/253-2739*

Jamaican Patties, *5172 Allisonville Rd., 317/253-4006*

White Castle, *on the way to the airport, 5501 West 38th St., 317/298-8821*

---

weekends. Lunch Mon–Fri, dinner Tue–Sat. ⌖ (Downtown)

RESTAURANT AT THE CANTERBURY
123 S. Illinois St.
317/634-3000
$$$
You'll feel cosseted in this fine restaurant, which has only 12 tables. Superbly prepared and presented foods, such as lamb on butterscotch and black beans, tingle all your taste buds. One savvy businesswoman said, "No one ever turns me down when I suggest a meeting over lunch at the Canterbury." A fixed price menu changes weekly. Breakfast, lunch, dinner. ⌖ (Downtown)

RUTHELLEN'S
825 N. Pennsylvania Ave.
317/631-7884
$$
Located just across the street from the library, this new restaurant is making its mark with eye-catching decor and zesty dishes. The atmosphere is peaceful and vaguely Victorian. A nonsmoking section is not available. Closed Monday. Lunch Tue–Fri, dinner, Sunday brunch. ⌖ (Downtown)

ST. ELMO STEAK HOUSE
127 S. Illinois St.
317/635-0636
$$$
Established in 1902, this is the best-known restaurant in the city and beyond. Over the years, the permanently famous and the temporarily prominent have praised the succulent steaks and perfect shrimp cocktails. Refined waiters in tuxedos provide seamless service. Make a reservation, requesting a table near the bar. Dinner. ⌖ (Downtown)

NORTH

AMALFI
1351 W. 86th St.
317/253-4034
$$$
This restaurant is a family affair for Arturo DiRosa, his three brothers, and their mother. Insiders know that Mama DiRosa personally makes the appetizers, the bread, the soups, the calamari, and the rich lemon biscotti. If bell peppers stuffed with veal are not on the menu, ask if the chef will prepare it for you anyway. Closed Sunday. Lunch Mon–Fri, dinner daily. ⌖ (North)

AMBROSIA
915 Westfield Blvd.
317/255-3096
$$$
Gino Pizzi perfected his recipe for superior Italian dining at Ambrosia, his first restaurant (he owns several other restaurants in Indianapolis, including Sangiovese). *Gamberi*, pasta della Mama, and calamari cooked to perfection are some of the best dishes from an excellent menu. The atmosphere is relaxed and upscale; diners can eat outside in warm weather. Reservations are recommended on weekends. Dinner. ⌖ (North)

ARNI'S
3443 W. 86th St.
317/875-7034
$$
Cycles of all sorts dangle from the ceiling of this restaurant: a bicycle built for five, a 1948 Indian motorcycle, a few Harleys, and some fantasy creations, such as a bicycle with oranges for wheels and a banana for the seat. Adults and children linger over Arni's burgers and salads as they try to iden-

NORTH INDIANAPOLIS

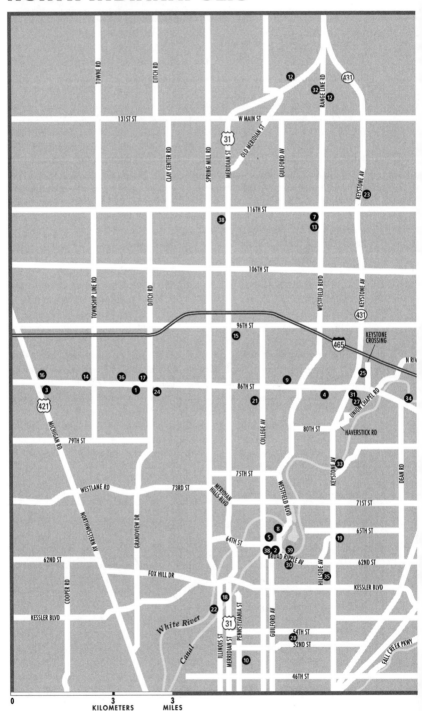

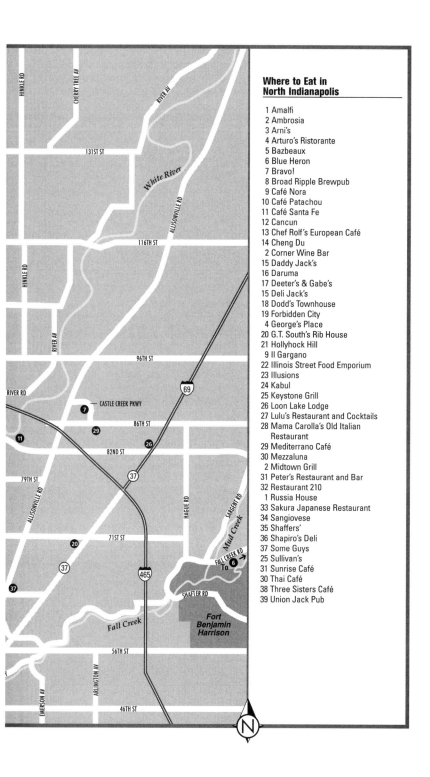

Where to Eat in North Indianapolis

1 Amalfi
2 Ambrosia
3 Arni's
4 Arturo's Ristorante
5 Bazbeaux
6 Blue Heron
7 Bravo!
8 Broad Ripple Brewpub
9 Café Nora
10 Café Patachou
11 Café Santa Fe
12 Cancun
13 Chef Rolf's European Café
14 Cheng Du
2 Corner Wine Bar
15 Daddy Jack's
16 Daruma
17 Deeter's & Gabe's
15 Deli Jack's
18 Dodd's Townhouse
19 Forbidden City
4 George's Place
20 G.T. South's Rib House
21 Hollyhock Hill
9 Il Gargano
22 Illinois Street Food Emporium
23 Illusions
24 Kabul
25 Keystone Grill
26 Loon Lake Lodge
27 Lulu's Restaurant and Cocktails
28 Mama Carolla's Old Italian
   Restaurant
29 Mediterrano Café
30 Mezzaluna
2 Midtown Grill
31 Peter's Restaurant and Bar
32 Restaurant 210
1 Russia House
33 Sakura Japanese Restaurant
34 Sangiovese
35 Shaffers'
36 Shapiro's Deli
37 Some Guys
25 Sullivan's
31 Sunrise Café
30 Thai Café
38 Three Sisters Café
39 Union Jack Pub

tify the contraptions overhead. Lunch, dinner. ♿ (North)

ARTURO'S RISTORANTE
2727 E. 86th St.
317/257-4806
$$$

Owner and chef Patrick Aasen and his wife, Beth, work hard to make Arturo's an especially hospitable eatery. Local regulars praise specialties such as chicken breast with artichokes and pistachios. The restaurant is also known for its zesty sauces, warm home-baked bread, and exquisite tiramisu. Patrons flock in for dinner, but at lunchtime you can partake for less without the crowds. Lunch Mon–Fri, dinner daily. (North)

BAZBEAUX
832 E. Westfield Blvd.
317/255-5711
$$

See full listing under Downtown. ♿ (North)

BLUE HERON
11699 Fall Creek Rd.
317/845-8899
$$–$$$

With a wall of windows and three tiers of dining space facing Geist Reservoir, this restaurant serves splendid views with meals year-round. Chicken salad, wood-grilled anything, hamburgers, and milk shakes are good. Sunday brunch is a good choice for families. A magician roams from table to table, amazing diners with his sleights of hand. Lunch and dinner Mon–Sat, Sunday brunch. ♿ (North)

BRAVO!
8651 Castle Creek Pkwy.
317/577-2211
$$–$$$

Bravo serves some of the best Italian food in town. Don't forgo the bread and olive oil, and top off dinner with raspberry cheesecake. The atmosphere is noisy but festive. If you're bothered by smoke, sit far from the bar at the Castle Creek location. The Lake Circle location is lighter and airier. No reservations are accepted. Lunch, dinner. Additional location is at 2658 Lake Circle Dr., 317/879-1444. (North)

BROAD RIPPLE BREWPUB
842 E. 65th St.
317/253-2739
$$

Opened in 1990 by British-born John Hill, this brewpub was the city's first, complete with an antique headboard-turned-bar and leaded-glass windows. The brewpub serves a solid selection of beers, many made on-site, including several with names evocative of the locale, such as Monon Porter, named after the train line that once ran only yards away, and White River Wheat. British menu items, including Scotch eggs, fish 'n'

St. Elmo Steak House, p. 59

Dan Francis for St. Elmo Steakhouse

Local Java

The Abbey Coffee House, *771 Massachusetts Ave., 317/269-8426 (Downtown); 74 W. New York St., 317/1870 (Downtown); and 6334 N. Guilford Ave., 317/251-0551 (North) (A fourth Abbey is slated to open near IUPUI by presstime. It and the North Abbey will serve breakfast.)*

Barnes & Noble Café, *3748 E. 82nd St. 317/594-7525 (North)*

Border's Books & Music, *8765 River Crossing Blvd., 317/574-1775 (North)*

Cath Inc., *222 E. Market St. (in the City Market, Downtown), 317/634-0600 and 705 E. 54th St., 317/251-2677 (North)*

Cornerstone Coffee, *651 E. 54th St., 317/726-1360 (North)*

Hubbard & Cravens, *4930 N. Pennsylvania St., 317/251-5161 (North)*

Java U, *905 Indiana Ave., 317/684-1560 (Downtown)*

KC's Coffee & Tea, *3965 E. 82nd St., 317/842-0545 (North)*

Lulu's Electric Cafe, *1460 W. 86th St. (North Willow Commons), 317/879-1995 (North)*

M.T. Cup, *314 Massachusetts Ave., 317/639-1099 (Downtown)*

Monon Coffee Co., *920 E. Westfield Blvd., 317/255-0510 (North)*

---

chips, and shepherd's pie, are the best. Reservations are not accepted. Lunch Mon–Sat, dinner daily. ♿ (North)

CAFÉ NORA
1300 E. 86th St.
317/571-1000
$$$

Good for lunch and dinner, this restaurant is clean, quiet, and intimate. Fish is a specialty, and there are several vegetarian choices and a wide range of other heart-healthy items, along with steaks and chicken.

Closed Sunday. Lunch Mon–Fri, dinner daily. ♿ (North)

CAFÉ PATACHOU
4911 N. Pennsylvania St.
317/925-2823
$–$$

Since it opened in the 1980s, Café Patachou has been one of the north side's most popular gathering spots. From the moment the first cup of coffee is poured in the morning, diners gather to nibble thick slabs of sourdough toast slathered with butter and cinnamon sugar and to savor the

Loon Lake Lodge, p. 68

omelet of the day. By noon, they are noshing on the generous sandwiches. Weekend lines move fairly quickly. There's a play area for children. No reservations are accepted. Breakfast, lunch. & (North)

CAFÉ SANTA FE
2948 E. 82nd St.
317/576-0022
$$
Red napkins folded to resemble chili peppers catch your eye as soon as you walk into this Southwestern-style eatery. The blue-corn enchiladas and burritos are the most popular items; the grilled New Mexican chili relleno is a good appetizer choice. The daily special is written on the blackboard. Closed Sunday. Lunch, dinner. & (North)

CANCUN
13710 N. Meridian St.
Carmel
317/580-0995
$$
Both locations of Cancun pass the lit-

mus test for superior Mexican cuisine: fresh, flavorful guacamole and salsa. *Taquitos Mexicanos* are consistently good. The portions are enormous, and the service is fast and friendly. Reservations are not accepted on weekends. Lunch, dinner. Additional location is at 511 S. Rangeline Rd., Carmel, 317/580-0333. & (North)

CHEF ROLF'S EUROPEAN CAFÉ
11588 Westfield Blvd.
Carmel
317/815-9990
$$–$$$
Elegant, yet cozy, this restaurant is true to its name, with Italian, French, German, and Swiss dishes filling the menu. Swiss chef Rolf Meisterhans came to Indianapolis via Aspen, Colorado, and has earned a solid reputation for his flavorful and consistently tasty cuisine. The luncheon buffet will satisfy hearty appetites, and Wednesday's German buffet is popular. Closed Sunday. Lunch Mon–Fri, dinner daily. & (North)

CHENG DU
2402 Lake Circle Dr.
317/879-9988
$$

This family-owned restaurant offers some of the city's tastiest and most unusual Chinese fare. The Crab Rangoon appetizer and the shrimp with cashew nuts are especially good. The menu includes plenty of choices for vegetarians. The service is friendly and efficient. Closed Monday. Lunch, dinner. & (North)

CORNER WINE BAR
6331 N. Guilford Ave.
317/255-5159
$$$

Inside and out, the Corner Wine Bar brings Britain to Broad Ripple. The restaurant is a top people-watching spot during the summer, when tables are set outside under an awning. The interior is cozy. Try the rich cheese-crock appetizer flavored with pecans and Guinness; the beef stew is also very satisfying. As one would expect, the bar has a good wine list. Closed Sunday. Lunch, dinner. Not easily wheelchair accessible. (North)

DADDY JACK'S
9419 N. Meridian St.
317/843-1609
$$–$$$

Daddy Jack's offers traditional American fare: pasta, steaks, chicken, and stir-fry for dinner and hearty sandwiches, such as Reubens and hot browns, for lunch. Deli Jack's has an array of ingredients for sandwiches or subs, along with pizza, soups, and salads. Kona Jack's (the most expensive of the three) features seafood, including sushi. This trio has a devoted following from the north side. Lunch and dinner at Daddy Jack's Mon–Sat; lunch at Kona Jack's Mon–Fri, dinner Mon–Sat; lunch at Deli Jack's Mon–Sat. & (North)

DARUMA
3508 W. 86th St.
317/875-9727
$$$

At the city's original Japanese restaurant, the decor is engaging, with an antique Samurai warrior's costume guarding the entry. In keeping with traditional Japanese dining customs, shoes must be removed and seating is at low tables with wells beneath them. One of the most popular dishes is the combination dinner with filet mignon, teriyaki, and shrimp tempura. There is a sushi bar. Closed Sunday. Lunch Mon–Fri, dinner daily. & (North)

DEETER'S & GABE'S
1462 W. 86th St.
317/876-1111
$$

An intimate restaurant with German flair, Deeter's & Gabe's consistently offers tasty fare. Hearty, flavorful German dishes are the specialty, but the restaurant serves lighter fare, as

If you want to be assured of a kosher meal, head for Sadie's, in the Jewish Community Center, 6701 North Hoover Rd., 317/726-5455. Dishes include favorites like Thai chicken and turkey chili. You can even pick up carryout. Call for hours. (North)

well. The restaurant exudes warmth, and the wait staff is solicitous. The mainly older clientele always seems to be having a nice time. The beer and wine lists are extensive. No reservations are accepted, but the management will find a table for large groups who call ahead. Lunch Mon–Sat, dinner daily. & (North)

DELI JACK'S
9435 N. Meridian St.
317/818-1413
A spin-off of Daddy Jack's, just a few doors south, Deli Jack's serves an array of sandwiches and subs, along with pizza, soups, and salads. Aunt Jean's Eggs Benedict is a breakfast favorite, as are pancakes; homemade desserts vary each week. Closed Sunday. Breakfast, lunch. & (North)

DODD'S TOWNHOUSE
5694 N. Meridian St.
317/257-1872
$$
Dodd's, situated in a historic farmhouse built in the 1800s, offers traditional American food such as fried chicken and steak. The menu also features heart-smart items, such as fish. The servings are generous, but diners can order smaller portions. No alcohol is served. Closed Monday. Lunch Tue–Fri, dinner daily, Sunday brunch. (North)

FORBIDDEN CITY
2605 E. 65th St.
317/257-7388
$$
Probably the best-known Asian restaurant in the city, Forbidden City serves Szechwan and Mandarin cuisine. Cashew chicken, general's chicken, and green-pepper beef are all tasty. Lunch specials, which include soup, an egg roll or chicken

wings, rice, crispy noodles, a main dish, and a fortune cookie, are a good value (between $4 and $5). Forbidden City has several other locations around town. Closed Monday. Lunch, dinner. & (North)

GEORGE'S PLACE
2727 E. 86th St.
317/255-7064
$$$
Even those who avoid beef are tempted by George's steaks and filets, finalists in the contest for the city's best beef (a sure winner has never been declared). Patrons choose their meat off a cart, and some items are cooked tableside. The dining room is large, but the seating is intimate. Reservations are strongly recommended on weekends. Closed Sunday. Dinner. & (North)

G. T. SOUTH'S RIB HOUSE
5711 E. 71st St.
317/849-6997
$$
When you hear Indianapolites arguing about who has the best ribs in town, this unassuming spot is always among the contenders. You don't go for the atmosphere (as one regular says, "There is none."); you go for the food. Ribs, pulled-pork sandwiches, and Brunswick stew are specialties. The barbecue sauce has the right amount of kick. The staff is friendly and efficient. Closed Sunday. Lunch, dinner. & (North)

HOLLYHOCK HILL
8110 N. College Ave.
317/251-229
$$
When Deborah Paul, the editor-in-chief and publisher of *Indianapolis Monthly*, has guests from L.A. "who have had their fill of juice bars and

California Café Bar and Grill in Circle Centre, p. 55

Wolfgang Puck," she takes them here. The fried chicken is first-rate. Dinners, which include an appetizer, a beverage, and dessert, are served family style, with hearty bowls of mashed potatoes, cooked-to-death green beans, and more. The atmosphere evokes memories of an earlier Hoosierdom, with waitresses in gingham uniforms and decor just this side of the fifties. White hair may predominate, but this is still a multigenerational restaurant. Smoking is not allowed. Reservations are strongly recommended and are essential for holidays. Closed Monday. Dinner. &. (North)

IL GARGANO
Nora Plaza, 1300 E. 86th St.
317/843-0226
$$ –$$$

When Italian Antoinette Bonfitto married an American, she brought a slice of her home region, Gargano, to Indy. Dishes such as fettuccine with peppers and artichoke hearts are loaded with zesty, rich flavors. The calamari and tiramisu are quite good. Poster-sized family photos add charm to this comfy restaurant. Reservations are recommended on weekends. Closed Monday. Lunch Tue–Fri, dinner daily. &. (North)

ILLINOIS STREET FOOD EMPORIUM
5500 N. Illinois St.
317/253-9513
$–$$

This cozy restaurant draws people from around the city, in large part because of its baked goods: the croissants, cookies, brownies, cakes, and pies are irresistible. The sandwiches are hearty and the pancakes are outstanding. Diners order food and drinks at one counter and pick up drinks at another—a bit confusing. No reservations are accepted. Closed Sunday. Breakfast, lunch, and dinner. &. (North)

ILLUSIONS
969 Keystone Way
Carmel
317/575-8312
www.illusionsrestaurant.com

If you're a David Letterman fan, stop by Atlas Super Market, 5411 North College Ave., 317/255-6800 (North). Letterman bagged groceries here during high school. There's a good deli for carryout.

$$–$$$

Illusions entertains adults and children with hocus-pocus and dinner. Choose among cleverly named entrées, such as Alakazam (lamb chops) and Houdini's Escape (rib eye), and enjoy the entertainment as first-rate magicians roam from table to table. Closed Sunday. Dinner. & (North)

KABUL
8553 Ditch Rd.
317/257-1213
$$

The owners of Kabul expertly prepare and proudly serve the complex cuisine of their native Afghanistan (which is similar in many respects to Indian food). The restaurant's signature soup, served with every entrée, is a spicy, rich beef broth with noodles. Portions are generous. Closed Sunday and Monday. Dinner. & (North)

KEYSTONE GRILL
8650 Keystone Crossing
317/848-5202
$$$

Seafood is the specialty at this upscale restaurant. The Norwegian salmon is succulent, and the Maryland crab cakes, grilled tuna, and mahimahi are exceptional. This is a popular spot for expense-account luncheons. The Keystone Grill is not the place to bring your kids: No one under 18 is allowed to eat here. Lunch Mon–Sat, dinner daily. Sunday brunch. & (North)

LOON LAKE LODGE
6880 E. 82nd St.
317/845-9011
$$$

The décor in this northwoods-style lodge is welcoming and whimsical. The walls are made from hewn wood and the fireplaces are large. Animated bears on a log try to get honey from a hive; a skunk pops out of a wading boot; the twinkle lights above the bar are actually shaped like the constellations. But the Loon Lake Lodge offers diners more than just eye candy; the food is flavorful and handsomely presented. Game dishes, including elk and mountain trout, are a specialty. Lunch, dinner. & (North)

LULU'S RESTAURANT
AND COCKTAILS
8487 Union Chapel Rd.
317/251-5858
$$–$$$

This vibrant, upbeat restaurant is as cosmopolitan as its sister, the Midtown Grill; owner Hamada Ibrhim has a flair for design. The warm colors are intended to create an atmosphere reminiscent of the Caribbean. The food is contemporary American, and there's not a dull item on the menu, which changes regularly. Desserts, too, are great. Closed Sunday. Lunch, Mon–Fri, dinner daily. & (North)

MAMA CAROLLA'S
OLD ITALIAN RESTAURANT

1031 E. 54th St.
317/879-9988
$$

Walk into Mama Carolla's through the 54th Street door and you'll find yourself in a warm waiting area with soft lighting and a fireplace; come in through the parking lot and you're in the noisy bar. The building is divided into several rooms, each with a different ambience. The food is superb: the rich cream and zesty tomato-based sauces are delicious. This restaurant is always crowded and does not take reservations. Closed Sunday and Monday. Dinner. & (North)

MEDITERRANO CAFÉ
Pavilion at Castleton
5941 E. 86th St.
317/595-0399
$$

The strip-mall exterior of this restaurant is unremarkable, and the interior décor is an odd mixture of casual and formal. But the delightful soups, dolmas, hummus, kabobs, and baklava more than compensate for the lack of ambience. No alcohol is served. Closed Sunday. Lunch, dinner. & (North)

MEZZALUNA
927 Broad Ripple Ave.
317/255-9300
$$–$$$

Whether you choose to make a meal out of appetizers or leap to the pastas and other entrées, you'll find an enticing selection of innovative Italian fare at Mezzaluna. Pasta primavera with lots of garlic, penne alla vodka, and fish specials are reliably wonderful. House wines by the glass are good and inexpensive. The personable waiters and waitresses like to point out their own favorites. In warm weather diners can eat out-

side. Reservations are accepted for parties of six or more only. Closed Sunday. Lunch, dinner. (North)

MIDTOWN GRILL
815 Westfield Blvd.
317/253-1141
$$$

With big-city style and sophistication, the Midtown Grill offers some of the best contemporary cuisine in town. The restaurant's innovative chef brings in flavors from around the world. You might dine on walnut-encrusted rack of lamb, steak, or sea bass with couscous. The decor is contemporary and stylized. There's outdoor dining in warm weather. Lunch Mon–Fri, dinner daily. & (North)

PETER'S RESTAURANT AND BAR
8505 Keystone Crossing Blvd.
317/465-1155 or 800/479-0909
$$$

Always in vogue, Peter's is renowned for its distinctive Midwestern cuisine. The menu changes seasonally, but there's always fish, beef, and fowl. Although pricey, the salads are superb, as is the bread. Ice creams, sorbet, and other desserts are made on-site. During warm weather, diners enjoy a screened-in verandah and an outdoor cocktail area. Décor is contemporary and sophisticated. Closed Sunday. Dinner. (North)

RESTAURANT 210
210 N. Range Line Rd.
Carmel
317/582-1414
$$

A charming old house, with a back deck for outside dining, provides a warm and cozy setting for this upscale eatery. The menu changes monthly, but the items are consistently good (and best at dinner).

Soups are particularly tasty. This would be a fine choice for a romantic dinner or for a larger party to celebrate a special occasion. Closed Sunday. Lunch Mon–Sat, dinner Tue–Sat. &. (North)

RUSSIA HOUSE
1475 W. 86th St.
317/876-7990
$$

Vareniki (stuffed dumplings) and cabbage rolls are specialties here, and the owner is particularly proud of his stroganoff. Try an Estonian beer. The front room features traditional Russian decor; the back room has a cottage look. Closed Sunday. Dinner. &. (North)

SAKURA JAPANESE RESTAURANT
7201 N. Keystone Ave.
317/259-4171
$$

Widely considered the best sushi bar in town, Sakura has an extensive menu that includes dishes from several Asian countries. Diners often stand in a line that goes out the door for lunch and dinner. Sushi-lovers should try the Hoosier roll and the soft-shell crab roll. Smokers and nonsmokers aren't well separated in this small space. Although there is no dress code, blue jeans and t-shirts are rare. Sakura also owns Sakura Ocean Grill, 1206 West 86th Street, 317/848-8901, which is a larger restaurant with a similar menu; the original location seems, though, to be more popular. Closed Monday. Lunch Tue–Sat, dinner daily. &. (North)

SANGIOVESE
4110 E. 82nd St.
317/596-0731
$$$

The flavors of Tuscany predominate in this elegant yet casual restaurant. The risotto, rack of lamb, and breast of duck are stellar. In warm weather diners can eat outside. Closed Sunday. Lunch Mon–Fri, dinner daily. &. (North)

SHAFFERS'
6125 N. Hillside Ave.
317/253-1404
$$$

If you thought fondue had gone away with Herman's Hermits—surprise! This eatery has kept the cooking pots heated through the first and second incarnations of bell bottoms. Diners cook their food at their tables. The superior wine list, which features more than 300 wines, has won national awards. Lunch Mon–Fri, dinner daily. &. (North)

SHAPIRO'S DELI
2370 W. 86th St.
317/872-7255
$

This is cafeteria-style comfort food at its best, and long lines prove it. (Don't worry, they move swiftly.) Potato pancakes with applesauce, liverwurst, corned beef on rye, and more are served in satisfying portions. Your first bite of homemade macaroni and cheese will bring back the tastes of childhood. The brisket is always tops. Pass up desserts at the head of the line; they're not as good as they look. Reservations and charge cards are not accepted. Breakfast, lunch, dinner. &. (North)

SOME GUYS
6235 Allisonville Rd.
317/257-1364
$$

Founded by former Bazbeaux employees, this restaurant serves marvelous pizza. Try the four-cheese pizza with pecans or the barbecued-chicken

Sullivan's

pizza. The pasta dishes, often overlooked and in Paul Bunyan portions, are also good. The decor is unimaginative. There's often live music during the weekend. Reservations are not accepted. Closed Monday. Lunch, dinner. & (North)

SULLIVAN'S
Keystone at the Crossing
3316 E. 86th St.
317/580-1280
$$$
The ambience at Sullivan's is reminiscent of an era of martinis, cigars, bravado, and the heavyweight champ himself, John L. Sullivan. Diners are pampered with complimentary parking and an attentive wait staff. As might be expected of a Texas-based chain (there are nine Sullivan's scattered across the country), the specialty is big, succulent steaks. Try mashed potatoes with horseradish (two or three people can split this side dish and, for that matter, any other side order). The martinis are excellent. Closed Sunday. Dinner. & (North)

SUNRISE CAFÉ
3309 E. 86th St.
317/253-8266
11452 N. Meridian St.
Carmel
317/575-9323
$
The 86th Street location is cozy and bright, while the Meridian Street location is open and subdued. Both have scrumptious food. The Eggs Benedict, the hash browns, and the cinnamon rolls are all winners. Bread for sandwiches is freshly baked. Reservations are accepted for large parties only. Breakfast, lunch. & (North)

THAI CAFÉ
1041 Broad Ripple Ave.
317/722-1008
$$
Pad Thai and *thom yum gai* are finally wriggling their ways into the Indianapolis culinary lexicon thanks to this centrally located, first-rate restaurant and its typically Thai menu. The chefs here will make dishes in varying degrees of spiciness, so tongues need not be afire. Coconut milk, curry, peanuts, and cilantro, common in the Thai diet, delight local diners as well. Reservations are accepted for groups of six or more only. Closed Tuesday. Lunch Mon and Wed–Sat, dinner daily. & (North)

THREE SISTERS CAFÉ
6360 Guilford Ave.
317/257-5666
$
Tuck your *New York Times* crossword puzzle under your arm and head to Three Sisters for a leisurely breakfast. This inviting restaurant in an old Victorian offers many vegetarian dishes and a great selection of home-baked

Best Views in Town

1. **Eagle's Nest**, the rotating restaurant atop the Hyatt Regency, 1 South Capitol Ave., 317/632-1234. Offers panorama views of the city. (Downtown)
2. **Corner Wine Bar**, 6331 North Guilford Ave., 317/255-5159. Situated on the prime people-watching corner in Broad Ripple. (North)
3. **Rick's Café Boatyard**, 4050 Dandy Tr., 317/290-9300. Provides sunset views over Eagle Creek; need we say more? (West/Southwest)

muffins, breads, and scones. Closed Monday. Breakfast, lunch, dinner. & (North)

UNION JACK PUB
924 Broad Ripple Ave.
317/257-4343
$$
This British-style pub has consistently good pizzas, sandwiches, and other pub fare. Reservations are not accepted on weekends. Lunch, dinner. & (North)

WEST/SOUTHWEST

BYNUM'S STEAKHOUSE
3850 S. Meridian St.
317/784-9880
$$–$$$
Bynum's prepares some of the best steaks in town, in addition to creative seafood dishes—including succulent swordfish steak and a gargantuan 24-ounce lobster tail. Locals swear by this place. The decor is rustic, with hewn cedar walls, butcher-block tables, and captain's chairs. You'll know

that you've arrived when you see steers in the yard. Lunch, dinner. & (West/Southwest)

CHANTECLAIR
Holiday Inn Select at the Airport
2501 S. High School Rd.
317/243-1040
$$$
Back in 1969, when Indy's restaurant choices were meager, Chanteclair opened to great fanfare, and the restaurant is still earning praise. In 1998 it won the award for the best restaurant in the Holiday Inn chain worldwide. Waiters prepare dishes such as Caesar salad and crêpes Suzette tableside. The formally dressed wait staff is loyal: many of them have been around for 20 years. A strolling violinist adds charm. Closed Sunday. Dinner. & (West/Southwest)

CHEZ JEAN RESTAURANT FRANÇAIS
8821 S. State Rd. 67
Camby
317/831-0870
$$$

Indianapolis's original French restaurant is improbably attached to a 1950s motel in an even more improbable rural-industrial area. Chez Jean now has plenty of competition, but it still tops the list for traditional French cuisine. A current favorite is fillet in white wine cognac with mushrooms, topped with a lobster tail. The ersatz decor is overwhelming and charming all at once. Chez Jean is ideal for those who want to practice French. Dinner Tue–Sat, Sunday brunch. ⚒ (West/Southwest)

FORBIDDEN CITY
3837 N. High School Rd.
317/298-3588
$$
See full listing under North. ⚒ (West/Southwest)

GERMAN AMERICAN KLUB
8602 S. Meridian St.
317/888-6940
$$
Located in German Park, this restaurant was once a private club for the German community. Today, anyone can stop by for traditional German cuisine. The setting is casual, and the restaurant also serves American fare. Closed Sunday and Monday. Dinner. ⚒ (West/Southwest)

GINZA
5380 W. 38th St.
317/298-3838
$$$
At this Japanese steakhouse, the staff is having as much fun as you are as they prepare your meal tableside. There's also a sushi bar. The lunch menu, which has many of the same dishes as the dinner menu, only in smaller portions, is also the children's dinner menu. Lunch, dinner. ⚒ (West/Southwest)

INDIA PALACE
4213 Lafayette Rd.
317/298-0773
www.indyshopping.com
$$
Despite its odd location in a strip mall north of Lafayette Square, this restaurant has a steadily growing clientele. Ingredients such as coconut, raisins, curry, and mango are used to create exotic treats. Basmati rice dishes, including rice pudding, are favorites. Try a mango milk shake. There's a $5 minimum charge for dinners. Lunch, dinner. ⚒ (West/Southwest)

IRON SKILLET
2489 W. 30th St.
317/923-6353
$$
Pan-fried chicken is the first choice for diners at this family-style restaurant, around since 1953. Pike, steak, and salmon are also on the menu, and all include extras. Closed Monday and Tuesday. Lunch Sunday, dinner daily. ⚒ (West/Southwest)

MAJOR TOOLEY'S PUBLIC HOUSE
7445 W. 10th St.
317/271-6262
$$
Homemade soups and sandwiches are popular in this pub-style restaurant, along with pasta, steaks, and fresh salads. Reservations are not accepted. Lunch, dinner. ⚒ (West/Southwest)

RICK'S CAFÉ BOATYARD
4050 Dandy Tr.
317/290-9300
$$
Located on the shore of Eagle Creek Reservoir, Rick's offers some of the best scenery in town and a contemporary menu that includes pizza baked in

E/SE AND W/SW INDIANAPOLIS

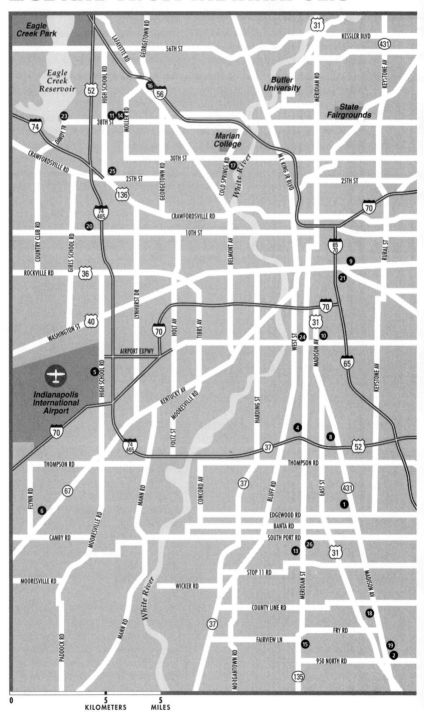

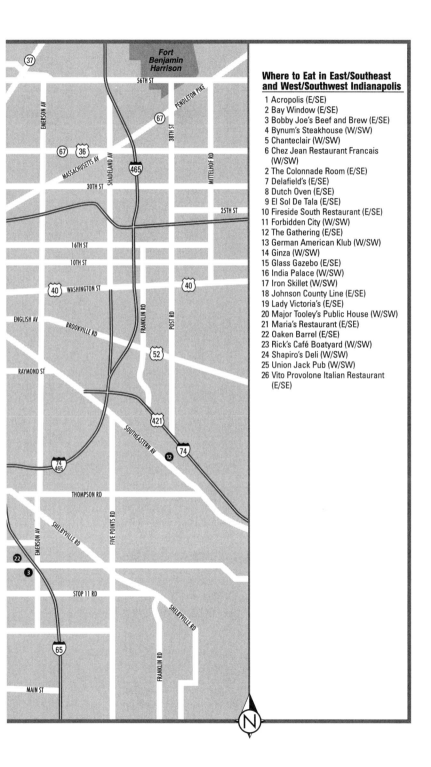

Where to Eat in East/Southeast and West/Southwest Indianapolis

1 Acropolis (E/SE)
2 Bay Window (E/SE)
3 Bobby Joe's Beef and Brew (E/SE)
4 Bynum's Steakhouse (W/SW)
5 Chanteclair (W/SW)
6 Chez Jean Restaurant Francais (W/SW)
2 The Colonnade Room (E/SE)
7 Delafield's (E/SE)
8 Dutch Oven (E/SE)
9 El Sol De Tala (E/SE)
10 Fireside South Restaurant (E/SE)
11 Forbidden City (W/SW)
12 The Gathering (E/SE)
13 German American Klub (W/SW)
14 Ginza (W/SW)
15 Glass Gazebo (E/SE)
16 India Palace (W/SW)
17 Iron Skillet (W/SW)
18 Johnson County Line (E/SE)
19 Lady Victoria's (E/SE)
20 Major Tooley's Public House (W/SW)
21 Maria's Restaurant (E/SE)
22 Oaken Barrel (E/SE)
23 Rick's Café Boatyard (W/SW)
24 Shapiro's Deli (W/SW)
25 Union Jack Pub (W/SW)
26 Vito Provolone Italian Restaurant (E/SE)

a wood-burning oven, pasta, and steaks. Blending black beans, fresh veggies, sour cream, and a bit of cantaloupe, the chef has concocted an unusual black bean soup. You may spot a player for the Indianapolis Colts here; their training facility is moments away. Head here for the view and accept good food as a bonus. Reservations are not accepted. Lunch, dinner, Sunday brunch. ♿ (West/Southwest)

SHAPIRO'S DELI
808 S. Meridian St.
317/631-4041
$
See full listing under North (this is the original location). (West/Southwest)

UNION JACK PUB
6225 W. 25th St.
317/243-3300
$$
See full listing under North. ♿ (West/Southwest)

EAST/SOUTHEAST

ACROPOLIS
1625 E. Southport Rd.
317/787-8883
$$
Start with *tiropita* or *saganaki*, a flaming cheese dish. Undecided? Try the sampler, which has tastes of everything, with enough left over for your doggie bag. Of course, there's Ouzo at the bar, as well as Greek beers and wines. When the belly dancer comes in gyrating (Friday and Saturday), you'll forget your gyros and begin clapping with the crowd. Acropolis is a good family choice. Reservations are accepted for parties of six or more. Closed Sunday. Lunch, dinner. ♿ (East/Southeast)

BAY WINDOW
202 W. Main St.
Greenwood
317/882-1330
$
One of the darlings of downtown Greenwood, the Bay Window has been serving tasty and prettily presented luncheons since 1983, including homemade soups and quiche. Decorated with antiques, the restaurant is pleasant and restful. Charge cards are not accepted. Closed Sunday and Monday. Lunch. ♿ (East/Southeast)

BOBBY JOE'S BEEF AND BREW
4425 Southport Crossings Way
317/882-2333 (BEEF)
$$
Born and bred in Indianapolis, Bobby Joe was known nationwide as Bob Collins, sportswriter. Journalism awards, sports memorabilia, photos, and more decorate the walls. Specialties and heart-healthy items are noted on the menu. No one under 21 is allowed in the restaurant. Reservations are not accepted. Lunch, dinner. ♿ (East/Southeast)

THE COLONNADE ROOM
230 W. Main St.
Greenwood
317/887-6980
$$$
New in 1998, the Colonnade Room brings fine dining to Greenwood. A marble entryway and subdued, warm colors set the tone for an elegant evening. The menu has a continental and French flair, with a variety of main courses, including salmon, pork medallions, and a wonderful selection of melt-in-your-mouth chicken dishes. The menu changes seasonally. Closed Sunday and Monday. Dinner. ♿ (East/Southeast)

TRIVIA

What's Hoosier cooking? According to native Carl Huckaby, named 1996 Chef of the Year by the American Culinary Federation, it's fried biscuits with apple butter, persimmon pudding, and farm cooking, such as corn, pork chops, and chicken and dumplings.

DELAFIELD'S
Vista Village, 50 Airport Pkwy.
317/882-5282
$–$$
Delafield's satisfying soups and sandwiches make the restaurant a particularly good choice for lunch. The decor is pleasant but plain. Save room for coffee and dessert—all the choices are top-notch. Closed Sunday and Monday. Breakfast Saturday, lunch, dinner. ⑇ (East/Southeast)

DUTCH OVEN
4004 S. East St.
317/784-0305
$
The Dutch Oven is the place where baked goods are created for all the restaurants in the Laughner's cafeteria chain. The aroma is intoxicating. The big, airy dining room is welcoming to families, and the restaurant serves traditional fare, such as hamburgers, country-fried steak, and BLTs. This is a good place to bring a family for an inexpensive meal. Reservations are not accepted. Breakfast, lunch, dinner. ⑇ (East/Southeast)

EL SOL DE TALA
2444 E. Washington St.
317/635-8252
$$
El Sol De Tala lies just east of the parking lot where the limousines topped with giant chickens are parked. Inside you'll find a business crowd eating fresh, authentic Mexican dishes. Piquant guacamole is made several times a day. The tostados and tamales are tasty. Lunch, dinner. ⑇ (East/Southeast)

FIRESIDE SOUTH RESTAURANT
552 E. Raymond St.
317/788-4521
$$$
At noon, executives cloistered in downtown office towers slip away to the south side and eat hearty American food at the Fireside. Steaks on sizzling platters, fried oysters, and beef Manhattan are favorites for lunch and dinner. The local crowd claims the Fireside (named in 1939 after President Roosevelt's chats) is the best of the best. The same family has owned the restaurant since 1946. Closed Sunday. Lunch Mon–Fri, dinner daily. ⑇ (East/Southeast)

THE GATHERING
8814 Southeastern Ave.
317/862-5545
$
You'll tool down a country road to find this little tearoom in Wanamaker. It's where the bridge clubs gather for chicken salad, tasty soups, and bread pudding with whiskey pecan sauce. Customers love being fussed over by the waitresses. No liquor is served, and the restaurant is nonsmoking.

Lunch Tue–Fri and the first Saturday of each month. ♿ (East/Southeast)

GLASS GAZEBO
385 N. State Rd. 135
Greenwood
317/888-6151
$

In a yellow building trimmed in white latticework, the Glass Gazebo started as a tearoom and gift shop but is now staking its reputation on its cuisine. Chicken crêpes are a favorite for lunch and brunch, while heavier fare, such as prime rib and coconut-breaded shrimp, is offered on the dinner menu. Lunch Mon–Sun, dinner Thu–Sat. ♿ (East/Southeast)

JOHNSON COUNTY LINE
1265 N. Madison Ave.
Greenwood
317/887-0404
$$–$$$

Although this restaurant specializes in prime rib and steaks, it also offers plenty of seafood and a few vegetarian items. The dessert specialty is a flaming European chocolate fondue, served with marshmallows, pound-cake, and fruit. The décor is rustic. Dinner. ♿ (East/Southeast)

LADY VICTORIA'S
201 N. Madison Ave.
Greenwood
317/849-0487
$

This cheerful tearoom is fittingly located in quaint Greenwood. The menu offers such standard items as grilled chicken Caesar salad, roast beef sandwiches, and club sandwiches. The desserts are mostly homemade and tempting. Upstairs there's a stash of gift items for sale. Closed Sunday. Lunch. ♿ (East/Southeast)

MARIA'S RESTAURANT
1702 Southeastern Ave.
317/685-9061
$

Like many of the city's authentic Mexican restaurants, Maria's isn't in a prime location. Fresh ingredients and

Corner Wine Bar in Broad Ripple, p. 65

The Indianapolis Project

**T
i
P**

Twenty years ago, you'd be hard pressed to find a restaurant open after 10 p.m. Today, you can dine 24 hours a day at Modern Times, Urban Truck Stop, 5363 North College Ave., 317/253-7876. The diverse menu includes Dan Quayle's Potato Omelet, royal Moroccan couscous, and espresso drinks.

food prepared to order attract downtown businesspeople and Mexican Americans from the neighborhood. The service is okay. Access to the bathroom is outside, and there isn't a nonsmoking section. Lunch, early dinner (closes at 6 p.m.) Mon–Sat. (East/Southeast)

OAKEN BARREL
50 N. Airport Pkwy.
Greenwood
317/887-2287
$$
First and foremost a brewpub, the Oaken Barrel is shipping its beer to bars and restaurants around the state, and the brew master has won a national award for Razz-Wheat. Ribs are the most popular menu item (cleverly illustrated). The fries are good, too. The 18-and-over crowd flocks to the outside beer garden during the summer; there's also a brew house. Lunch, dinner. & (East/Southeast)

VITO PROVOLONE ITALIAN
RESTAURANT
8031 S. Meridian St.
317/888-1112
$$

Tucked in a strip mall behind an Amoco station, Vito Provolone presents simple choices—lasagna, spaghetti with meatballs, chicken Marsala—but the flavors are complex and satisfying. There's a selection of gourmet (but not daring) pizzas. The atmosphere is friendly and casual, and the service is attentive. Weekend reservations are accepted for parties of eight or more only. Lunch Mon–Fri, dinner daily. & (East/Southeast)

Hot New Restaurant

This restaurant is making a BIG splash in Indy's downtown restaurant landscape. **Agio**, *located at 635 Massachusetts Avenue, 317/488-0359, combines fine food and art. The bent is Italian, with treats such as cioppino and penne primavera, but their steaks and filets are also superb.*

Artsgarden

5

SIGHTS AND ATTRACTIONS

Most Indianapolis sights are in the downtown area, making Indy an easy city to tour. In the city center, you can see war memorials galore and an abundance of sports-related facilities, including Market Square Arena and Pan Am Plaza. The latter was built to commemorate the Pan American Games held in Indianapolis in 1987 and flies the flags of the 38 nations that participated in the games. Once you roam beyond downtown, you'll find elegant homes to tour, neighborhoods to explore, and more.

Begin your visit at the Indianapolis City Center (listed on page 84), where you can see a diorama of downtown and find brochures about the area's attractions. Employees have the inside track on what's happening and can help you plan your visit.

DOWNTOWN

ATHENAEUM
401 E. Michigan St.
317/630-4569
Designed by Bernard Vonnegut (grandfather of noted author and Indianapolis native Kurt Vonnegut), the Athenaeum, originally called *Das Deutsche Haus*, was once the center of the city's German life. Begun in 1893 and completed in 1898, this grand example of German Renaissance revival architecture has been undergoing restoration work since

1991. It houses the Rathskeller (the city's oldest restaurant), a branch of the YMCA (the city's oldest functioning gymnasium), a beer garden with a stylish band shell, and the American Cabaret Theatre. The building is mentioned in several Kurt Vonnegut works and is the setting for scenes in the movies *Going All the Way* and *Eight Men Out*. Beyond poking around on your own after dinner or before a show, you can schedule a tour by calling the above number in advance and selecting option one. ♿ (Downtown)

DOWNTOWN INDIANAPOLIS

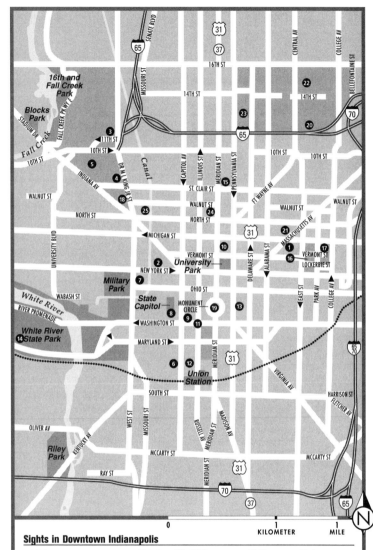

Sights in Downtown Indianapolis

1 Athenaeum
2 Bethel African Methodist
   Episcopal Church
3 Crispus Attucks Museum
4 Heritage Learning Center
5 Historic Ransom Place
   (shaded area)
6 Indiana Convention
   Center and RCA Dome
7 Indiana Historical Society
8 Indiana State Capitol
   Building
9 Indiana Theatre

10 Indiana World War
   Memorial
11 Indianapolis Artsgarden
12 Indianapolis City Center
13 Indianapolis City Market
14 Indianapolis Zoo
15 Indianapolis-Marion
   County Public Library
16 James Whitcomb
   Riley Home
17 Lockerbie Square
18 Madame Walker
   Theatre Center

19 Monument Circle
20 Morris-Butler House
21 Murat Centre
22 Old Northside (shaded
   area)
23 President Banjamin
   Harrison Home
24 Scottish Rite Cathedral
19 Soldiers and Sailors
   Monument
25 USS Indianapolis
   Memorial

Morris-Butler House, p. 88

HERITAGE TOURISM CORRIDOR
Between Indiana Ave., Central Canal, and 16th St.

This area of Indianapolis is rich in structures that were and are important to the city's African American community. The best known of the sights is the **Madame Walker Theatre Center** because it continues to play a significant role in the city's cultural life.

But there are other sights as well, including the **Crispus Attucks Museum**, 1140 Dr. Martin Luther King Jr. Street, 317/226-4613, and the **Bethel African Methodist Episcopal Church**, 414 West Vermont Street, 317/634-7002, which was organized in 1836 and moved to this site in 1869.

The area is also home to **Historic Ransom Place**, a vibrant African American neighborhood during the early part of this century. It is listed on the National Register of Historic Places not for its architecture but for its ethnic heritage. Today, visitors can tour the area by taking a walking or driving tour; yard markers explain each building's place in local history.

The **Heritage Learning Center**, 830 Dr. Martin Luther King Jr. Street, 317/632-2340, is an African American heritage museum and headquarters for the corridor. This makes it an ideal starting point for a corridor visit. In addition to touring the museum home, with its antique furniture and other items of historical interest, visitors can grab a corridor brochure and route map here. Although the center is open daily, call ahead. (Downtown)

INDIANA CONVENTION CENTER AND RCA DOME
100 S. Capitol Ave.
317/237-3663 (DOME)
www.iccrd.com

With a hope and a prayer for a pro football team and a real need to expand its convention center, Indianapolis broke ground for the then–Hoosier Dome when the Colts were still ensconced in Baltimore. Today, the dome, staggering in size, is booked with conventions, concerts, and even a church service or two, in addition to being home to the Colts. On days when the stadium is not in use, you can tour the stadium portion of the complex, beginning with a show (complete with lasers and confetti) at the Indianapolis City Center. Call ahead for the tour schedule. Tours Mon–Sat 11, 1, 3; Sun 1, 3. Price: $5 adults, $4 children 5–17 and seniors, $2 show only. &
(Downtown)

INDIANA HISTORICAL SOCIETY
450 W. Ohio St.
317/232-1882
www.indianahistory.org

Slated to open in June 1999, this building has a pleasing facade of Indiana limestone, granite, and brick, with an airy, inviting interior. Visitors

Movie Lover's Tour

Indianapolis may not be in great demand as a location for shooting movies, but a fair amount of filming has taken place in Indy over the years. Below is a list of films that were partially shot in town and the locations where the filming took place. Unless an address is shown, directions are given under the location's listing elsewhere in this book.

Going All the Way *(1997, screenplay by Indianapolite Dan Wakefield): Athenaeum, Fountain Square, Herron School of Art, the Indiana Transportation Museum, and the Red Key Tavern, 5170 North College Ave.*

Roommates *(1995): Bush Stadium*

Eight Men Out *(1988): Athenaeum, Bush Stadium, Federal Court Building, 46 East Ohio St., Propylaeum, 1410 North Delaware St.*

Hoosiers *(1985): Hinkle Fieldhouse at Butler University*

Winning *(1969): Indianapolis Motor Speedway*

will be welcome to explore the society's research library, where one will be able to peruse rare manuscripts, photographs, and more, and to tour the Sounds of Indiana room, honoring Hoosier musicians from Cole Porter to John Mellencamp. A gallery will display changing exhibits featuring famous Hoosiers, including Tecumseh, Madame Walker, and Eugene Debs. A gift shop will sell things Hoosier and historical, notably the Indiana Historical Society's own books. On the canal level of the building, a café will be open to the public. Open Tue and Thu 10–8, Wed, Fri, and Sat 10–5, Sun noon–5. Library closes daily at 5. Free. ⓖ (Downtown)

INDIANAPOLIS ARTSGARDEN
Intersection of Washington and Illinois Sts.
317/631-3301
www.indyarts.org
Operated by the Arts Council of Indianapolis, the glass-encased Artsgarden is an ideal place to discover what is happening in the local art community and perhaps catch a free performance. Since its opening in 1995, hundreds of performances and exhibitions have been held each year in the 12,500-foot-square space, which is connected to Circle Centre mall. The Artsgarden is also home to Ticket Central, which sells tickets to events put on by local arts and cultural organizations. Open Mon–Sat

9–9, Sun 12–6. Free. (See Chapter 11 for more information.) ♿ (Downtown)

INDIANAPOLIS CITY CENTER
Pan Am Plaza, 201 S. Capitol Ave.
317/237-5206 or 800/323-4639 (INDY)
www.indy.org

Start your visit right by starting it here. With the help of city-savvy volunteers, maps, and hundreds of brochures, you can plan excursions throughout Indianapolis. There's a model of downtown that lets visitors push buttons to light up selected sights. Souvenir shoppers will salivate over the Indy-related trinkets on sale here. RCA Dome tours depart from here. Information about statewide attractions is also available. Open Mon–Fri 10–5:30, Sat 10–5, Sun noon–5. Free. ♿ (Downtown)

INDIANAPOLIS CITY MARKET
222 E. Market St.
317/634-9266

Farmers sold their produce and meat at this market when the building was erected in 1886. Then, as today, citizens must have appreciated the enormous windows that wash the interior with light. At first the market had a companion building—a hunk of its ruin stands today in the spacious plaza, which is dotted with outdoor diners at noontime in warm weather. Since its renovation in the mid-seventies, City Market has been humming with vendors, some of whom sell fresh produce. You can also grab a sandwich, cappuccino, and souvenirs. From June through October in the late morning/early afternoon, the market becomes a farmers market, featuring exclusively Hoosier-grown produce. From June through November, performances are given on the plaza in the late morning/early afternoon (indoors when it's raining).

Open Mon–Sat 6–6; hours for individual stands vary. ♿ (Downtown)

INDIANAPOLIS-MARION COUNTY PUBLIC LIBRARY
Central Library, 40 E. St. Clair St.
317/269-1700
www.imcpl.lib.in.us.org

The first Indianapolis Public Library opened in 1873, and its volumes were shuffled from building to building until they came to rest, in 1917, in today's Central Library. The property, once called St. Clair Square, was in part donated by the altruistic James Whitcomb Riley. Built for the then-stunning price of more than half a million dollars, the library was widely viewed as one of the finest in the country. Since then, there have been additions, but the massive building retains its majestic feel. Today, the library (and its many branches) hosts films, lectures, and art retrospectives, in addition to lending tapes, films, paintings, and,

See the wildlife at the Indianapolis Zoo.

© Rich Clark

oh yes, books. Open Mon–Fri 9–9, Sat 9–5, Sun 1–5. Free. (For more information, see also Chapters 7 and 8.) ♿ (Downtown)

INDIANAPOLIS ZOO
1200 W. Washington St.
317/630-2001
www.indyzoo.com

You can talk to the animals at this zoo, where creatures great and small thrive in their own habitats. The zoo is divided into five areas: Forests, Waters, Deserts, Plains, and Encounters. The dolphin show attracts the biggest crowd, so get there early to get a good seat (or head over to one of the zoo's four restaurants; they're much less crowded during the dolphin shows). Times for dolphin shows, in addition to times for other zoo events, are posted at the front gate. If you're short on time, put the World of Waters building high on your list. If you have time to spare, squeeze in a trip to the new, lush White River Gardens, which is part of the zoo complex but charges a separate entry fee. Open Apr–May and Sep–Nov, 9–4 weekdays, 9–5 weekends; June–Aug, 9–5 daily; Dec–Mar, 9–4 daily. Admission: $9.75 adults, $7 seniors, $6 ages 3–12 Mar–Oct; $5.50 adults, $4 seniors, $4 ages 3–12 Nov–Feb. Parking $3. Admission is $4 for everyone the first Tuesday of each month. (For more information, see Chapters 6 and 8.) ♿ (Downtown)

INDIANA STATE CAPITOL BUILDING
200 W. Washington St.
317/233-5293

Built in 1882 on the site of the 1835 State House, this building, vaguely reminiscent of the U.S. Capitol, has long wings on the north and south, short ones to the east and west, and a rotunda in the middle. A massive 1988 renovation corrected more than 100 years of cobbled alterations and restored lost features. The Supreme Court is the only chamber of the building that has stayed substantially the same since 1888, when the building was completed. You can show yourself around by picking up a tour pamphlet at the information desk by the north entrance, or you can call the number above to schedule a guided tour, which lasts about an hour. (Young visitors get a state coloring book.) The lucky get to peek into the governor's office, with its state-seal rug. Note that all the exterior doorknobs are embossed with the state seal, too. You are welcome to sit in the galleries any time the General Assembly is in session. Tours and office hours Mon–Fri 8:30–4:30. Free. ♿ (Downtown)

INDIANA THEATRE
140 W. Washington St.
317/635-5277 or 317/635-5252 (box office)

When this movie palace was built in 1927, it had it all: a 3,200-seat auditorium, bowling alleys, a luncheonette, a barbershop, billiard rooms, and more. The structure was crowned with the Spanish village-style Indiana Roof Ballroom, with a 40-foot domed ceiling, complete with stars and moving clouds. Spared the wrecking ball in 1979 and put on the National Register of Historic Places, the building underwent a several-year, multimillion-dollar remodeling and restoration. The decorative exterior, the entrance lobby, the grand lobby (note the elaborate staircase and fountain), and the roof retain many of their original features. The old auditorium has been divided into three stages to accommodate the

Indiana Repertory Theatre. To tour the building, call for an appointment. Free. (For more information, see the Indiana Repertory Theatre listing in Chapter 11.) Ꭽ (Downtown)

INDIANA WORLD WAR MEMORIAL
431 N. Meridian St.
317/232-7615
www.ai.org/iwm

The newly renovated Indiana World War Memorial pays tribute to the soldiers of both world wars, the Korean War, and the Vietnam War, although when it was completed in 1931, it was dedicated to only World War I veterans. The memorial includes a military museum (recently redesigned and vastly improved) that tells the story of Hoosier veterans. There's a recreated bunker from Vietnam, a helicopter from Korea, a navy Terrier missile, and more. You can learn about Hoosiers who made a name for themselves in the military: the former governor's wife who flew fighter planes in World War II, one of the first black naval officers in the country, and the Hoosier who was the real-life Rosie the Riveter. The Shrine Room on the top floor presents an awe-inspiring tribute with marble columns soaring up to a star-studded sky. There are 20 vivid-blue stained-glass windows towering above a frieze depicting a scene from World War I. The walls are inscribed with the names of more than 145,000 soldiers.

The war memorial is the centerpiece of the Indiana War Memorial Plaza Historic District, a five-block area that includes University Park, the American Legion Mall, and Veteran's Memorial Plaza. For more information about these sights, see Chapter 8. The USS *Indianapolis*

Memorial (see listing below) and the Soldiers and Sailors Monument (see listing below under Monument Circle) are also part of the district. Open Apr 15–Oct 14, Wed–Sun 11–7; Oct 15–Apr 14, Wed–Sun 9–5. Free. Ꭽ (Downtown)

JAMES WHITCOMB RILEY HOME
528 Lockerbie St.
317/631-5885

A grand Victorian Italianate home, perhaps the finest in Lockerbie Square, stands as a tribute to the Hoosier bard James Whitcomb Riley (1849–1916). Preserved rather than restored, the home became a museum in 1922, with a collection including Riley's desk, easy chair, books, top hat, and a self-portrait in pencil. Take particular note of unusual features: the continuous first-floor-to-attic stairwell balustrade, the baseboard drawers in Riley's room, and the speaking tubes in the upstairs hallway, used to communicate with the staff in the kitchen. This is a must-see for Victorian-architecture devotees. Open Tue–Sat 10–3:30, Sun noon–3:30. Admission: $3 adults, $2 seniors, 50¢ students ages 7–17. (Downtown)

LOCKERBIE SQUARE
Between Michigan, Davidson, New York, and New Jersey Sts.

You can step back into the Victorian era when you stroll through charming Lockerbie. Immaculately restored homes with gingerbread gone mad and brick alleys and a cobblestone street make this neighborhood a visual feast. New construction takes over where original structures couldn't be or weren't saved. Even a dinky handyman's special in this neighborhood is exorbitant. Notable structures include the **James Whitcomb**

Tour Operators Pick Top-Notch City Sights and Surprises

Ted Stumpf, Accent on Indianapolis—"I've lived here all my life, but not until I began working in this business did I realize that Indy has so much history and so many interesting things to see. The War Memorial, the American Legion Mall, and the Scottish Rite are always exciting."

Stella Teague, American Sightseeing Indianapolis—"My favorite sight is Crown Hill Cemetery. There is so much intrigue there."

Phil Campbell, 500 Tours, Inc.—"I don't believe that a lot of people realize the unique architecture of our city. And they are amazed about how clean the city is."

Carol Willian, Gray Line of Indianapolis—"People are surprised by our history and new growth. I've heard comments on the very clean, safe downtown, and everyone comments on the Meridian Street corridor, how gorgeous the trees and homes are."

Heather Pierce, Landmark Tours—"Probably one of the most unnoticed attractions is the Shrine Room at the Indiana War Memorial. One of our tour operators has people look down at the stairs all the way up and then has them look up when they get to the Shrine Room. She calls it the 'whammy' because it will take your breath away. Another one is the Indiana State Museum, which is wonderful and it's free."

Peggy Best, Yellow Rose Carriages—"On my personal list, the top four sights would be Conner Prairie, the Scottish Rite (unique and so gorgeous), the Children's Museum, and the Zoo."

Riley Home and the old **Indianapolis Glove Company** on Park Avenue, renovated into condominiums. The square has been on the National Register of Historic Places since 1973. (Downtown)

MADAME WALKER THEATRE CENTER
617 Indiana Ave.
317/236-2099
www.mmewalkertheatre.org
This 1927 architectural masterpiece

is a multipurpose cultural showcase and home to many educational arts-outreach programs and businesses. The crown jewel is the theater, with its exotic and lavish African and Egyptian motifs, painstakingly restored in the late eighties. The building is named for Madame C. J. Walker, one of the city's prominent black leaders in the early part of this century and the country's first black female millionaire. She made her fortune creating and popularizing hair-care products for African American women. Although Walker didn't live to see the center's completion, she planned the building to give African Americans their own elegant theater. And elegant it is. Plans are in the works to open a heritage center on the first floor; currently, artifacts are on display on the fourth floor. Although individual tours are not available, the staff members will answer any questions you might have. Open Mon–Fri 9–5. Free. & (Downtown)

MONUMENT CIRCLE
Meridian and Market Sts.

When Alexander Ralston was planning Indianapolis, he placed a circle in the center of Mile Square. By the mid-1800s, the space in the center of what was then called Circle Street was a park ringed by churches (five of them) and residences. By the time the 284-foot Soldiers and Sailors Monument was dedicated in 1902, the neighborhood had become commercial. Now ringed by spit-and-polished businesses—with brick streets, broad walks, and landscaping—Monument Circle is the emblem of Circle City.

Of the five churches, only **Christ Church Cathedral**, built in 1857, 317/

636-4577, still stands. Visit in the late afternoon, when sunlight streams in the Resurrection stained-glass window at the west end of the nave. This early English Gothic gem has many other lovely stained-glass windows and an exceptional white-marble baptismal font.

Hilbert Circle Theatre, located at 45 Monument Circle, 317/262-1100, the second-oldest building on the Circle (built in 1916), was originally a movie and entertainment palace, noted for its elaborate facade and interior molding. Following a long, slow decline, the theater was renovated and reopened in 1984 as home to the Indianapolis Symphony Orchestra. The ornate 10-story building adjacent to the cathedral is the Columbia Club, built in 1925. (Downtown)

MORRIS-BUTLER HOUSE
1204 N. Park Ave.
317/636-5409
www.historiclandmarks.org

The quintessential Victorian home, the Morris-Butler House envelops you in the 24-karat-gold end of a gilded age. Built by John Morris in 1865, when wealthier citizens were moving north of Downtown, the home has lavish plasterwork and 16-foot ceilings. The Butler family bought the house in 1881 and lived there until 1959. When the Historic Landmarks Foundation bought the home in 1962, the original furnishings were gone. To restore the home and fill it with fittingly elegant objects, philanthropist Eli Lilly and others opened their pocketbooks. Many of the nineteenth-century Hoosier School paintings came from local attics. There are a few family relics, including Mrs. Morris's wedding fan and Mr. Butler's spectacles. Treasures include three

Soldiers and Sailors Monument, p. 91

T. C. Steele paintings, a pier mirror, a Wooten desk, and gold-leaf valances in the dining room. In the children's room, note the 1883 puzzle of the United States labeling Oklahoma as Indian Territory. At the end of 1998, 13 of the home's 16 rooms were open to the public; by 2000, all will be open. Special displays are exhibited at Christmas and during February.

Because Park Avenue is cut off by the interstate, to get to this home from downtown, you need to take Alabama or Delaware north to 13th Street and turn east to Park. Tours last 30 minutes; the last one is conducted at 3:30. Open Tue–Sat 10–4, Sun 1–4. Closed Dec 23–Jan 11. Admission: $5 adults, $4 seniors, $2 children ages 6–16. & (Downtown)

MURAT CENTRE
502 N. New Jersey St.
317/822-0662

For those not familiar with the Shriners, the Middle Eastern–style temple in the Massachusetts Avenue Arts District is a surprising sight. A minaret snakes into the sky,

and a towering, tiled desert scene is splashed across a portion of the exterior. But in Shrinedom, the motif is standard. The largest of the Shrine temples in North America, the Murat also has the most members. The temple was built in three phases: the plush theater in 1910, the exotic Egyptian Room in 1923, and the Shrine Club in 1969. If you go inside, the theater, with its gleaming new bar (believed to be the longest one in the state), and the Egyptian Room are must-sees. To tour the building, call the number above and ask for Lloyd B. Walton, the public relations director and the man with the best stories of the temple's history and its paranormal happenings. Hours vary, depending upon show schedules. (For more information, see Chapter 11.) & (Downtown)

OLD NORTHSIDE
Between I-65, 16th, Pennsylvania, and Bellefontaine Sts.

Old Northside was one of the city's most fashionable neighborhoods from about 1870 until the onset of World War I. Residents included Benjamin Harrison and Lyman Ayres, founder of the L. S. Ayres department store chain. But the wealthy moved north of 38th Street in the early twentieth century, and by the sixties, the neighborhood was run-down. In the seventies, a revitalization effort began, and today more than 70 percent of the homes are renovated. Driving through, you can marvel at highly decorative styles, such as Gothic revival and Italianate. The oldest home, built in 1836, is 1306 North Park. If you call ahead, you can stop in **Kemper House**, 1028 North Delaware Street, 317/639-4534 (ask for Kemper House). Owned by the state's preservation powerhouse, Historic Landmark's Foundation, the building is open weekdays from 9 to 5 and is one of the finest examples of high Victorian architecture in the state. Two rooms are elegantly restored and furnished, complete with beautifully carved fireplaces, soaring ceilings, and elaborate moldings. (Downtown)

PRESIDENT BENJAMIN HARRISON HOME
1230 N. Delaware St.
317/631-1898
www.surf-ici.com/harrison
Built in 1874 and remodeled in 1895, the stately Italianate home reflects the Harrisons' sophisticated tastes. Eighty-five percent of the furnishings that visitors see belonged to the family. New technology has revealed original paints and wallpapers, some of which have been recreated. Treasured possessions include Harrison's

---

An Empress and Her Empire

Born in Louisiana to former slaves, Sarah Breedlove (1867–1919) was orphaned at seven, married at 14, and widowed at 20. She spent 18 years as a laundress and then, with $1.50 in savings, started her own business making hair-care products for African American women. In 1906 she married Charles Joseph Walker (which is how Sarah became C. J.), who helped her promote her business. In 1910 she settled in Indianapolis, where she built her factory. At one point, she employed about 20,000 people in various capacities.

A philanthropist and civil rights advocate, Walker was widely admired. Although she planned the Walker Building and Walker Theatre, she didn't live to see them built. Her daughter, A'Lelia (best known for her role in the Harlem Renaissance), completed the fantastic building in 1928. It incorporates artifacts and ideas that the two women collected during extensive travels through Africa.

inaugural Bible; a Tiffany vase given to Harrison and his second wife, Mary; the White House china designed by Harrison's first wife, Caroline; and a nineteenth-century version of the Nordic Track. There are also a number of original paintings by Caroline Harrison. The third floor has a museum with plenty of memorabilia and information about Harrison, our 23rd president and grandson of the ninth. The first floor, which is wheelchair accessible, has a gift shop with items related to Indiana and to the presidency. The carriage house renovation will be completed in 2000. Open Mon–Sat 10–3:30, Sun 12:30–3:30. Usually closed first three weeks of January. Admission: $5 adults, $4 seniors, $1 students ages 7–16. On Mother's Day and Father's Day, parents accompanied by kids get in free. (Downtown)

SCOTTISH RITE CATHEDRAL
650 N. Meridian St.
317/262-3100
www.aasr-indy.org
You don't have to know the Masons' secret handshake to get an outstanding tour through one of the city's premier architectural wonders. The approximately one-hour tours are led by knowledgeable Masons through this Tudor-Gothic building, designed by George Schreiber, an architect and member of the Scottish Rite. Schreiber labored over the design for five years, incorporating Masonic symbolism into the tiniest details. The exterior and the name lead you to expect a traditional cathedral inside. Instead, the interior contains a ballroom, an auditorium, a library, and other rooms where the Masons gather.

Notice the craftsmanship and the sense of whimsy in the artwork here.

The Indianapolis Project

Scottish Rite Cathedral

For instance, on one of the many richly colored stained-glass windows in the main floor lobby, two angels demonstrate the uses of electricity: one talks on a telephone and the other holds a microphone. To appreciate the grandeur of the ballroom and its 200-light, 2,500-pound crystal chandelier, view it from the balcony and imagine the gowned women and tux-clad men whirling below. The cathedral's bell tower houses one of the largest carillons in the country (the bells weigh in at 56,372 pounds). Don't miss the Stone Room, which contains a wall of stones sent from all the states in the country in 1929, when the building was completed. There's a cafeteria in the mezzanine that serves lunch. Tours Mon–Fri 10–3. Free. ♿ (Downtown)

SOLDIERS AND SAILORS MONUMENT
Monument Circle

Murat Theatre in the Mural Centre, p. 89

317/232-7615
www.ai.org/iwm
Indiana's tribute to its Civil War soldiers was a long time in coming. In
1865 Governor Oliver Morton called
for a memorial, but the funds weren't
raised and the monument wasn't
completed until 1902. The original
cost was just shy of $600,000; the re-
cent restoration exceeded $11 mil-
lion. It's the city's maypole. On its
steps, performers entertain, politicians pontificate, and celebrations
begin and end. In the winter, it becomes a towering Christmas tree
with more than 4,000 lights. At press
time, a world-class Civil War museum was scheduled to open at the
base of the monument, replacing
older ho-hum exhibits. Hours: Apr
15–Oct 14 Wed–Sun 11–7; Oct
15–Apr 14 Wed–Sun 10–6. To view
the city from its epicenter, take the
elevator or climb up 330 steps to the
top. The lower level is wheelchair
accessible. Open Apr 15–Oct 14
Wed–Sun 11–7, Oct 15–Apr 14
Wed–Sun 9–5. Open Memorial Day,
Labor Day, Veteran's Day, and July

4th; closed all other major holidays.
Free. (Downtown)

USS INDIANAPOLIS MEMORIAL
Indianapolis Canal Walk
317/232-7615
www.ai.org/iwm
This 21-ton granite memorial stands
in commemoration of the brave
crew of the USS *Indianapolis*. Torpe-
doed by a Japanese submarine in
1945, the ship sank, killing many of
its company of 1,198 instantly but
leaving about 800 floating in the
western Pacific. While lack of food
and water took its toll, the sharks
were the greatest terror. Swimming
around and below the men, sharks
picked off the crew one by one. By
the evening of the third day, no more
than 400 survived. On the fourth day,
the men were spotted, and due to
the courage of Adrian Marks, a 28-
year-old navy pilot from Frankfort,
Indiana, 318 men were saved. (For
in-depth information about the USS
Indianapolis, check out the exhibit at
the Indiana World War Memorial.)
This memorial is at the north end of

the Canal Walk, on the east bank by the Walnut Street footbridge. Lined by a walkway, the old Central Canal has been gussied up with fountains, decorative street lamps, murals, landscaping, and benches. Strollers amble, joggers trot, and many rent pedal boats during the summer. (For more information, see Chapter 8.) (Downtown)

NORTH

BROAD RIPPLE VILLAGE
Between White River, Evanston Ave., Kessler Blvd., and Meridian St.
317/251-2782
Once an incorporated town, Broad Ripple was also a summer retreat for Indianapolites, complete with an amusement park. Swallowed by the city, the Village, as it is called, is now a popular dining and shopping area (see chapter 9 for more information). At night, Broad Ripple's diverse restaurants, bars, and coffee shops attract crowds of lively folks. During the day, Monon Trail walkers start or stop here for a bite to eat or a cup of coffee. Children like to feed the ducks in the canal that runs through the Village. Beyond the commercial area, streets are lined with charming homes, small and large. Beautifica-

tion plans for the canal area are on the drawing board. At the east end of the village, just past McDonald's, a billboard for Ossip Optometry is framed in eyeglasses made of, well, junk, with giant fans for irises. Maps of the village are available through most local merchants. On warm weekend evenings, allow for time to find a parking space. (North)

CONNER PRAIRIE
13400 Allisonville Rd.
Fishers
317/776-6000 or 800/966-1836
www.connerprairie.org
Climb in a time machine and head for Prairietown, where it is perpetually 1836. Among the cast that populates the village, no one's heard of Abraham Lincoln, let alone Bill Clinton. There are no flashlights, toilets, or washing machines, just candles, outhouses, and washboards. Prairietown is one of three historic areas at 250-acre Conner Prairie. At the Pioneer Adventure Area, you can dip candles, churn butter, and play with nineteenth-century toys. The William and Elizabeth Conner Estate, which is on the National Register of Historic Places, was built in 1823 by a prosperous businessman and presents a different view of life in 1836. In 1999, the building through which visitors enter was redone to include

T i P

Head for the highest point in Marion County for a stellar view of the city. You can see the Pyramids, Keystone at the Crossing, the skyline, and beyond. Your vantage point does demand some decorum—you'll be standing atop James Whitcomb Riley's grave in Crown Hill Cemetery. But the jolly bard would appreciate your enjoyment of the view.

Marty Davis

The Gothic Chapel at Crown Hill Cemetery

Many of the most prominent people in the city's history are buried here: Eli Lilly (founder of the drug company), Richard Gatling (inventor of the Gatling gun), Larry Conrad (an author of the 25th and 26th Amendments to the Constitution), President Benjamin Harrison, and more. There's an orphans' lot and a Confederate soldiers' lot. James Baskett, the actor who played Uncle Remus in Walt Disney's *Song of the South*, and John Dillinger, the infamous bank robber, are also interred here. (When you've found the general area for Dillinger's grave, look for the concrete bench that looks like logs; Dillinger's grave is to the right and behind it.)

Enter at Boulevard Place and 34th Street and get a free map of the cemetery by the Waiting Station (built in 1885), where, in slower times, relatives gathered prior to the funeral, or at the Mausoleum, north of 38th Street. For $5, you can buy a tour book that tells about the history of the cemetery and its permanent residents. From March through November, there are walking tours—usually on the third Sunday of the month—with themes such as celebrities, art and architecture, and the Civil War. Guided tours: $5 adults, $4 seniors, $2 children ages 17 and under. Grounds open daily Apr–Sep 8–6, daily Oct–Mar 8–5. Free. (North)

interpretive exhibits. Some buildings are wheelchair accessible. Open Tue–Sat 9:30–5, Sun 11–5. Admission: $9.75 adults, $8.75 seniors, $5.75 children ages 5–12. AAA members get a $1.50 discount. Tour of Conner Estate: $1.50. The village is closed from the end of November to March 31. (For more information, see Chapter 6.) (North)

CROWN HILL CEMETERY
700 W. 38th St.
317/925-8231
www.crownhill.org
Coming east on 38th Street from Michigan Road all the way to Boulevard Place, you will spot this cemetery, the third largest in the nation. Dedicated in 1864, the cemetery has expanded over the years, crossing to the north side of 38th Street via a tunnel. Crown Hill is the highest point in the cemetery and the county (James Whitcomb Riley is buried at the top), offering a grand vista. If you're not interested in the grave, visit for the view alone.

HOOK'S AMERICAN DRUG STORE MUSEUM
Indiana State Fairgrounds
1180 E. 38th St.
317/924-1503
www.hookamerx.org
Founded in 1900, Hook's was one of the oldest drugstore chains in the country until it was bought out by

According to Hook's American Drug Store Museum, you can make your own cough syrup the old-fashioned way by melting rock candy and horehound drops and, if you choose, adding a dollop of lemon and bourbon.

Revco in 1994. Now this museum store is the only Hook's left in the nation. Although it doesn't sell prescription drugs, you can pick up Rolaids, sunscreen, cough drops, and other modern sundries—items that come in handy for the hordes who come to the state fairgrounds. The store also sells a collection of nostalgic items: Victorian greeting cards, horehound drops, wooden toys, and more. The big attraction, though, isn't the items for sale; rather, it's the ambience, a recreation of a mid-1800s drugstore, including an antique soda fountain. In 2001, the museum will move to larger quarters downtown. Open Fri–Sun 11–4. Free. Fri–Sun, the fairgrounds charges $2 per car, but bring your parking ticket into the museum to get a rebate. ♿ (North)

J. I. HOLCOMB OBSERVATORY AND PLANETARIUM
Butler University
4600 Sunset Ave.
317/940-9333
www.butler.edu
This solid Indiana limestone building houses one of the largest telescopes east of the Mississippi, but the instrument doesn't touch the building. The telescope mount is secured to its own concrete structure to minimize vibrations created by activity in the building. Weekend tours include a planetary show with laser lights

and a peep through a scope into the final frontier. Open Fri and Sat nights. Tour hours: 7 and 8:15 during the Butler academic year; 8 and 9:15 during the summer. Show prices: $2.50 adults, $1 seniors and children, $6 families. The observatory and planetarium are wheelchair accessible; weather permitting, staff will bring a scope out to the lawn. (North)

NORTH MERIDIAN STREET HISTORIC DISTRICT
North Meridian between 40th St. and Westfield Blvd.
This street features a number of elegant homes, including Booth Tarkington's former home at 4270 North Meridian. Most of the homes were built in the 1920s and 1930s, but the oldest dates to 1908 and the newest to 1997. Tudor revival, prairie, and American foursquare are among the styles represented. State law protects the homes from being substantially altered or demolished, and the street is now listed on the National Register of Historic Places. The current governor's mansion sits on extensive grounds (famous locally for the birdcage gazebo) at the northwest quadrant of 46th and Meridian. From 1945 to 1970, the governor occupied the home at 4343 North Meridian Street, which was built by the president of the Stutz Motor Car

GREATER INDIANAPOLIS

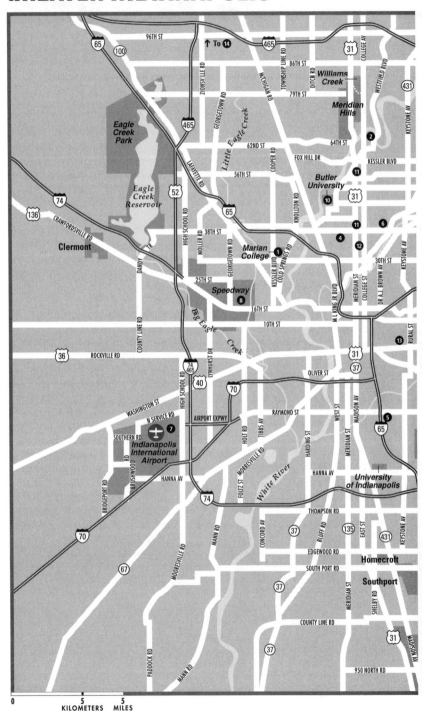

0   5   5
KILOMETERS   MILES

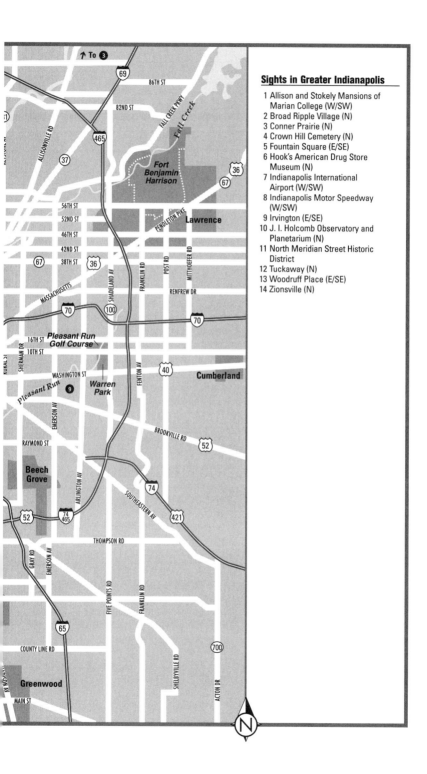

Sights in Greater Indianapolis

1 Allison and Stokely Mansions of
  Marian College (W/SW)
2 Broad Ripple Village (N)
3 Conner Prairie (N)
4 Crown Hill Cemetery (N)
5 Fountain Square (E/SE)
6 Hook's American Drug Store
  Museum (N)
7 Indianapolis International
  Airport (W/SW)
8 Indianapolis Motor Speedway
  (W/SW)
9 Irvington (E/SE)
10 J. I. Holcomb Observatory and
   Planetarium (N)
11 North Meridian Street Historic
   District
12 Tuckaway (N)
13 Woodruff Place (E/SE)
14 Zionsville (N)

Chocolaholics stop here: Catering to our sweet nature, perhaps, Godiva Chocolatiers opened its first airport shop in Indianapolis International Airport in 1998.

Co. Its regal limestone, wrought-iron fence, and large carriage houses are the most outstanding features. (North)

TUCKAWAY
3128 N. Pennsylvania St.
317/926-0251

Walt Disney, Duncan Hines, George Gershwin, Eleanor Roosevelt, Carole Lombard, and scores of other luminaries visited Tuckaway between 1920 and 1941, drawn by a nationally known and fascinating couple: George Meier, a women's apparel designer, and his wife, Nellie, a palm reader. In 1972 Ken Keene Jr. bought the home from Meier's niece, along with all the memorabilia—scores of letters and photographs from celebrities, palm prints in clay, newspaper clippings, correspondence, and Meier-designed gowns. Although not original to the home, which was built in 1906, furnishings are appropriate to the time and elegance of the Meiers' lifestyle. Tuckaway is listed on the National Register of Historic Places. And, beware, the house is reportedly haunted. Call to schedule a tour time. $5 adults. (North)

ZIONSVILLE
SR 334 and Zionsville Rd.
317/873-3836
www.bremc.com/Zionsville

Nestled in the far northwestern corner of the metropolitan area, Zionsville will charm you with its tree-lined streets, beautifully preserved old homes, brick Main Street, restaurants, and quaint shops. Aside from cruising the streets, touring the P. H. Sullivan Museum (see Chapter 7), and popping into Munce Art Center for a quick look, the main pastimes are shopping and dining. For antique lovers, Zionsville is nirvana. The Chamber of Commerce, located at 35 South Elm and open weekdays from 10 to 3, has a visitor's guide, a shopping and dining guide, brochures for local attractions, and a stash of souvenirs with the Zionsville logo emblazoned upon them. One particularly good brochure, *This Old Zionsville House*, details an interesting walking tour of town. (North)

WEST/SOUTHWEST

ALLISON AND STOKELY MANSIONS OF MARIAN COLLEGE
Marian College Campus
3200 Cold Spring Rd.
Allison Mansion, 317/955-6120
Stokely Mansion, 317/955-6110

Marian College sits on land that once comprised the estates of three of the four founders of the Indianapolis Motor Speedway: James A. Allison, Carl G. Fisher, and Frank Wheeler. Of these three once-opulent homes, the most interesting to see is the Allison Mansion, completed in 1911. The exterior melds Prairie School with Lombardy Villa, while the interior blends a variety of European styles. Rooms worthy of note include the music room, the white-marble aviary, the library, and the 25-foot-square bathroom upstairs.

Built in 1912, Frank Wheeler's Mediterranean villa, complete with a seven-car garage, an artificial lake and island, and a Japanese teahouse, was sold to William Stokely, of Stokely-Van Camp Co., in 1937. There are several lovely molded ceilings and much beautiful paneling and tiling. The oval main dining room and the adjacent small octagonal dining room are charming. Unfortunately, there's little left to see at the Fisher Mansion; part of the home burned and the remainder has been turned into classrooms. The Allison and Stokely Mansions are open for guided tours by appointment; the latter is wheelchair accessible on the first floor only. Open Mon–Fri 8–noon and 1–4:30. Tour price: $2. (West/Southwest)

Uncorked Tours

Indiana's strict blue laws say you cannot buy carryout liquor on Sunday. Then, there's the fine print that says you may buy carryout wine from a small winery. So, on Sunday, the wineless can visit the area's wineries. There are three that welcome guests:

Chateau Thomas Winery, *6291 Cambridge Way, Plainfield (I-70 and State Hwy. 267), 317/837-9463 or 888/761-9463, www.chateauthomas.com. This winery offers free tours and tastings of 18 wines, plus a winery gift shop. Open Mon–Thu 10–9, Fri–Sat 10–10, Sun noon–7.*

Easley's Winery, *205 North College Ave., 317/636-4516. Free wine tasting is available, but there's no tour for walk-ins. To get a tour ($12 per person), gather a group of at least 12 and call ahead. Fourteen table wines and some specialty wines are for sale, along with wine-related gifts. Open Mon–Fri 9–6, Sat 9–5, Sun noon–4.*

Gaia Wines, *608 Massachusetts Ave., 317/634-9463. A quickie tour (free) takes you to the production area, where you soak in the wine-making process. For $5, you can participate in a tasting after the tour. You can quaff 13 varieties of wine. A gift shop sells everything from wine to gourmet food to grape-shaped soap. Open Mon–Wed 11–6, Thu–Sat 11–8, Sun noon–6.*

INDIANAPOLIS INTERNATIONAL AIRPORT
2500 S. High School Rd.
317/487-7243
www.indianapolisairport.com
You can watch big jets and little planes take off and land from the park on Pierson Drive (north of the airport), the park on South Perimeter Road, or from the observatory, which tops the "V" where concourses B and C split. In 1997 the airport added 19 chic stores in concourses B and C. (West/Southwest)

INDIANAPOLIS MOTOR SPEEDWAY
4790 W. 16th St.
317/484-6747 (museum)
317/481-8500 (corporate offices)
www.indyracingleague.com
To most, Hulman is the name most closely associated with the Indianapolis Motor Speedway, but the famous two-and-a-half-mile oval was actually conceived and built by Carl Fisher, an early automobile promoter and entrepreneur. The

first race was held in 1911, and the track was paved in brick later that year, earning it the nickname "The Brickyard."

Today, only the start/finish line is bricked, for nostalgia's sake. Two races are held at the track: the Indianapolis 500 on the Sunday of Memorial Day weekend and the Brickyard 400, a stock-car race, in August. At press time modifications to the track were in the works to add Formula One racing. When the track isn't in use, you can cruise around on a bus at something well below warp speed. In addition to the big vrroooom track, there's the Hall of Fame Museum (see Chapter 7 for more information) and an 18-hole championship golf course. If you do nothing else, drive along Georgetown Road between 16th and 30th Streets to get a glimpse of the sheer size of the Speedway. Museum is open daily 9–5. Bus ride and museum each: $3 adults, $1 children ages 6–15. Free admission to track, except in May and August, when prices vary. (West/Southwest)

Indianapolis Motor Speedway

The day before she was killed in a plane crash, Carole Lombard had her palm read in Indianapolis by internationally acclaimed palmist Nellie Simmons Meier. Meier warned Lombard not to take a plane and to go straight to the train station. Eager to return home from her war-bond drive efforts to her husband, Clark Gable, Lombard ignored the warnings.

EAST/SOUTHEAST

FOUNTAIN SQUARE
Virginia Ave. at Shelby St.
If you take Virginia Avenue southeast from downtown, you'll run smack into Fountain Square. You'll recognize it by—you guessed it—the fountain, *Pioneer Family*, placed here in 1914. From 1889 until 1914, a water nymph graced the square. Before that, mules drank from a trough. The Fountain Square building, once renowned for its theater and today the centerpiece of the neighborhood, is newly renovated. Currently there's a twentieth-century artifacts shop, a grand old diner, and duckpin bowling in the building, which dominates the lopsided square. The restored theater, 317/686-6010, with its 40-foot dome and twinkle lights, normally hosts private events, but you can tour it by calling ahead to schedule a time. Driving back toward downtown, you'll get a five-star view of the skyline. (East/Southeast)

IRVINGTON
Between 10th St., Arlington Ave., Brookville Rd., and Emerson Ave.
www.spvi.com/irvington
One of Indianapolis's early suburbs, Irvington has a distinct character, clearly defined by its meandering streets—in contrast to the city's clas-

sic grid pattern. Although the community was planned in 1870, only a handful of homes remain from that era; most extant homes were constructed in the first three decades of this century. For a good look at the eclectic home styles in the neighborhood—including Queen Anne, Italianate, and Craftsman—cruise down South Audubon Road from Washington Street to Oak Avenue. At press time, the area tour book was out of print, but you can get a map by e-mailing a request to Diebold@tcon.net.

Arts and Crafts movement fans should drive by 59 North Hawthorne (north of Washington Street), one of two homes in the state known to have been designed by Gustav Stickley. Also, be sure to drive by the Benton House, 312 South Downey Avenue, 317/357-0318, built in 1873. Its mansard roof, cupolas, and towers are eye-catching. On the third Sunday of the month, the mansion is open for tours (open 2–4, admission: $1). (East/Southeast)

WOODRUFF PLACE
East of Arsenal Technical High School between E. 10th and E. Michigan Sts.
Plotted in 1872 and once a separate town, Woodruff Place was a model of Victorian gentility. Following World War I, wealthier families

moved to the north side of the city, and a gentle decline began that lasted until the early 1970s, when new residents began renovating the old homes and the neighborhood was listed on the National Register of Historic Places. Woodruff Place wasn't incorporated into the city until 1962, and its old town hall still stands. Self-contained and set off by stone walls, the neighborhood has three streets, West, Middle, and East Drives, which are connected by Cross Drive. Each intersection has a roundabout with a fountain in the center (the three oldest fountains in the city are here), and the north-south drives are divided by grassy esplanades decorated with fountains and statuary. (East/Southeast)

TOURING

Most Indy tour companies schedule tours for groups only; two offer regular tours once a week, but they cancel if a minimum number of participants don't sign up ahead of time. Carriage rides are available on demand but don't offer the depth of a guided tour.

ACCENT ON INDIANAPOLIS
233 McCrea St., Ste. 501
317/632-8687
Accentindy@aol.com
Although Accent has done group tours for years, it has just begun offering individual tours each Thursday, with reservations required by Tuesday. The three-hour tour, which leaves from the Indianapolis City Center at noon, covers downtown and then heads out

to the Motor Speedway, the only stop on the tour. Tours are canceled if fewer than 10 people sign up. Price: $20 adults.

AFRICAN AMERICAN HERITAGE TOURS
133 W. Market St., #162
317/425-9921
This company gives gospel tours, Underground Railroad tours, and jazz tours, among others. If you have a group of 10, you can call to book your own tour; otherwise, you can call to find out about tagging along with a scheduled tour. Price: $10 per person.

GRAY LINE OF INDIANAPOLIS
9075 N. Meridian St.
317/573-0699
This company offers a tour every Wednesday. About 80 sights are included, with stops at the Indianapolis City Center and the Motor Speedway. Reservations must be made by the Monday before the tour, and tours are canceled if too few people sign up. Tours begin at the Hyatt Regency Hotel at 9 a.m. and last until around noon. Price: $20 adults, $15.50 seniors, $11 children ages 3–11.

LANDMARK TOURS
340 W. Michigan St.
317/639-4646
www.historiclandmarks.org
Operated by Historic Landmarks, these tours are foot-powered. The tours must be scheduled in advance and require a minimum of eight people. Groups can design their own tours. The critters tour, for example, explores creatures on buildings and in statuary. Price: $5 adults, $2 children.

6

KIDS' STUFF

Indianapolis packs in big fun for kids. Over the past couple of years, Indy Parks and Recreation has been upgrading all of its playground equipment and adding new equipment in some spots. The department has also built several splendid aquatic centers, hot spots for hot weather. There's a thriving children's library program and a community of kid-friendly businesses. The centerpiece of the fun is the Children's Museum, the largest of its kind in the world. Plus, there are toy stores, bookstores, and restaurants eager to attract young patrons.

ANIMALS AND THE GREAT OUTDOORS

EAGLE CREEK PARK
7840 W. 56th St.
317/327-7110
www.indygov.org

One of the largest city parks in the country, Eagle Creek offers an abundance of family activities. Visitors can hike on the park's more than 10 miles of trails, tour the nature center and arboretum, and, in the winter, cross-country ski. The park borders Eagle Creek Reservoir, which has a sandy beach and many boating opportunities, and it has its own five-acre lake, where families can fish. Four playgrounds, including one on

the beach, provide fun for youngsters. Parking: $2 per vehicle, $3 on weekends and holidays, 25¢ for each additional passenger over six people. (West/Southwest)

GARFIELD PARK
2450 S. Shelby St.
317/327-7220
www.indygov.org

Garfield Park has a sensational outdoor aquatic center. The adjacent play area features swings, a climber, and a ladder-shaped loopy climber. The park has many other attractions as well, including a greenhouse and a sunken garden. Open dawn until dusk. Free. (For more information, see Chapter 8.) (East/Southeast)

HOLLIDAY PARK
6349 Spring Mill Rd.
317/327-7180
www.indygov.org

For youngsters, this park rates two thumbs up and five stars. It's the city's best for kids and the only one that has equipment that older children will enjoy. Toddlers have a special enclosed area with swings, several small climbers, and plenty of sand. Two giant slides and a monster-sized spider web appeal to the boldest children. There's another set of equipment that draws the three-to-eight-year-olds, and there are plenty of swings for everyone.

Behind the play area, trails drop down into the woods and run along the east end of the park and beside White River. Children also enjoy walking around the park's "ruins" and fountain. A nature center, scheduled to open in the fall of 1999, will offer a number of family activities. (For more information, see Chapter 8.) Open dawn until dusk. Free. (North)

INDIANAPOLIS ZOO
1200 W. Washington St.
317/630-2001
www.indyzoo.com

This new zoo opened along the banks of the White River in 1988. Here, flora and fauna of all shapes and sizes thrive in habitats that are separated into five areas: Forests, Waters, Deserts, Plains, and Encounters. The zoo focuses on entertainment and learning by presenting shows, talks with animal keepers, and narratives about animals and their habitats.

Show schedules, including schedules for the dolphin show and the Camp Zoorific Magic Show, are posted at the front gate. Particularly in summer, families should head for the dolphin show about 20 minutes early to get good seats. In summer, animals are most active early in the day, before the sun shines full strength. For more information, see Chapter 5. Open Apr–May and Sep–Nov Mon–Fri 9–4, Sat and Sun

Memorable Meals

For happy meals, take kids to spots where there's entertainment along with the food.

*At **Blue Heron**, 11699 Fall Creek Rd., 317/845-8899, a magician entertains during Sunday brunch.*

***Fazolis** (many locations) features Tony the Tomato, who passes out balloons at dinnertime and talks to children. Call the location near you to find out which nights Tony will be there.*

*At **Illusions**, 969 Keystone Way, Carmel, magicians entertain nightly. The five locations of **O'Charley's** offer bargain meals for kids and balloon sculptures during Sunday brunch.*

Catch the dolphin show at the Indianapolis Zoo.

9–5; Jun–Aug daily 9–5; Dec–Mar daily 9–4. Admission: Mar–Oct $9.75 adults, $7 seniors, $6 children ages 3–12; Nov–Feb $5.50 adults, $4 seniors, $4 children ages 3–12; first Tue of each month $4 per person. Parking: $3. ♿ (Downtown)

KRANNERT PARK
605 S. High School Rd.
317/327-7375
www.indygov.org
This park has the city's most popular outdoor aquatic center, with a curly slide and other water-play attractions. Additionally, there's a playground, hiking trails, and fishing. The recreation center has a gym and an indoor pool. Open dawn until dusk. Free. (Southwest)

RITCHEY WOODS
NATURE PRESERVE
10410 Hague Rd.
Fishers
317/924-5431, ext. 3826
Nature trails crisscross the pristine 126 acres of Ritchey Woods. The Chil-

dren's Museum, which owns the preserve, organizes guided walks and other programs, and the full-time naturalist can answer questions. Open Apr–Oct Wed–Sun 10–5. Admission: $2; free to Children's Museum members. (North)

MUSEUMS AND LIBRARIES

CHILDREN'S MUSEUM
3000 N. Meridian St.
317/924-5431 or
800/208-5437 (KIDS)
www.childrensmuseum.org
Surely the cheeriest place in Indianapolis, the Children's Museum (the largest in the world) draws in children from all over the city and elsewhere with its multitude of attractions. There's a planetarium, a dinosaur dig area, a mummy's tomb (complete with a real mummy), an area where children learn about people and cultures around the world, and an area designed especially for preschoolers. The museum

Traveling Tykes

Debbie Blackwell Smith knows Indianapolis. This former media relations director for the Indianapolis Project also once worked for Conner Prairie and for the mayor, so when she had triplets, she knew where to entertain them. As Smith says, "When you have three, you have to sing and dance fast!"

Indy parks—Holliday Park's playgrounds are unlike any place else in the city. We take the beautiful paths down to the White River. And there is no better place to walk than along the Monon Trail and Canal in Broad Ripple.

Children's Museum—Scienceworks is a hit, as are the carousel and the trains.

Airports—At Indianapolis Aviation, 9913 Willowview Rd., Fishers, 317/849-0840, on a bright, beautiful day, there's lots of action. You can see pilots practicing landing and taking off. You are so close that the pilots wave.

Monument Circle and Downtown—We try to identify things, like bison, carved on the monument, and we always go for the Strawberry Festival. We stop by the Wyland mural (on St.Clair between Pennsylvania and Delaware) and count the dolphins. My kids like the model at City Center where they can make things light up.

Fire stations—Stop at any one of them! Kids receive coloring books, stickers, and badges; they also learn not to play with matches.

Uncle Bill's Pet Center—At Uncle Bill's (four locations), you can touch and hold snakes, frogs, turtles, puppies, kittens, birds, and mice. It's great on a rainy day.

Mike's Car Wash—Kids love the Disney and Sesame Street characters here (11 locations).

Indiana State Museum at Christmas time—The old L. S. Ayres Christmas displays are wonderful, with toy soldiers and a train you can ride.

The call-a-story booths are located at the Indianapolis–Marion County Public Library branches, p. 108

levers, and scamper through an underground burrow.

This museum can occupy families for a full day and more. An array of food options, including both healthy foods and McDonald's, is available in the large, market-style restaurant. The large gift shop has a superior selection of toys. The entrance and parking lots are one block west of the museum on Illinois Street, marked with bright blue lamp posts and street signs topped with the museum's dinosaur mascot. Open Labor Day–Feb, Tue–Sun 10–5; Mar–Aug, daily 10–5. Admission: $8 adults, $7 seniors, $3.50 children ages 2–17; there is a separate charge for the IWERKS Cine-Dome; free on Martin Luther King Day, Presidents' Day, and on the first Thursday of the month 5–8 p.m. Most exhibits are wheelchair accessible. (North)

also features a turn-of-the-century carousel, which runs all day, and a splendid new train exhibit, complete with a full-sized train. The museum's Lilly Theater presents superb children's shows, and there are special exhibits. IWERKS CineDome, a theater with a three-story screen, shows specially designed films. At Science Works, in the Dow Science Center, children can scale a rock wall, frolic in a large water-play area, experiment with pulleys and

CONNER PRAIRIE
13400 Allisonville Rd.
Fishers
317/776-6000 or 800/966-1836
www.connerprairie.org

What games did children play in 1836? What was learning like in a one-room schoolhouse? Families learn this and more as they explore Prairietown, a typical Hoosier farming community of the early nineteenth century. The costumed "townspeople" can't be tricked

T i P

For a-maze-ing fall fun, you can head for Waterman's Farm Market, 7010 East Raymond St., 317/357-2989. In addition to hay, cornstalk, and cornfield mazes, the u-pick farm offers pony rides, pumpkin picking, and scarecrow making.

For up-to-the-minute listings of children's activities around town, pick up a copy of *Indy's Child*, a free monthly paper with a comprehensive calendar. You'll find it at Marsh Supermarkets, libraries, specialty shops, and other places where kids hang out, as well as online at www.indyschild.com.

into talking about modern times. They declare that Andrew Jackson is president and stare blankly at the mention of computers. Conner Prairie is of most interest to older children, although there's a small playground to occupy younger kids. (For more information see chapter 5.) Open Tue–Sat 9:30–5, Sun 11–5. Closed from the end of Nov–Mar 31. Admission: $9.75 adults, $8.75 seniors, $5.75 children 5–12; $1.50 discount to AAA members. Some buildings are wheelchair accessible. (North)

EITELJORG MUSEUM OF AMERICAN INDIANS AND WESTERN ART
500 W. Washington St.
317/636-9378
www.eiteljorg.org

The Eiteljorg Museum is in an eye-catching, distinctly Southwestern-style building with a totem pole. Before you begin a tour, stop at the admission desk and pick up the *Family Guide*, which suggests fun activities and poses questions that help kids appreciate what they see.

Each Saturday, activities are scheduled for families. Participants may hear a storyteller, make a craft, or watch a demonstration of weaving. (For more information see Chapter 7.) Open Tue–Sat 10–5, Sun noon–5. Open Mon 10–5 Jun–Aug. Admission: $5 adults, $4 seniors, $2 students and children ages 5–17. ♿ (Downtown)

INDIANAPOLIS-MARION COUNTY PUBLIC LIBRARY
Central Library, 40 E. St. Clair St.
317/269-1700 or 317/269-1717
(call-a-story line, 24 hours)

In the Riley Room for children, young book lovers can busy themselves among the stacks, sit in a car-shaped chair, or climb into a cozy phone booth to use the library's popular call-a-story line. There's a special room for storytelling. Every branch library has great children's programs as well. Each has a different theme: Winnie the Pooh at Lawrence, Wind in the Willows at Shelby, and a clubhouse at small Fountain Square. All branches feature call-a-story. There are a variety of age-specific activities held year-round at the libraries. Children's movies show weekly during the summer and on school holidays. (For more information see Chapter 5.) Central Library open Mon–Fri 9–9, Sat 9–5, Sun 1–5. Free. ♿ (Downtown)

INDIANA STATE POLICE YOUTH EDUCATION AND HISTORICAL CENTER
8500 E. 21st St.
317/899-8293 or 888/477-9688

One of only seven such museums nationwide, this facility opened in 1994, entirely funded by donations. From the name, one would imagine this is a no-nonsense museum, but the collection is unusual and fun to look at, from an exhibit on Indiana's own John Dillinger to information on bicycle safety to miniature police cars from every state in the union. Car lovers will linger around the sizable collection of restored police vehicles, dating to 1937. You can sit in a police car and turn on the lights, siren, and radio for a real-life experience. (For more information see Chapter 7.) Open Mon–Fri 8–11 and 1–4. Free. ♿ (East/Southeast)

MUSEUM OF MINIATURE HOUSES AND OTHER COLLECTIONS
111 E. Main St.
Carmel
317/575-9466
For little folks and all who like things small, this museum is a delight. Tiny rooms of varying scale and in many styles offer scenes where the tiniest

Indoor Escapades

Bad weather needn't ruin vacation fun. The places listed below are made for indoor action.

Discovery Zone—There are four locations in town, but the best one is 3720 East 82nd St., 317/577-1565. It features climbers, tubes, arcade games, and very casual dining.

Greatimes—Located at 5341 Elmwood Ave. (on the south side, near the I-465 Beechgrove exit), 317/780-0300, Greatimes offers arcade games, climbing tubes and balls, and dining. Outside, there are two miniature golf courses, two go-cart tracks, bumper boats, and other play equipment.

Indiana World Skating Academy—Located at Pan American Plaza, 201 South Capitol Ave., 317/237-5555, this is an excellent ice-skating rink.

Indy Island Aquatic Center—This is a city-owned indoor water park with slides and more, 8575 East Raymond St., 317/862-6867, www.indygov.org. LaShonna Bates Aquatic Center, at 1450 South Reisner Street, 317/327-7340, is a smaller water park.

McDonald's Indoor Playlands—This is a choice that never fails. Locations include: 8907 East 116th St., Fishers, 317/842-0013; 15101 U.S. 31 North, Carmel, 317/844-4166; 3021 Southeastern Ave., 317/631-3484; 9833 Fall Creek Rd., 317/849-3011; 121 Marlin Dr., Hwy. 135, Greenwood, 317/882-8097; 7229 East Washington St., 317/353-2771; 7236 West 10th St., 317/247-1415.

A "garden" at the Indianapolis Children's Museum, p. 105

details do count. Exhibits change every six months; the gift shop sells miniature furniture, accessories, and more. Open Wed–Sat 11–4, Sun 1–4. Closed the first two school weeks of January. Admission: $2 adults, $1 children. ♿ (North)

PUPPETS AND THEATER

ASANTE CHILDREN'S THEATRE
P.O. Box 22344
317/638-6694
Asante Children's Theatre explores African and African American history and culture through the dramatic arts. The company stages three productions a year and produces the African Folktale Festival. Actors ages 12 to 23 perform the mostly original scripts centering around history and social issues. Performances are at the Walker Theatre. The African Folktale Festival is free. ♿ (Downtown)

JUNIOR CIVIC
Indianapolis Museum of Art
1200 W. 38th St.
317/924-6770
www.civictheatre.org
A branch of the Indianapolis Civic Theatre, Junior Civic is geared for aspiring thespians, with programs offered year-round. If you are visiting Indianapolis in June, the troupe stages a children's favorite, such as *Charlotte's Web,* starring an all-kids cast. Civic also produces a family show each holiday season. (For more information see Chapter 11.) Call for ticket prices and show times. ♿ (North)

PEEWINKLE'S PUPPET STUDIO
25 E. Henry St.
317/535-4853 or 800/849-4853
Peewnkle@aol.com
www.nashvilleindiana.com/
attractions/puppet/show.html
New in 1998, this pint-sized theater— it seats 50—is the Indianapolis home to the Melchior Marionettes and Peewinkle, an adventurous gnome.

TRIVIA

A rag doll in Johnny Gruelle's mother's Indianapolis attic inspired him to create Raggedy Ann and Raggedy Andy. Although Gruelle moved away in 1907, when he was 17, he always considered the city home, which may be why his warm, endearing stories have that heartland feel.

These wonderful puppets and their skilled puppeteers have been delighting youngsters for two generations in a variety of venues in the city and at the Melchior Marionette Theatre in Nashville, Indiana. Seasonal performances, including the holiday show and the Slightly Haunted Puppet Theatre at Halloween are special favorites; reservations are essential. Ticket prices vary depending on the show. ♿ (Downtown)

STORES KIDS LOVE

COOKIE CUTTERS
3906 E. 82nd St.
317/842-7753
Cookie Cutters is the place for chopping kids' locks. While waiting, children play on a climber and with video games. Kids choose their chair—a car, plane, or tractor—and watch videos or play video games while a stylist grooms them. Other services include manicures and first-cut packages. This bright, cheery shop makes parents and kids happy. Open Mon–Fri 10–8, Sat 10–5. Standard haircut: $11.95. Additional Cookie Cutters locations can be found at 2320 E. 116th St., Carmel, 317/574-0399, or on 7791 U.S. 31, S. Indianapolis, 317/885-7752. (North)

KIDS INK
5619 N. Illinois St.
317/255-2598
199 N. Madison Ave.
Greenwood
317/882-1090
The best in children's literature lines the shelves at Kids Ink, and knowledgeable clerks can help you make the right choices. In addition to books, the store has a selection of Brio and other toys, games, and puzzles. Hours vary by store. (East/Southeast)

KITS AND KABOODLE
Keystone at the Crossing
8701 Keystone Crossing
317/574-3333 or 800/252-8697 (TOYS)
www.kitsandkaboodle.com
From its founding in 1978, Kits and Kaboodle has had a knack for spotting and stocking the hottest toys. In fact, they're so good at it that *USA Today* has consulted them when the paper is monitoring toy fads. Whether they're looking for Madame Alexander dolls or Stomp Rockets, kids will be eager to empty the shelves. While parents shop, young ones stay occupied with toys set out for them. This is a toy shop that offers superior quality and selection, with 7,000-plus items. Open Mon–Fri 10–9, Sat 10–9, Sun noon–5. (North)

MY MOTHER'S DOLL SHOP
10 N. Main St.
Zionsville
317/873-4338
This shop of collectibles elicits oohs
and aahs from big and little girls alike.
Elegant dolls in exquisite clothes
deck the shelves. You can bring dol-
lies home well provisioned with
dainty furniture and accessories.
Open Mon–Fri 10–6, Sat 10–5. Open
Sun 1–4 in Dec. (North)

7

MUSEUMS AND ART GALLERIES

Yeah, we know already Indianapolis isn't New York . . . or Chicago . . . or Paris or London for that matter. And residents of another city might feel embarrassed if their city had only a handful of museums and a sprinkling of galleries. But we've got a right to be proud of one of the oldest and the seventh-largest art museum in the country and of the world's largest children's museum. What's more, Indy has a growing art scene backed by impressive resource centers and nonprofit groups, and a calendar brimming with art fairs, gallery openings, and exhibits. And in Indy you'll discover small treasures of museums—one-of-a-kind finds that will occupy you for a weekend afternoon and perhaps teach you something new.

The future holds good news for Civil War buffs, sports fans, and supporters of the Indiana State Museum. The Colonel Eli Lilly Civil War Museum, which will focus on the experiences of Indiana natives during that period, will be completed in 1999. Two museums will open their doors as the new millenium dawns: The NCAA Hall of Champions Museum is scheduled for completion in 2000, and the Indiana State Museum will move to its new home in White River State Park in 2001.

ART MUSEUMS

EITELJORG MUSEUM OF AMERICAN INDIANS AND WESTERN ART
500 W. Washington St.
317/636-9378
www.eiteljorg.org
Had to cancel that trip to Santa Fe?

No problem. Once inside the Eiteljorg, you'll discover a collection that rivals those of the most renowned Southwestern art museums. The museum features works by Georgia O'Keeffe, Frederick Remington, and contemporary artists, as well as a collection of Native American crafts and artifacts. The gift shop contains Oaxacan art,

113

fetishes, dream catchers, and silver jewelry—at reasonable prices. With all this, who needs New Mexico? Open Tue–Sat 10–5, Sun noon–5. Museum is closed Mon except during summer (Jun–Aug). Admission: $5 adults, $4 seniors, $2 students and children 5–17. ᕽ (Downtown)

INDIANAPOLIS MUSEUM OF ART (IMA)
1200 W. 38th St.
317/923-1331
www.ima-art.org

World-famous artworks, from paintings by the old masters to contemporary African works, are housed in four pavilions on the museum's grounds. But the museum is more than a collection of great works. It also serves as a bustling center for cultural, social, and community activities. The museum hosts lectures, poetry readings, classes, storytelling, special family days, concerts, and movies. Also on-site are the Indianapolis Civic Theatre, restaurants, and shopping (from art to used clothing to exotic plants). But back to art—the museum features the largest collection of J. M. W. Turner watercolors and drawings outside Great Britain, the Eli Lilly Collection of Chinese Art, the W. J. Holliday Collection of Neo-Impressionist paintings, and a comprehensive collection of Asian art. Open Tue–Wed, Fri–Sat 10–5; Thu 10–8:30; Sun noon–5. Free (except for selected exhibitions). ᕽ (North)

NATIONAL ART MUSEUM OF SPORT
850 W. Michigan St.
317/274-3627

Since being moved to Indianapolis in 1990, this collection of sports-related

Top Art Fairs

Broad Ripple Art Fair—More than 200 artists, dozens of food booths, and music performances keep the crowds enthralled at this fair in May.

Penrod Arts Fair—This one-day fair features food, music, dance, and nearly 300 exhibitors on the grounds of the Indianapolis Museum of Art the first Saturday after Labor Day.

Talbot Street Art Fair—Part of Talbott St., next to the Herron School of Art, is blocked off to allow room for 200 to 250 art exhibitors at this bustling art fair that typically takes place during the second weekend of June.

Indian Market—More than 90 exhibitors (many are Native American) display their skills at this weekend event held at the Eiteljorg in June.

Indiana Medical History Museum

fine art has nearly tripled in size. It is considered the largest of its kind in the country. But what else would you expect from a city designated the amateur sports capital of the United States? The collection features more than 750 paintings, prints, photographs, and sculptures by such well-known sports artists as Winslow Homer and George Bellows. Sports represented range from primitive games to tennis, football, basketball, and auto racing. Open Mon–Fri 8–5. Weekend hours vary. Free. ♿ (Downtown)

SCIENCE AND HISTORY MUSEUMS

CRISPUS ATTUCKS MUSEUM
1140 Dr. Martin Luther King Jr. St.
317/226-4613
This new museum on the grounds of Crispus Attucks Middle School, a national historic landmark, pays tribute to the achievements of African Americans, particularly to the achievements of former students of the

school. More than 30 exhibits in four galleries focus on local, state, and national African American history and on African history. One gallery is dedicated to the history of basketball at Crispus Attucks, alma mater of famed sports hero Oscar Robertson. Guided tours are available, and the museum makes a popular field trip for grade-school classes. Open Mon–Fri 10–2. Free. ♿ (Downtown)

INDIANA MEDICAL HISTORY MUSEUM
Old Pathology Building
3045 W. Vermont St.
317/635-7329
www.imhm.org
The Indiana Medical History Museum is perhaps too morbid for some people's tastes (although the occasional physician finds it the perfect site for a wedding reception). After all, autopsies were performed daily (a small building in back is called the Dead House) on the grounds of what was once the Central State Hospital for the Insane. The imposing structure, built in 1896 and perfectly preserved,

Love at the IMA

It started as a Christmas card more than three decades ago. Today, the large block letters that spell "LOVE" with the "O" askew have become an icon for the Indianapolis Museum of Art—much to the chagrin of promoters who want visitors to appreciate the museum for more than the celebrated sculpture. Although it is indeed one of the most visible—and visited—features on the museum's grounds, the monumental, three-ton statue is just one of the museum's 50 works by artist Robert Indiana, who took the name of his home state as his last name.

Indiana created the first of many versions of his LOVE image in 1964, as a study for a Christmas card for the Museum of Modern Art. The design became the museum's most popular Christmas card ever, and the image brought its artist enormous commercial success. The LOVE painting, a number of sculptures, and 38 prints by the artist are also part of the collection at the IMA.

houses more than 15,000 medical artifacts and features displays about the study of mental illness until the 1960s. Various laboratories, the amphitheater, and the autopsy room are open for guided tours. The oldest remaining building of its kind (it's on the National Register of Historic Places), it was featured in the movies *Eight Men Out* and *Going All the Way.* Open Wed–Sat 10–4. Admission: $5 adults, $1 children ages 6–18. Some exhibits are not wheelchair accessible. (West/Southwest)

INDIANA STATE MUSEUM
202 N. Alabama St.
317/232-1637
www.ai.org\ism

Hoosier history is recounted in a variety of ways at the Indiana State Museum—from the perspectives of prehistoric animals to those of twentieth-century high school basketball fanatics. You can stroll down a turn-of-the-century Main Street, visit the Radio Hall of Fame, or relive the African American experience through a living history troupe in Freetown Village. The Rotunda features the 212-pound bronze Foucault Pendulum, similar to the one at the Smithsonian. The museum is scheduled to move to a new location, surrounding the IMAX Theater in the downtown White River State Park area, by 2001. Open Mon–Sat 9–4:45, Sun noon–4:45. Free. ♿ (Downtown)

INDIANA TRANSPORTATION MUSEUM
Forest Park on State Rd. 19
Noblesville
317/773-6000
www.itm.org
Train lovers won't want to miss this museum. Artifacts are displayed in train cars or original railroad buildings. The museum features one of five operating mainline steam engines in the country, and visitors can ride a 1920s-era trolley. And special theme trips, aboard a 1930s car originally built for the Santa Fe Railroad, run virtually every weekend from May through October. Open Memorial Day–Labor Day, Tue–Sun 10–5. Open weekends Apr, May, Sep, Oct 10–5. Admission: $3 adults, $2 children. Some exhibits may not be wheelchair accessible. (North)

P. H. SULLIVAN MUSEUM AND GENEALOGY LIBRARY
225 W. Hawthorne St.
Zionsville
317/873-4900
An elaborate Victorian hair wreath, featuring intricate weavings of more than 100 identified contributors, is one of the most unusual items at the P. H. Sullivan Museum. The small but intriguing museum was founded in

More Love at the IMA

Okay, it's not really a singles-only event. But the museum's First Fridays give the unattached a great opportunity to meet people while they're listening to jazz and looking at art. Held the first Friday night of each month except January, the event, featuring hors d'oeuvres, a cash bar, and a lively atmosphere, draws as many as 1,000 attendees a night. Admission for First Friday, which the museum has hosted for more than a decade, is $7 ($4 for members).

Another popular social event hosted by the IMA—for singles and otherwise—is the Summer Nights Film and Concert series, which is held on the concert terrace. Films are shown on Fridays and concerts on Tuesdays; both begin near sunset, but the crowds are waiting even before the gates open at 6 p.m. It has become a tradition to arrive early and dine al fresco before the entertainment begins. Dinners range from chicken in a bucket to elegant affairs complete with tablecloths, candelabras, and champagne. Concert ticket prices vary but are typically under $20; movie tickets are $5 ($3 for members).

An Art Writer's Checklist of Indy's Best

"The Indianapolis cultural canvas is awash with great galleries and alternative spaces to view art," says Julie Pratt McQuiston, the former editor of *Arts Indiana* magazine and a highly regarded art critic. "From the largest institution to the smallest gallery space, it's all here." And here, she offers a number of must-sees for the art lover in Indianapolis.

1. **The Indianapolis Museum of Art**—It's known for its permanent collections of J. M. W. Turner watercolors and paintings by T. C. Steele, 317/923-1331.

2. **Eiteljorg Museum of American Indians and Western Art**—Be sure to catch the biannual New Art of the West exhibit, 317/636-9378.

3. **The Stutz Building**—This historic automobile-factory-turned-artists'-haven hosts at least two open houses each year and houses a number of studios.

4. **Ruschman Art Gallery**—One of the city's longest-standing commercial spaces for contemporary art, this gallery features high-quality works by well-known Indiana and regional artists, 317/634-3114.

5. **Massachusetts Avenue**—This area is considered to be Indy's art district. It is home to a number of galleries, not to mention theaters, nightlife, and a winery.

6. **Indy Installation Fest**—This biannual festival devoted to installation art is sponsored by 4 Star Gallery, 317/686-6382.

7. The **Arts Council of Indianapolis**—This is a great source of arts information, 317/631-3301. They offer maps showing public sculptures in the city.

1823 by the great-granddaughter of the first white settler in Boone County. Furniture, quilts, costumes, and old photographs, including an 1855 portrait of William Zion, for whom the city of Zionsville was named, reveal intimate details of local history. The museum's genealogy library contains more than 4,000 volumes and 70,000 surname cards. Open Tue–Sat 10–4. Free. ⅁ (North)

OTHER MUSEUMS

CHILDREN'S MUSEUM
3000 N. Meridian St.
317/924-5437 or 800/208-5437
www.childrensmuseum.org
The Children's Museum calls itself the "do-seum" because so many of its exhibits are interactive. You can perform scientific experiments, climb a rock wall, ride a restored carousel,

touch live animals, participate in an archaeological dig, and explore a cave. Listed in *Family Fun* magazine as the number-one family museum in the country and identified by the American Association of Museums as one of the 20 most-visited museums of any kind, the Children's Museum attracts nearly a million visitors a year.

More than 100,000 items are on display in 10 major galleries—including the SpaceQuest Planetarium, the ScienceWorks gallery, and the three-story-high IWERKS CineDome. (For more information see Chapter 7.) Open Labor Day–Feb, Tue–Sun 10–5; Mar–Aug, daily 10–5. Admission: $8 adults, $7 seniors, $3.50 children ages 2–17. The museum is free on Martin Luther King Day, Presidents' Day, and on the first Thursday of the month from 5–8. Most exhibits are wheelchair accessible. (North)

INDIANAPOLIS MOTOR SPEEDWAY HALL OF FAME MUSEUM
4790 W. 16th St.
317/484-6747
www.indyracingleague.com

On the site of the celebrated Indianapolis Motor Speedway, this museum recounts the history of the "greatest spectacle in racing" since its inception in 1911—when the fastest cars in the world took all day to complete the race. The museum exhibits more than 30 cars that have won the Indy 500, as well as other race memorabilia and historic photos. Every half-hour a film about the history of the Indy 500 is shown in the Tony Hulman Theatre. Antique and classic cars—many by Indianapolis automakers such as Stutz and Duesenberg—are on display. The facility that houses the museum is a national

historic landmark. Open daily 9–5. Admission: $3 adults, $1 children ages 6–15. & (West/Southwest)

MUSEUM OF MINIATURE HOUSES AND OTHER COLLECTIONS
111 E. Main St.
Carmel
317/575-9466

You don't have to be a little girl to be fascinated by the dozens of miniature houses displayed here. The oldest house is from 1861, but the museum features primitive pioneer dwellings, majestic Victorian mansions, a Mexican hacienda, and the metal, molded-furniture habitats of the late 1950s. The collection even includes a whimsical "grunge bathroom," with ring-around-the-bathtub and dirty towels. For the aficionado, a small (of course) gift shop sells hard-to-find items for the well-appointed dollhouse, including miniature Christmas tree lights, oriental carpets, and Monopoly games. Open Wed–Sat 11–4, Sun 1–4. Admission: $2 adults, $1 children, free for kids under 10. Some of the exhibits

Archaeological dig exhibit at the Children's Museum

Indianapolis Children's Museum

Tiny Treasures, Priceless Value

Listed below are small museums found within other sightseeing at-tractions or institutions such as hospitals and government centers. And, best of all, none charge admission!

*The **National Track and Field Hall of Fame**, 1 RCA Dome, 800/323-4693, contains exhibits that commemorate the accomplishments of Jim Thorpe, Jesse Owens, Wilma Rudolph, and other track-and-field greats. Open Mon–Fri 9–4:30.*

***Wishard Memorial Hospital Nursing Museum**, 1001 West 10th St., 317/630-6233, features uniforms, equipment, photographs, and displays, including a hospital room from 1940, where scenes from the movie Hoosiers were filmed. Open Wed 9–2, or by appointment.*

*At **Hook's American Drug Store Museum**, 1180 East 38th St. (Indi-ana State Fairgrounds), 317/924-1503, www.hookamerx.org., you can order a root beer float at the soda fountain, then look at fasci-nating displays of dental equipment and obstetric tools that look like torture devices, as well as jars of elixirs concocted for ailing Hoosiers of the past. Open Fri 11–4.*

*The **American Legion Headquarters Museum**, 700 North Pennsyl-vania St., 317/630-1200, is housed in a national historic land-mark. This museum features military dioramas, historic flags, and more than 2,500 posters from World Wars I and II. Open Mon–Fri 8–4:30.*

*The **Indiana State Police Youth Education and Historical Center**, 8500 East 21st St., 317/899-8293, is recognized as one of the finest police museums in the country (it was recently rated num-ber three). This nonprofit museum contains law-enforcement memorabilia, police vehicles, and historical artifacts. There's also an exhibit about notorious native John Dillinger. Open Mon–Fri 8–11, 1–4.*

are in small rooms with several steps and may not be wheelchair accessible. (North)

GALLERIES

Members of the Indy art community bemoan the lack of a healthy art market in the city. Despite such a pronouncement from the pros, those of us who "may not know art but know what we like" will likely be satisfied with the number of galleries and variety of styles and media offered. Listed below are a few of the largest, oldest, or most well-known galleries, as well as Indy neighborhoods with high concentrations of galleries and art studios.

EDITIONS LIMITED GALLERY OF FINE ART
4040 E. 82nd St.
317/842-1414
Editions Limited represents more than 100 artists, both local and international, and features an eclectic array of media and styles—from the avant-garde to traditional landscapes. The gallery, in business for more than 25 years, is owned by John Mallon and directed by Marta Blades, who offers free art consultations for individuals and businesses. Open Mon–Fri 9–5, Sat 10–3, or by appointment. (North)

HERRON GALLERY
1701 N. Pennsylvania St.
317/920-2420
www.herron.iupui.edu
Located on the campus of the Herron School of Art, this 3,000-foot-square noncommercial facility (smaller than a museum, larger than a commercial gallery) specializes in contemporary art and features exhibits that rotate every month. The exhibits, less than a

quarter of which are devoted to student and faculty work, include works in all media from artists around the country. The Herron Gallery invites the public to all show openings, which are frequently attended by the artists, and welcomes school classes and groups. The gallery will be celebrating its 100th birthday (in 2002) in a new home—it is scheduled to move to the site of the IUPUI law school before the turn of the century. Open Mon–Wed 10–5, Thu noon–8, Fri–Sat 10–3. Free. (North)

INDIANAPOLIS ART CENTER
820 E. 67th St.
317/255-2464
www.indplsartcenter.org
Much more than a gallery, this nonprofit organization is the city's largest art facility, providing unmatched resources for the community. It offers more than 200 studio art classes (for beginners and professionals alike), workshops, lectures, and talks each semester and maintains an extensive book and video library. The Art Center features exhibits of contemporary

Robert Indiana's LOVE statue at IMA, p. 114

Indianapolis Museum of Art

Indy's Hearts of Art

Massachusetts Avenue—Lights flickered and dimmed during the early 1990s, when support for the arts was uncertain, but the area of Massachusetts Ave. is experiencing a revival of sorts, as coffee shops, performing arts facilities, and boutiques move into the vicinity. Noteworthy galleries in the neighborhood include 4 Star Gallery, 653 Massachusetts Ave., 317/686-6382, which features cutting-edge exhibits, and Dean Johnson Gallery, 646 Massachusetts Ave., 317/634-8020, which shows works by talented local artists.

Downtown—The Stutz Gallery, 1036 N. Capitol Ave. 317/684-9471, is in the historic Stutz Business Center, and is a co-op rotation gallery featuring several artists. Other artists and galleries have studios and showrooms there as well.

Fountain Square—At presstime, Phil Campbell was planning to move his Hot House Art Gallery from its former location in the Faris Building to the old G.C. Murphy building (1043 Virginia Ave.) in the Fountain Square neighborhood. A Herron graduate and artist, Campbell represents 12 artists. Readers of Nuvo newsweekly voted Hot House "Best Art Gallery" in 1998.

Broad Ripple—At the north end of this community is the Hoosier Salon Gallery, 6434 N. College Ave., 317/253-5340, which has sponsored exhibits since 1925 and continues to feature Hoosier artists. Sharing the same building is Byron and Sons Gallery, 317/257-6714, which buys and sells paintings by nineteenth- and twentieth-century Indiana artists such as T. C. Steele and William Forsyth. Also specializing in art from this period, Hoosier and otherwise, is the Winthrop Art Gallery, 6224 Winthrop Ave., 317/255-1127, the city's oldest gallery. The Center for the Creative Arts Gallery, 6263 Carrollton Ave., 317/255-9633, features works from active state artists (who own and operate this co-op facility).

artists in all media, but it particularly supports and promotes state and regional artists. In addition, the facility sponsors the popular Broad Ripple Art Fair in May. The facility's Basile Gallery Gift Shop sells art on consignment. The Art Center, incidentally, was designed by city native and world-acclaimed architect Michael Graves. Open Mon–Fri 9–10, Sat 9–6, Sun noon–3. Free. &. (North)

RUSCHMANN ART GALLERY
948 N. Alabama St.

317/634-3114
Mark Ruschmann has successfully weathered the ups and downs of the art market during the 15 years he has owned a gallery in Indy. His gallery features contemporary artwork by 40 regional and nationally known artists in all media, and specializes in indoor and outdoor sculpture. Novice art lovers are encouraged to come in to learn more about art. Works are available for as little as $200 and as much as several thousand dollars. Open Tue–Sat 11–5. (Downtown)

Indy Parks

8

PARKS, GARDENS, AND RECREATION AREAS

Alas, Indy has no majestic mountains, craggy coasts, or vast expanses of canyon. But what the city lacks in dramatic scenery, it makes up for in quiet surprises, like serene gardens and sun-drenched plazas tucked away in downtown corners and walking paths meandering along waterways or weaving through neighborhood parks.

Indy Parks and Recreation alone manages nearly 150 parks from nature preserves to modern recreation complexes. In addition, Indy Parks is developing a system of trails, or linear parks, that will eventually link 175 miles of neighborhoods, parks, and recreational, historical, and natural areas. In the meantime, neighborhood parks are liberally sprinkled throughout the city. Sadly, we simply cannot mention them all here—but rest assured, you're never far from a shaded park bench, a sun-washed patch of grass, or a winding trail in Indianapolis. (For a complete listing of parks and more information, call Indy Parks and Recreation at 317/327-0000.)

Each place listed in this chapter is strollable—featuring areas or trails for purposeful walking or aimless wandering. Moreover, each place provides benches, steps, picnic tables, or lush lawn—so you can relax and take in the pleasant surroundings.

ALBERT AND SARAH RUBEN HOLOCAUST MEMORIAL GARDEN
6701 Hoover Rd.
317/251-9467
In this garden next to the Jewish Community Center, a brick walkway leads you on a journey through 5,000 years of Jewish history, and leads to the Holocaust memorial. The JCC, which includes a children's playground, an athletic field, a day-camp area, and a large pavilion, is a membership facility

(for more information see Chapter 10), but the public is welcome to visit the memorial and the walkway. Open dawn until dusk. Free. (North)

BROAD RIPPLE PARK
1610 Broad Ripple Ave.
317/327-7161
A fitness trail for wooded walks (you can use the equipment or just enjoy a stroll) leads to the edge of White River. Crawl down the bank for a view of boaters (there's a public boat launch nearby) or throw in a fishing line. There's a large sheltered picnic area, tennis courts, a playground, and an outdoor pool. Open dawn until dusk. Free. (North)

BROOKSIDE PARK
3500 Brookside Pkwy., S. Dr.
317/327-7179
Offering wooded trails that wind along the brook as well as open areas for kite flying and Frisbee playing, this eastside park is a perfect escape for area residents. There are also playgrounds, a basketball area, a recreation center, and an outdoor pool.

During warm weather, the neighborhood association hosts frequent festivities. Open dawn until dusk. Free. (East/Southeast)

CAPITOL COMMONS
Washington and Capitol Sts.
It's hard to believe that a few years ago, this picturesque corner was a parking lot. Today, the cars are hidden in an underground garage, and downtown workers and visitors can stroll through the trim gardens sandwiched between the Westin Hotel and the Indiana Convention Center. A large fountain mesmerizes weary shoppers who stop to rest on its park benches. Free. (Downtown)

EAGLE CREEK PARK
7840 W. 56th St.
317/327-7110
Eagle Creek Park is without question the finest park managed by Indy Parks and Recreation. It is one of the largest municipal parks in the country, with more than 4,000 acres of woodlands, an abundance of wildlife, and a 1,300-acre reservoir. The peaceful trails and

---

Best Spots for Winter Activity

Eagle Creek Park features 10 miles of marked cross-country trails (you can rent ski equipment there).

Southeastway Park draws cross-country skiers and sledders with its mix of open, wooded, and hilly terrain.

Ellenberger Park and *Perry Park* offer indoor ice-skating from October to April.

For those who prefer the frosty outdoors, there's ice-skating on *Eagle Creek*'s pond. Call 317/327-7139 to confirm whether or not the pond is frozen.

Most Romantic Spots for Weddings

Garfield Park—*Couples can choose between the gazebo in the conservatory or the 1920s pagoda.*

Indianapolis Museum of Art—*Construction scheduled for 1999 will limit opportunities—but the outdoor gardens are popular choices for warm-weather weddings. The betrothed will undoubtedly be disappointed to learn that they'll not be able to exchange "I do's" in front of the museum's famed LOVE statue. The front terrace and sculpture court are tented.*

University Park—*It may be the city's best-kept secret—since no one's ever requested it for a wedding site. But its tree-shaded plaza, profusion of flowers, and lovely gilded fountain offer a charming setting for nuptials.*

Eagle Creek Park—*The Hide-A-Way and Eagle's Crest are two wooded areas popular for weddings. Each includes a house with a kitchen and bride and groom rooms, as well as indoor accommodations if the weather turns bad.*

Indianapolis Canal Walk—*The best spots are the Vermont Street Plaza, with two grand staircases, and the Walnut Street Basin, with gently rolling slopes and landscaped paths. Contact Indy Parks and Recreation for information, 317/327-0000.*

Crown Hill Cemetery—*No joke! The Gothic Chapel and the Waiting Station are buildings that could be on top of a wedding cake.*

White River Gardens—*Scheduled for completion in 1999, the Wedding Garden will be bordered by hedge mazes and brightened by an 1899 heritage garden.*

---

tranquil scenery are unsurpassed in the area. Some of the best spots are Lilly Reflecting Pond, complete with lilypads and cool, stone benches; Lilly Lake, with paddle boating; the newly renovated nature center; the marina; and countless trails and open areas with playgrounds and picnic shelters.

(For information about the activities offered at the park, see Chapter 10.) Open dawn until dusk. Parking: $2 per vehicle; $3 on weekends and holidays. (West/Southwest)

ELLENBERGER PARK
5301 E. St. Clair St.

317/327-7176

Ellenberger Park is always abuzz with activity. With 45 acres of wooded rolling landscape, the park offers a serene retreat. Outdoors there are walking trails, picnic sites, playground areas, campfire pits for cookouts, six tennis courts, and a swimming pool. There's also a recreation center where you can buy food. Open dawn until dusk. Free. (East/Southeast)

FORT HARRISON STATE PARK
5753 Glenn Rd.
317/591-0904

In what was probably one of the quickest takeovers in history, Fort Benjamin Harrison witnessed a peaceable retreat by the armed forces and reopened as a state park in 1996. The park is now home to endangered wildlife rather than military troops, and its nearly 1,750 acres attract families and nature-lovers to playgrounds, picnic areas, three small lakes (with fishing), and wooded hiking trails. Other features include an 18-hole golf course, a paved trail for bicyclists and in-line skaters, and a saddle barn with guided trail rides. Open dawn until dusk. Parking: $2 for in-state cars; $5 for out-of-state cars. (East/Southeast)

GARFIELD PARK
2450 Shelby St.
317/327-7220

One of the city's oldest parks, Garfield Park was called Southern Park until 1881, when it was renamed in commemoration of the assassinated President Garfield. It features a newly restored conservatory with a 15-foot waterfall and a greenhouse that contains exotic blooms and tropical plants. Flower shows and other events are scheduled throughout the year. Outdoors are a charming pagoda, built

in the 1920s, and a sunken garden. The park also has an outdoor aquatic center, a center for performing arts, biking and walking trails, and a new family center. Open dawn until dusk. Free. (East/Southeast)

HOLCOMB GARDENS
Butler University
4600 Sunset Ave.
317/940-9352

You'll swear you stumbled onto a royal English estate when you see these spectacular gardens. A length of lawn (large enough for a croquet game) rolls like an emerald carpet between two manicured rows of hedges and blooming flowerbeds. At one end is a fountain featuring, appropriately enough, a statue of Persephone, goddess of vegetation. The garden's stone and wooden benches offer visitors a chance to rest. The Central Canal runs tranquilly along the side of the gardens—cross a bridge and wander along the Canal Tow Path. Open dawn until dusk. Free. (North)

Persephone at Holcomb Gardens

Holcomb Gardens

The "Ruins" at Holliday Park

It started in 1958: New York City's venerable St. Paul Building was scheduled for demolition. Its facade featured a compelling sculpture depicting the three races—which had been designed by renowned sculptor Karl Bitter. Rather than raze this work of art, the building owners promoted a contest, to design a new setting for the statues. Contenders included Hoosier artist Elmer Taflinger.

Perhaps it was meant to be—after all, the sculpture was constructed of Indiana limestone. Or maybe the judges were genuinely impressed by Taflinger's grand plan for a "Constitution Mall." Taflinger won the contest, and the statues, weighing 100 tons and valued at $150,000, began their journey to Indianapolis.

The trip was to prove a rocky one. Funding problems slowed the project. To aggravate matters, the artist stubbornly insisted that all details of his plan be followed, including a fountain that would pulse a 40-minute message in Morse code.

The next 20 years were a staccato series of stops and starts for the completion of the "Ruins," as they came to be called. Taflinger alternately lobbied, pressured, and pleaded for funding that eventually accumulated to more than $250,000. Although the artist did make some compromises (the Morse-code fountain was never implemented), park manager John Schaust insists that today's park is basically true to Taflinger's original plans.

Happily, Taflinger lived to see the completion of his dream. In 1978 the parks department dedicated Holliday Park and Taflinger's "symbolic lesson in history." He died in the early 1980s, but his presence lives on in the park. Literally. If you examine the west side of the facade closely, you'll discover old Elmer's silhouette carved into the center of a wreath.

HOLLIDAY PARK
6349 Spring Mill Rd.
317/327-7180
Ready for a walk and can't decide between a formal-garden ambience and a rugged, lost-in-the-woods experience? At Holliday Park, you can have both. Scheduled for completion

in the fall of 1999 are butterfly and hummingbird gardens, a prairie preserve, and a new nature center. Some pretty sophisticated playground equipment entertains kids as well as adults, who seem unable to resist the temptation of a giant, octopus-like slide. Deeper into the park are hilly, marked trails that lead down to White River, where children and parents splash in the shallow water. (For more information see Chapter 6.) Open dawn until dusk. Free. (North)

INDIANAPOLIS CANAL WALK
Ohio and West Sts.
Indianapolis

With antique streetlights lining the way, tidy landscaping, and the soothing sound of fountains and geysers, the Indianapolis Canal Walk seems like a stroll along Paris's Rive Gauche. This stretch of walkway below street level runs from St. Clair Street to the White River. (Plans are in the works to extend it north to 11th Street.) The USS *Indianapolis* Monument is at the north end of the walkway. Along the walk are plenty of benches, picnic areas, and

Monument Circle at Christmas, p. 130

Rob Banayote/The Indianapolis Project

colorful murals. You can rent pedal boats at the Washington Street end from April to October (weather permitting). Free. (Downtown)

INDIANAPOLIS MUSEUM OF ART
1200 W. 38th St.
317/923-1331

While the museum's collections are indeed impressive (see Chapter 7 for

TRIVIA

The House of Blue Lights

Searching the secluded woods surrounding a far eastside estate has been a rite of passage for nearly three generations of teenagers. True, some are just looking for a romantic place to park. But many, enthralled by stories whispered in the light of a campfire or at a slumber party, are hoping for a glimpse of a glass casket bathed in ghostly blue light. Here, as the oral tradition goes, a mad widower was said to keep the body of his long-dead wife. The man was Skiles Test. And although no casket, body, or blue lights were ever found on his estate after his death in 1964, the legend lives on—and local security continues to shoo away the curious who roam the densely wooded Skiles Test Park late at night.

TRIVIA

Bugfest at Southeastway Park draws bug lovers like, well, flies. Each August, attendees learn about, look for, and eat bugs.

more information), its grounds are works of art in themselves. Trails meander to quiet spots for reflection. The historic Oldfields gardens add color throughout the grounds. There's a wheelchair-accessible garden and a greenhouse where you can purchase plants you admired on your walk.

The new Ravine Garden, which opened in spring 1999, features three pools and thousands of trees, shrubs, and plants, and recreates a historic garden that was once on the estate in 1930. Of course, there are marvelous sculptures at every turn, including the renowned *LOVE* statue by native artist Robert Indiana. Grounds open daily dawn until dusk; greenhouse Tue–Sat 10–5, Sun 12–5. Free. (North)

KRANNERT PARK
605 S. High School Rd.
317/327-7375

A tranquil, tree-shaded pond is the picturesque focal point of this westside park. A playground area attracts young families, while the pond lures fishing aficionados of all ages. The park is perfect for strolling, picnicking, or simply sitting and unwinding on park benches or large boulders near the water. Krannert Park also has a recreation facility with an indoor pool and aquatic center. Open dawn until dusk. Free. (West/Southwest)

MILITARY PARK
West and New York Sts.
317/634-4567

The most park-like component of the White River State Park complex, Military Park features a shady grove of mature trees that shelters picnic areas and park benches. The oldest park in Indianapolis, it was the site of the first state fair in 1836 and, in the 1860s, a staging area for Union troops—which earned the park its inclusion on the National Register of Historic Places. Today, it's a popular place for events such as the AIDS walk in October and Jazz in the Park during the summer. Open dawn until dusk. Free. (Downtown)

MONUMENT CIRCLE
Meridian and Market Sts.
317/232-7615

According to Bill Sweeney, executive director of the War Memorial, there's nothing better on a warm summer day than to grab a hot dog, sit by the fountain on Monument Circle, and watch the world go by. The fountains and pools that encircle Soldiers' and Sailors' Monument provide plenty of nooks and crannies for weary shoppers, sightseers, and workers. The monument is worth a winter trip as well, when it is transformed into the city's largest Christmas tree. (For more information see Chapter 5.) Free. (Downtown)

PERRY PARK
451 E. Stop 11 Rd.
317/888-0070

The emphasis at Perry Park is on sports activities (it's one of two parks that offer indoor ice-skating in the winter), but there are lots of escape-and-wander options, including 10 acres of woods to explore. A few trails wind around picnic areas, a shelter house, playgrounds, and benches. The open areas are perfect for exercising the dog or stretching out on a blanket. Open dawn until dusk. Free. (East/Southeast)

RIVER PROMENADE
801 W. Washington St.
317/233-2434
A half-mile of limestone-lined walkway extends from the Washington Street Bridge to White River Parkway, winding behind the Indianapolis Zoo.

Many of the giant blocks of native stone feature etchings of famous buildings, such as the Empire State Building, that were built with Indiana limestone. A rose window made of polished limestone is an intriguing attraction along the way. In 1992 the Promenade won a prestigious design award from the American Society of Landscaping Architecture. Open dawn until dusk. Free. (Downtown)

RIVERSIDE PARK
2420 E. Riverside Dr.
317/327-7171
Once the site of the first city zoo (built in 1899), Riverside Park is Indy's second

You Call This a State Park?

White River State Park is not your typical state park. It has a fitness center, a ballpark, two museums, and a bigger-than-life 3-D movie theater, not to mention the Indianapolis Zoo.

Dedicated in 1979 and located in the heart of Indy's urban center, White River State Park has flowered as the result of a state and community investment of more than $57 million. In addition to the zoo, the park's attractions include:

- *Victory Field Baseball Park, home of the Indianapolis Indians*
- *National Institute for Fitness and Sport, a state-of-the-art fitness facility and research center*
- *Eiteljorg Museum of American Indians and Western Art*
- *Military Park (There had to be picnic tables here somewhere!)*
- *River Promenade, running behind the zoo*
- *IMAX 3-D movie theater*
- *Indiana State Museum (2001)*
- *White River Gardens (summer 1999)*
- *NCAA Headquarters (late 1999)*
- *NCAA Hall of Champions Museum (2000)*

The "Ruins" at Holliday Park, p. 128

largest. Within its perimeters are an aquatic center, three golf courses, and the Kuntz Memorial Soccer Stadium. The park also provides playgrounds and areas for walking, biking, and picnicking. Miles of natural greenway connect destinations throughout the park. There's also a small pond surrounded by trees, benches, and picnic tables. Open dawn until dusk. Free. (West/Southwest)

SOUTHEASTWAY PARK
5624 S. Carroll Rd.
317/861-5167

Nature is the focus of this park's activities and design 188 acres of fields, woodlands, wetlands, and flood plains offer endless opportunities for exploration and escape. Marked trails allow for solitary wanderings, but the park organizes a number of environment-oriented guided hikes—as well as some more unusual events, such as the Creek Stomp and Bugfest. Shelters are available for picnics. Hayrides are popular in the fall, and sledding is a big draw in winter. Open dawn until dusk. Free. (East/Southeast)

VETERANS MEMORIAL PLAZA
Meridian and North Sts.
317/232-7615

Part of a five-block area that encompasses the Indiana World War Memorial, the plaza is divided into three separate areas. University Park is decorated with a fountain, flowers, and monuments. Obelisk Square also has a fountain, as well as a mini-Washington Monument. On a breezy day, the sounds from the fountain vie with the snapping of the 50 flags just north of the obelisk. The American Legion Mall sinks into a lawn that invites strollers, sunbathers, and Frisbee players, providing a view of city landmarks such as the Vietnam Memorial and the Scottish Rite Cathedral. Free. (Downtown)

WHITE RIVER GARDENS
White River State Park, on the
grounds of the Indianapolis Zoo
317/630-2001

Scheduled for completion in summer 1999, this new addition to the White River State Park complex will boast three acres of gardens and as many as 1,000 varieties of plants and flowers. A greenhouse will feature seasonal blooms, tropical plants, and butterflies. Hedge gardens, sunken gardens, aquatic gardens, sculptures, and quiet corners will offer visitors a serene setting to while away the time. A resource center will be available for gardeners, and the Wedding Garden will offer a romantic setting for nuptials. Free. (Downtown)

**WILLIAM S. SAHM PARK
AND GOLF COURSE
6800 E. 91st St.**

**Fishers
317/327-7161**

Indy's far-north suburbs are growing at an alarming rate, but this 155-acre park, with wooded trails and sports facilities (golf course, sand volleyball, tennis courts, and soccer fields), provides a prescription to counter the madness. An aquatic center is scheduled to open next year. A shady grove of trees shelters benches, fitness stations, and picnic sites. Broad, grassy areas feature playgrounds. Open dawn until dusk. Free. (North)

9

SHOPPING

Just as there has been a huge increase in the number of restaurants in the city in the past 20 years, the number of stores has grown dramatically. Between Keystone at the Crossing and Castleton, in particular, locals gaze in bewilderment at the vast array, wondering how so many stores can compete.

There are nationally and regionally known chain stores on every side of town, ensuring satisfaction for inveterate and reluctant shoppers alike. You can be sure that wherever there's a Target, the city's favorite discount store, there's some good shopping nearby.

Plenty of national companies Brookstone, Gap, Smith & Hawkens, Victoria's Secret have set up shop in Indy, but many of the city's stores are unique to Indianapolis or Indiana. Those are the stores listed here.

SHOPPING DISTRICTS

Broad Ripple

No area of town comes close to matching the eclectic mixture of shops in Broad Ripple. You can buy tailored dresses and lake-cottage casuals at The Depot or fun but up-scale clothes at Marigold's. There are guitars to strum and baubles to buy, classic accessories at The Shop and adorable ones at Periwinkle. There's a Christian bookshop, a health-food store, a perfumery, and more. If you stay in the heart of the retail district, you'll miss bargains and fun, such as The Little House and Urban Gypsy. Shop till you drop, then reward yourself at the Broad Ripple Trophy Center. Admire your prizes while sipping or supping at one of Broad Ripple's too-many-to-count eateries.

ARTZY PHARTZY
918 Broad Ripple Ave.
317/257-1688

A favorite among teens and 20-some-things, this shop is full of hot, hip clothes, accessories, wigs, Beanie Babies, and fun trinkets. The eclectic assortment at Artzy Phartzy makes it an ideal place to shop for something out-of-the-ordinary or a gag gift. (North)

THE DEPOT
900 E. 64th St.
317/253-3768
In a neighborhood known for funki-ness, this shop stands out. It sells classic clothes, from dressy to cottage casuals. It is actually inside the old train depot, right beside today's Monon Trail. (North)

MARIGOLD'S
6323 N. Guilford Ave.
317/254-9939
Marigold's offers fashionable and exciting clothes at reasonable prices. The space is small, but the variety is good. The sales staff is friendly. (North)

SCRIBBLES
808 Broad Ripple Ave.
317/251-2331
For those who love to put pen to paper, this shop has a selection of high-quality stationery (including a full Crane line), lovely journals, and more. Party invitations are a specialty. *ER!* fans, take note: "Jerry's" mom, Patricia Benrubi, is one of the store's owners. (North)

TURANDOT DECORATIVE ARTS
912 Westfield Blvd.
317/255-5969
An elegant shop that stays ahead of the game by featuring the absolute latest in trends. This shop is packed with one-of-a-kinds, such as baubles, accessories, and clocks, that beg to be whisked home. A broad price range gives the shop added appeal. (North)

Castleton

If you can brace yourself for the traffic, you can bring home about anything you want from Indianapolis's largest shopping area. An auger, an alligator belt, a bow tie, boxing gloves, a Beatles CD, a chandelier, a camera, a canoe . . . you probably can't order an elephant, but, then again, we've never tried. The big draws are the many nationally known stores here, including Toys R Us, Pier One, Linens and Things, Shoe Carnival, and Half-Price Books. The mall at the center of this complex has just been expanded, making its Ayres store the finest in town and adding Von Maur, an upscale retailer, which filled the void left by Montgomery Wards and ratcheted up the quality level at the mall. Parking is generally easier on the north side of the mall.

GRAHAM'S CRACKERS
5981 E. 86th St.
317/849-5300
www.grahamscrackers.com
Begun as a small nutcracker shop, this store has grown and added a grand variety of gifts, collectibles, and greeting cards. A purveyor of Department 56, famous for its miniature holiday villages, the shop displays ceramic villages year-round. (North)

KITTLE'S HOME FURNISHINGS
8600 Allisonville Rd.
317/849-5300
www.kittles.com
This enormous store, newly redesigned, carries contemporary and traditional furniture and accessories to suit almost any taste. There are other locations in the city, but this is the largest. (North)

TIP

For a truly personalized gift and an adventure in creativity, head to Olivia's Painted Cup, Nora Plaza, 1300 East 86th St., 317/574-7990. At this ceramics shop, you can make your own pottery, with the help of artists on staff.

Clearwater

Eager to take advantage of the up-scale shopping meccas created by the Fashion Mall and Keystone at the Crossing, local merchants moved to this area, just east of the White River. With each successful strip mall, a new one was built just a little farther east; now shops extend all the way to Castleton. Chains have moved in, too, including discount shoe store DSW Shoe Warehouse.

BEAR CREEK GALLERY AND TRADING POST
8659 River Crossing Blvd.
317/580-0882
A purveyor of Southwestern-style jewelry, artwork, furniture, and more, this store also offers classes, such as an overview on Kachina dolls for the beginner collector. Original works by many Native American artists are on display. (North)

HOUSEWORKS
3917 E. 82nd St.
317/578-7000
Houseworks sells high-quality contemporary furniture, lighting, and accessories, including Wassily chairs and Le Corbusier loungers. You can furnish your office at the store's newest addition (next door), At the Office. (North)

Keystone at the Crossing

Capitalizing on the success of the Fashion Mall, merchants have been opening shops across the road from the mall to the south and east. (Each of the areas has its own moniker, but if you can get to 86th and Keystone, you'll know you've arrived.) Some are chains—including Bed, Bath & Beyond; Old Navy; Kohl's; Zany Brainy; and a dandy Borders with a café—while others are one-of-a-kind, such a Theobald's and Two Magnolias.

DETAILS
8663 River Crossing Blvd.
317/571-9977
If it isn't beautiful or whimsical, owner Susie Beiman doesn't stock it. She sells artistic jewelry, distinctive home accessories, gifts, and a few pieces of furniture. (North)

HAND N' HAND CHILDREN'S SHOPPE
8639 River Crossing Blvd.
317/844-4263 (HAND)
This store specializes in children's bedding, accessories, and clothing (for kids up to age 14). Children enjoy crawling into the giant tree trunk while parents browse through the precious clothing. This is a great spot to splurge for an exceptional outfit. (North)

Deborah Simon's Top Ten Shopping Tips (Plus One)

"I guess shopping is in the blood," says Deborah Simon. And who would know this better than the senior vice president of Simon Property Group (which has developed shopping malls all over the country) and a member of the International Council of Shopping Centers?

1. **Keystone at the Crossing** has two of my favorite stores, **Pottery Barn**, 317/571-1591, and **Hold Everything**, 317/846-7611, and one of the best toy stores around, **Kits and Kaboodle**, 317/574-3333. (North)

2. **Circle Centre** has the coolest architecture of any mall anywhere and has captured the downtown market with its mix of shopping and food. (Downtown)

3. **Castleton Square** is the monster mall of Indianapolis, with all the mall stuff you need, the largest and most exciting **Galyan's**, and a new department store entry to Indiana, **Von Maur**. (North)

4. For beautiful jewelry and gifts, **G. Thrapp Jewelers**, 317/255-5555, is the best. Two stores down is **Charles Mayer**, 317/257-2900, which has nice home and gift items, and **Eckert Fine Art Gallery**, 317/255-4561, known for its Indiana artists. All these shops are at 56th and Illinois Sts. (North)

5. If you love fine linens, here's the secret—**Parkside Linen**, 317/844-1756, in Northview Mall. (North)

6. Beautiful children's clothing can be found at **Blue Bear**, 1488 E. 86th St., 317/848-2327, and **Hand N' Hand**, 317/844-4263. (North)

7. I love going to **Two Magnolias**, 8689 River Crossing Blvd., 317/843-1509, a favorite for gifts and home décor. (North)

8. I could spend most of my life in a bookstore, and **Borders**, at River Crossing, 317/574-1775, is the place to do it. A few doors down, I love going through **Bed, Bath & Beyond**, 317/843-0746. (North)

9. In **Broad Ripple Village**, you can find all sorts of oddities, and I don't mean just the people. (North)

10. If you really love antiques, drive to **Beauchamps**, 16405 Westfield Blvd., Westfield, 317/896-3717. (North)

11. Okay, I know that I was going to do just 10 items, but after this, you'll want some coffee, so stop in **Lulu's Electric Cafe**, 1460 W. 86th St., 317/879-1995, for the best brew in town. (North)

STUDIO V BOUTIQUE
8635 River Crossing Blvd.
317/843-2463
Studio V Boutique specializes in fashionable plus-sized clothing, which is rarely available in department stores. If an item in your size isn't on the rack, the store will get it for you, either through the manufacturer or through another retail store. (North)

TWO MAGNOLIAS
8689 River Crossing Blvd.
317/843-1509
Two Southern belles transplanted from Atlanta started this colorful, elegant store because they couldn't find their favorite Southern looks elsewhere. They offer antiques, lamps, handmade and hand-painted items, candles, pillows, and more. (North)

Nora Plaza Area

A series of strip malls stretch along 86th Street from just east of its intersection with Westfield Boulevard to about Guilford Avenue. Nora Plaza has a good variety of stores: Aronstam Fine Jewelers, renowned citywide; the Blue Bear, filled with children's clothing; Killybegs, an Irish shop; and Perry's Luggage and Gifts. In addition, Northview Mall, just east of Westfield Boulevard, contains several one-of-a-kind shops, including a favorite children's bookstore, Treehouse Tails.

THE ACCENT SHOP
1520 E. 86th St.
317/844-5112
This store carries an extensive selection of gifts, stationery, and more. There is a nice variety of seasonal items, such as Easter tablecloths and Fourth of July celebratory napkins. (North)

PARKSIDE LINEN
Northview Mall, 1756 E. 86th St.
317/844-1756
At this store, beds and tables are works of art. Bring in favorite linens

Two Magnolias

Two Magnolias

and pick out new pillows, shams, and other items. The focus is on fine linens, but there are some funky items, vintage linens, and more. (North)

SINFONIA
Northview Mall, 1730 E. 86th St.
317/843-0411 or 800/566-0411
About 90 percent of the music in this specialty shop is classical. Sinfonia carries only recordings that have been critically well received. Sales clerks, most of whom have degrees in music, are exceptionally knowledgeable. (North)

North Willow Commons

The shops in North Willow are primarily locally owned. Many of the stores are fairly upscale, but the prices are certainly not outrageous. Stein-Mart, a chain discount store, draws crowds, and there are plenty of places to dine. Because there's ample parking in this area and the traffic is not bad, shopping here is a leisurely experience.

ARNOLD'S MEN'S STORE
1484 W. 86th St.
317/875-8887
www.arnoldsmenstore.com
In business for more than 20 years, Arnold's sells upscale, contemporary men's fashions. Store employees will

alter your purchases in a day, press your shirts, and deliver your parcels to your home or hotel. Custom-made shirts and suits are available. (North)

COLLECTION 94
1478 W. 86th St.
317/872-9494
This store offers stylish women's clothing. The owner purchases only one or two of each item and keeps a list of who buys what for formal occasions to help avoid look-alike gowns. The prices are modest in comparison with prices at similar high-end stores in other large cities. (North)

LITTLE WOMEN
1470 W. 86th St.
317/872-0374
Grandmothers can't get enough of this store, full of elegant clothing for girls up to age 16 and little boys through size 4T. The store also carries embossed baby books and fairy-tale costumes. (North)

Old Towne Greenwood

Old Towne Greenwood is a charming area, with shops, including a number of antique stores, housed in old homes. Most of the stores are clustered around the intersection of Madison Avenue and Main Street. However, those who roam will be rewarded with such finds as the Southside Art

League Gallery, 299 East Broadway, 317/882-5562, and the gift shop Diversions, 1675 West Smith Valley Road, 317/865-9014.

ACCENTS
176 N. Madison Ave.
Greenwood
317/889-4863
Teddy bears, lace, baskets, Yankee candles, gourmet food items, and more fill every room of this cheery old home. Don't miss the upstairs, where there are more items, including children's things. (East/Southeast)

MAKING THYME HERB SHOPPE
199 N. Madison Ave.
Greenwood
317/889-4395
Head here for cracked rose hips, nettles, horseradish powder, lavender, frankincense, and myrrh. In addition to the herbs and spices, this shop sells mostly Hoosier-made products, Dillman Farms jellies, Bloomington jams, and soaps from Morgantown. Open Tue–Sat. (East/Southeast)

The Shoppes at 56th and Illinois

At this tiny intersection, there's hardly a store that isn't notable, including the meat market, hair salon, bookstore, and pet shop.

CHARLES MAYER & CO.
5629 N. Illinois St.
317/257-2900
Delicate porcelain, sturdy pottery, luxurious towels, furniture, and art are among the offerings at this nineties revival of a store that was one of the city's finest in the first half of this century. Fragrant lotions, adorable children's items, and gourmet soups make this a great place to buy a gift. (North)

TARKINGTON TWEED
5631 N. Illinois St.
317/253-6632
In this upscale store you'll find a fine selection of women's clothes and accessories, such as jumpers, high-style sweatsuits, slacks, dresses, and other casual wear. (North)

G.THRAPP JEWELERS
5609 N. Illinois St.
317/255-5555
The master jewelers at G. Thrapp create rare and exotic pieces. The store also carries crystal, Limoges boxes, and more. (North)

Speedway Super Center

This large strip center, located at 5852 Crawfordsville Rd., 317/243-8219, is convenient for shoppers who aren't necessarily looking for high-end, one-of-a-kind items. Stores include Old Navy, Kaybee Toys, Dollar Bills, Paul Harris, Factory Card Outlet, Kohl's, and Rainbow Apparel. This is a fine place to spend money while boasting about how much you've saved.

Zionsville

Roam up and down the sidewalks bordering Zionsville's brick main street, and you'll find many unusual little shops, including the sweet Children's Clothier. This quaint village is well known for its antique stores; there are at least 10 in town.

BROWN'S LAMP SHADE SHOP
315 W. Fifth St.
Zionsville
317/873-2284
Don't be fooled by the name. Although Brown's has hundreds of shades, it also carries antiques and

gifts. This is a charming spot to stop even if you are only browsing. (North)

**STACY LABOLT'S
FINE LADIES APPAREL
125 W. Sycamore St.
Zionsville
317/873-2087**
Those who love sweaters will be in their element at this shop. Labolt's also boasts a wide selection of travel clothes and accessories. (North)

NOTABLE BOOKSTORES AND NEWSSTANDS

Large chain bookstores like Borders Books & Music and Barnes & Noble unquestionably offer shoppers the broadest selections of books. But if you're looking for a specialty item, such as an out-of-print book, you'll probably find it at one of Indy's locally owned booksellers or newsstands.

**ARCHITECTURAL CENTER
BOOKSTORE
Majestic Building
47 S. Pennsylvania St.
317/634-3871**
If it has to do with design and use of space, you'll find a book about it here. Subjects include preservation, landscaping, and Prairie School style. (Downtown)

**BROAD RIPPLE BOOKSHOP
6407 Ferguson St.
317/259-1980**
Located in a nineteenth-century cottage that it shares with the Urban Gypsy, this bookshop deals in rare and out-of-print books. The book-savvy staff will help you find whatever you need. It's open only Thu, Fri, and Sat. (North)

**INDIANA NEWS
20 E. Maryland St.
317/632-7680**
The granddaddy of local newsstands, this store carries more than 5,000 different newspapers from around the world. The knowledgable staff members are a helpful resource. (Downtown)

**X-PRESSION BOOKSTORE
AND GALLERY
5912 College Ave.
317/257-5448**
X-Pression has the city's largest selection of African American literature. It also carries gifts. (North)

OTHER NOTABLE STORES

**BEAUCHAMPS ANTIQUES
16405 Westfield Blvd.
Westfield
317/896-3717**
With one of the broadest selection of European and American antiques and accessories in central Indiana, this shop is worth the 15-mile drive north. (North)

TRIVIA

Which stores offer the most family-friendly shopping in town? Paul Harris has playrooms for children at seven of its 12 local stores. Von Maur has the most accommodating bathrooms (spotless and spacious!) with a mother's room and a separate family room, where dads can take daughters.

COLLECTIONS ANTIQUES
111 E. 49th St.
317/283-5251
Beautifully appointed, this shop sells
one-of-a kind items, antiques, and accessories. Another antique store,
Hope's, is just across the street.
(North)

HARDWICKE'S PIPE
AND TOBACCO
24 N. Meridian St.
317/635-7884
For imported cigarettes, cigars,
pipes, and other items, including fine
pens, steins, and collectibles, this is
the place to go. There's a Hard-
wicke's in Broad Ripple as well.
(Downtown)

HENSELMEIER'S SADDLERY
AND WESTERN WEAR
1000 U.S. 31S
Greenwood
317/881-8225
Headed for a round up, a square
dance, or a dude ranch? Outfit yourself
at this big store with its broad selec-

tion of Western wear. Could anyone
stock more boots? (East/Southeast)

HOOSIER PEN COMPANY
Hyatt Regency
155 W. Washington St., Ste. 102
317/632-5712
www.hoosierpen.com
Beautiful pens, desk accessories, and
other gifts for the executive in your
life line the shelves here. The store
carries fine brands such as Mont
Blanc, Parker, Sensa, and Waterman.
(Downtown)

LUNA MUSIC
1521 W. 86th St.
317/875-5862
www.lunamusic.net
This store has a good selection and
an outstanding staff, who know the
trends and can get you anything from
the soundtrack for *Kiss Me Kate* to
the latest house techno. (North)

MIDLAND ARTS AND ANTIQUE
MARKET
907 E. Michigan St.

Circle Center, p. 146

Best Museum Shops

Don't forget to check out the treasures at the city's museum gift shops; our favorites are listed below.

Basile Gallery Gift Shop, *Indianapolis Art Center, 820 East 67th St., 317/255-2464*

Children's Museum Store, *3000 North Meridian St., 317/920-4606*

Indianapolis Museum of Art, *1200 West 38th St., 317/923-1331*

Better Than New Shop, *on the grounds of the IMA, 317/924-4951*

President Benjamin Harrison Home, *1230 North Delaware St., 317/631-1898*

Riley Museum Home Gift Shop, *528 Lockerbie St., 317/631-5885*

Trackside Gift Shop, *Indianapolis Motor Speedway Hall of Fame Museum, 4790 West 16th St., 317/484-6760*

White River Trader, *Eiteljorg Museum of American Indians and Western Art, 500 West Washington St., 317/636-9378 or 800/878-7978*

317/267-9005
Located just east of downtown, this old factory is home to about 100 vendors of antiques, art, and other collectible items. Eclectic describes the mix: old machinery, clothes, jewelry, furniture, and more. Be sure that you get to the upper floor. (East/Southeast)

PAUL HARRIS
11 S. Meridian St.
317/955-2100
www.paulharrisstores.com
Although this retailer was founded in Indianapolis in 1952, it didn't open this downtown flagship store until 1998. Four times as large as the chain's average shop, this store carries the full line of Paul Harris branded clothing,

designed for women on the go; accessories; and more. Prices are reasonable, and shoppers can find clothes for any occasion, from casual to business to formal. (Downtown)

REIS NICHOLS JEWELERS
Majestic Building
47 S. Pennsylvania St.
317/635-4467
www.betterdiamonds.com
The quality of this store's bracelets and pendants is exceptional. Founded in 1919, the shop is still owned by the founding family. There's a new location at Clearwater, 3535 East 86th Street, 317/255-4467. (Downtown)

SOLOMON/JONES ANTIQUES AND INTERIORS

1103 E. 52nd St.
317475-0203 or 888/238-0472
In this antique and traditional interior
design shop, no one hovers over you
as you peruse the art, furniture, and
accessories. Newly located along the
Monon Trail, this antique shop stocks
high-quality items, including art and
accessories. (North)

SPIECE
7435 N. Keystone Ave.
317/726-5200
This Indiana chain is known for its
Levis apparel, athletic shoes, and
sportswear. The shoe selection is
enormous. (North)

THE SPY SHOP
10059 E. Washington St.
317/842-0630
www.my-secret.com
CIA agent and James Bond wannabes
will find it all here: a tiny camera to at-
tach to your necktie, a guide to crack-
ing safes, a fake ink-pen microphone,
and more. The prices for many items
are steep, but it's fun to just look,
and there are even some items for
youngsters, such as squirt guns
masquerading as cigarette lighters.
(East/Southeast)

STOUT'S SHOE STORE
318 Massachusetts Ave.
317/632-7818
www.stouts@shoestore.com
If you want your kids to see how
your grandparents shopped for
shoes, stop by Stout's, around since
1886. Your payment travels to the office in a basket, as do your shoes,
where they are wrapped in brown
paper. Rockport, Hush Puppy, and
Easy Spirit are among the brands
carried. Youngsters get a kick out of
Ripley, the squawking blue parrot.
(Downtown)

SURROUNDINGS
1111 E. 61st St.
317/254-8883
Packed with treasures, this antiques,
art, and accessory shop is a visual
banquet. All the objects on display
show elegant and sophisticated
taste. Located in the back of the Mc-
Namara Florist building. (North)

TIM AND BILLY'S SALVAGE STORE
970 Fort Wayne Ave.
317/632-7161
www.architecturalantiques.net
For meticulous home restorers, this
drafty, dark old building is packed
with treasures, including faucets,
fireplace mantles, nuts, bolts, bird-
cages, and more. (Downtown)

VI WALKER SILVER
652 E. 52nd St.
317283-3753
www.viwalkersilver.com
Specializing in fine silverware, this
shop also carries china and other dining room accessories. If Walker
doesn't have the pattern or item you
want, she will do her best to track it
down for you. (North)

WELLS FLOWER AND GIFT HOUSE
2160 W. 86th St.
317/872-4267
In this sprawling shop, there's a room
(16 of them, in fact) for everything:
brass, tabletop items, kitchen accessories, children's clothes, stationery,
and much more. Flower arrange-
ments and greenhouse items are top
notch. (North)

MAJOR DEPARTMENT STORES

L. S. AYRES
Castleton Square Mall

Serendipitous Creations

A good idea goes far, and these local creations prove it.

CoasterStones—*Brothers Jay and Sandy Peacock bought a whetstone company in 1983. The nationally known stone coasters were created when their dad put his martini down on a stone and it absorbed moisture. For the name of the store nearest to you that carries the coasters, call Hindostone Products at 317/299-2200 or 800/288-2191.*

The Original Time Capsule Co.—*Jeff McCarty saved mementos from milestone events in his life and created these large, tin time capsules, figuring that everyone had as much trouble storing treasures as he did. Locally available at Graham's Crackers, Kits 'N' Kaboodles, the Museum Company, and elsewhere. Or you can call 317/729-8463 or 800/SAY-TIME.*

George F. Cram—*Back in 1867, this company started making maps, and it is still at it. Locally, you can find the maps at such spots as Odyssey Map Store, 902 North Delaware, 317/635-3837 or 800/972-1388. For other stores in Indy and around the country that carry the maps, call 317/635-5564 and ask for the commercial customer service.*

6020 E. 82nd St.
317/579-2900
Founded in Indianapolis by Lyman Ayres in the 1800s, this store is now part of the May Company chain and retains little of its Hoosier identity, although its goods remain reasonably priced. The newly renovated store at Castleton is the flagship shop in the city. Other locations include Glendale, 6101 North Keystone Avenue, 317/255-6611; Greenwood Park, 1251 U.S. Highway 31 North, 317/881-6781; and Lafayette Square,

3919 Lafayette Road, 317/293-8330. (North)

JACOBSON'S
Fashion Mall
8701 Keystone Crossing
317/574-0088
This upscale Michigan-based retailer is known for its inviting store and fine selection of clothing, shoes, gifts, housewares, and linens. The collections of designer clothes, shoes, and lingerie are particularly outstanding. (North)

LAZARUS
Castleton Square Mall
6020 E. 82nd St.
317/842-8880
A full-service department store with fashions, furniture, and more, this giant retailer gobbled up the old Wm. H. Block Company. Today, it is part of Federated Department Stores. Other locations include Greenwood Park, 1251 U.S. 31 North, 317/882-6244; Lafayette Square, 3919 Lafayette Road, 317/298-2213; Washington Square Mall, 10202 East Washington Street, 317/899-6213. (North)

NORDSTROM
Circle Centre
130 S. Meridian St.
317/636-2121
www.nordstrom.com
Rightfully renowned for good service, this large store trains clerks to put customers first and to find answers

Nordstrom at Circle Centre

Shawn Spence/The Indianapolis Project

and merchandise. The store has splendid fashions but limited housewares and no furniture; the shoe department has the best selection in town. (Downtown)

PARISIAN
Fashion Mall
8702 Keystone Crossing
Indianapolis
317/581-8200
This mid-market fashion retailer has a good selection, without the jammed racks and clutter in the aisles. There's also a downtown Parisian at Circle Centre, 1 West Washington Street, 317/971-6200. (North)

VON MAUR
Castleton Square Mall
6020 E. 82nd St.
317/594-1870
www.vonmaur.com
New to Indianapolis, this retailer established its reputation by caring for customers with such services as free gift-wrapping and free delivery anywhere in the United States. The stores are elegant, and the upscale clothing, shoes, and accessories are well displayed. There's also a Von Maur at the Greenwood Park Mall on 1251 U.S. 31 North in the East/Southeast. (North)

MAJOR SHOPPING MALLS

CASTLETON SQUARE MALL
6020 E. 82nd St.
317/849-9993
Major refurbishing in 1998 turned this dowdy giant into a chic big mama. The largest shopping mall in the city, in the midst of the largest shopping district in the city, this behemoth overflows with variety and style. Mall department stores include L. S. Ayres, Von Maur, Lazarus, JCPenney, and

Spas for a Shopping Pick-Me-Up

Sagging and flagging from power shopping? Revitalize yourself with a splurge at a spa.

Laser Skin Care Salon, *Circle Centre, 49 West Maryland, 317/266-1616, is downtown's answer for post-shopping relaxation and care. (Downtown)*

David and Mary, *Nora Corners, 1540 East 86th St., 317/844-6662, offers superb care at the spot that pioneered pampering in Indianapolis. (North)*

Phillipe's Spa and Juice Bar, *4635 East 82nd St., 317/578-9900, is the place to go for everything from manicures to nutritional consulting to yoga classes. (North)*

Sears. The new Galoyan's Trading Co. has added pizzazz with its four-story rock climbing wall and mega selections of sports gear and clothing. You can outfit yourself for a camping trip or a royal ball, decorate your home or equip your office, buy a camera or have a professional portrait made. Pregnant, short, tall, and small people will all find fashions here. Dining is casual and centered around a new food court near Galyan's. (North)

CIRCLE CENTRE
49 W. Maryland St.
317/681-8000

Circle Centre, a nationally acclaimed mall, has revitalized downtown shopping. The mall features two department stores, Nordstrom and Parisian, giant-sized versions of Limited, Limited Express, and Gap, and other nationally known stores, including Finish Line, Talbot's, Victoria's Secret, the Museum Company, Nine West, Structure, Sam Goody, the Disney Store, Doubleday Book Shops, and the Body Shop.

Not limited to chains, Circle Centre also contains Back Home Indiana, the best store in town to buy Hoosier-made and -related goods—including furniture, jewelry, books, coasters, foodstuffs, and more. Tarkington's offers a wide selection of food and wine gifts and has exquisite gift baskets. Circle Centre also has stores that sell athletic apparel emblazoned with logos of local teams.

Stop for a bite to eat at one of the restaurants, such as Bertolini's or California Café, or in the eclectic food court. Or stroll to the Artsgarden, where you may catch a free performance or learn something new about the city's arts offerings. (Downtown)

FASHION MALL
Keystone at the Crossing
8702 Keystone Crossing
317/574-3468

The Fashion Mall contains exclusive and upscale shops, and more than half of the stores can't be found anywhere else in the city. These shops include the Sharper Image, Williams-Sonoma, Mrs. Field's Cookies, the Mole Hole, Laura Ashley, Talbot's Kids, and Brooks Brothers. The mall's department stores, Jacobson's and Parisian, are both full of carefully selected merchandise. Eddie Bauer and Pottery Barn draw in the crowds.

Local shops include the Cheese Shop, a gourmet food store with samples; Abigail's, for prom queens, party-goers, and mothers of the bride; J. Shepard, the darling of the Pendleton and Susan Bristol set; Kits 'N' Kaboodle, a toy store; and J. T. Muesing, with fine china and more. There's sports apparel at All Stars and furs at Davidson's. On the second floor, a food court bridge spans the two sections of the mall. Parking garages, a Sheraton Hotel, and Westin Suites connect to the mall, which is in an office complex. There are other restaurants in the office park, so there's plenty here to buy and eat. (North)

GLENDALE CENTER
6101 N. Keystone Ave.
317/251-9281
Once the city's premier shopping destination, Glendale has struggled to find its place as upscale stores have moved to the Fashion Mall and Circle Centre. At press time, a new developer had purchased the mall and announced plans for a new 12-screen movie theater in the mall and a Lowes Homes Improvement Warehouse in the far reaches of the parking lot. Anchor L. S. Ayres has committed to staying and the developer promises at least four new retailers. A new entrance, two new restaurants, and a food court are also planned. The library may even open a branch in the lower level.

The Fashion Mall, p. 147

Many of the renovations will be completed by May 2000. (North)

GREENWOOD PARK MALL
1251 U.S. Hwy. 31N
Greenwood
317/881-6758
Located in the largest shopping area on the south side of Indianapolis, Greenwood has tremendous variety. L. S. Ayres, Lazarus, Sears, Service Merchandise, Von Maur, and JC Penney are all here. There's an array of national retailers, including Finish Line, Structure, Gap, and the Disney Store. There are plenty of eateries, including a new TGI Friday's. Children like the rides near Mr. Bulky. (East/Southeast)

LAFAYETTE SQUARE MALL
3919 Lafayette Rd.
317/291-6390
www.simon.com
When Lafayette Square was built in 1968, it was the first enclosed mall in the city and there were farms within blocks and a little airfield a mile or so to the west. Today, the mall sits

among apartment complexes and shopping strips. Renovated, the mall still has its pond and bridge. Stores include L. S. Ayres, Lazarus, JC Penney, Sears, and Waccamaw. Strip centers sprawl mainly to the west of this mall. (West/Southwest)

WASHINGTON SQUARE MALL
10202 E. Washington St.
317/899-4567
This mall, which has struggled with vacancies, is the site of a new Target superstore, scheduled to open in the summer of 1999. Kittle's, the city's premier furniture retailer, is also opening a large store here. L. S. Ayres, JC Penney, Lazarus, and Sears have stores at Washington Square. Smaller stores include Kaybee Toys, Frederick's of Hollywood, Custom Car Tag, and Wild Pair (shoes). (East/Southeast)

FACTORY OUTLET CENTERS

Although there are scores of discount stores in the city, Indianapolis has few outlet centers.

LOGO 7 OUTLET STORE
2333 Post Dr.
317/897-3776
This outlet store sells licensed sportswear for a wide range of professional sports—all created by this Indianapolis-based company. Outside of Indianapolis, the Logo 7 outlet center offers the largest selection of items. Another Logo 7 outlet is located at 5668 Georgetown Road, 317/388-1572. (East/Southeast)

10

SPORTS AND RECREATION

Indianapolis may not have the coastline for surfing or the altitude for skiing, but we do have the attitude for activity. We put our reservoirs, rivers, and creeks to use—whether boating, water-skiing, or fishing. We're saturated with swimming pools, teeming with tennis courts, and bursting with basketball hoops. We make use of every little bump and dip in our iceberg-flattened terrain, which is ideal for golf courses and trails for hiking, biking, and cross-country skiing.

In fact, for almost any leisure pursuit, Indy citizenry need go no farther than a nearby park. Forget swing sets and sandboxes. Instead, think sophisticated recreational complexes, aquatics centers, extensive systems of trails, athletic fields, golf, and more. And Indy offers plenty of state-of-the art fitness centers, as well.

Okay, so we have to catch our breath sometime. And when we do, we have plenty to watch—pro sports teams and events such as the Indianapolis 500 in May, the RCA Championships in August, and the Circle City Classic in October.

It would be hard to overstate how important sports are to the people of Indianapolis. Watching sports, managing sports organizations, and holding world-class sporting events are big businesses in Indianapolis. Since 1979 Indianapolis has hosted nearly 400 national and international sporting events, including the NCAA Final Four, the Pan American Games, the U.S. Olympic Festival, the U.S. Olympic Trials, and other National Governing Body (NGB) championships.

Several athletic governing bodies call Indianapolis home. These include USA Track and Field, USA Gymnastics, U.S. Synchronized Swimming, United States Diving, Inc., the U.S. Rowing Association, and the U.S. Canoe and Kayak Team. Indianapolis also offers world-class facilities for swimming (Indiana University Natatorium), track and field (Indiana University Track and Field Stadium), and bicycling (Major Taylor Velodrome). And every sports-minded native is eager to welcome the NCAA to its brand-new home when headquarters are completed, scheduled for the end of 1999.

Indianapolis moves to the beat of sports, whether it is the jet-engine roar of race cars blasting by at 230 m.p.h., the bounce of a basketball off Hoosier hardwood, or the splash of a world-class swimmer who hopes to represent her country in the Olympics.

RECREATION

Amusement Centers

Dozens of places in and around the city offer diversions such as putt-putt golf, paintball, virtual reality, and video games. **Greatimes**, *5341 Elmwood Avenue (East/Southeast), 317/780-0300, a full-service fun center, is ideal for families.* **Block Party**, *4102 Claire Drive (North), 317/578-7941, offers high-tech entertainment for adults. Paintball establishments include* **Dark Armies Paintball**, *2525 North Shadeland Avenue (East/Southeast), 317/353-1987;* **Splatter Zone**, *1747 Massachusetts Avenue (Downtown), 317/262-8838; and* **Gator Joe's Paintball**, *8180 Country Club Place (West/Southwest), 317/271-8050.*

GAMEWORKS STUDIO
Circle Centre, 49 W. Maryland St.
317/226-9267
There's a whole lot of shakin' going on—as shoppers at Circle Centre mall have discovered. The 27,000-foot-square complex provides a virtual reality—and game arcade on the mall's fourth level. The shaking is caused by the moving seats in the motion theater ($3 per movie). GameWorks, which took over the complex in 1999, offers the latest arcade games at 50¢ to $3 per game. Featured are traditional games (pinball and skee ball) as well as electronic games such as Indy 500, Deluxe Star Wars, and Rapid River

Challenge. Part owner Steven Spielberg is credited as the "creative direction" behind the chain. This is serious stuff—some companies send their executives here for team building. Remodeling, scheduled for early 1999, will bring new games, food, and possibly a new name. Open Sun–Thu 10–10, Fri–Sat to midnight. (Downtown)

RUSTIC GARDENS
GOLF DRIVING RANGE
1500 S. Arlington Ave.
317/359-8183
Established in 1930, this is the oldest miniature golf course in the city. It's not a putt-putt but a true miniaturized course—one-thirteenth the size of an 18-hole golf course—played on grass, with natural obstacles. On the course is an authentic homesteader's log cabin, built in 1832. In addition, there is a small petting zoo and a driving range. Open mid-Apr–mid-Oct Sun–Thu 10 a.m.–11 p.m., Fri–Sat 10 a.m.–midnight. Admission: $2.75 per person before 6 p.m., $4 per person after 6 p.m. (East/Southeast)

Bowling

Indy's more than a dozen bowling alleys keep bowlers busy; most offer plenty of lanes, electronic scoring, pro shops, snack bar, arcades, and beer. Some have bumper bowl.

ACTION BOWL
DUCKPIN BOWLING
1105 E. Prospect St.
317/686-6006
It's a riotous alternative to traditional bowling—using a downsized wooden bowling ball to aim at tiny pins—especially for those more familiar with gutter balls than strikes. Action Bowl has recently opened a second alley,

Atomic Bowl, featuring seven lanes and the turquoise and glass-block decor of the fifties. Reservations are strongly recommended. The rental rate is $18 per hour per lane; shoe rental is $1.50. Open Sun noon–6, Mon–Tue 11–10, Wed–Thu 11–midnight, Fri–Sat 11–1 a.m. (East/Southeast)

Bicycling

Ribbons of picturesque road wind throughout Indy and its environs, but few streets offer designated paths for cyclists. The good news is that, within a few years, the Indianapolis Greenways Project, a plan to link more than 175 miles of walking and biking trails throughout the city, will change all that. Already, the **Monon Rail-Trail** offers 10.5 miles of biking access on the city's north side, the **Fall Creek Trail** runs from 56th Street to Keystone Avenue on the east side, and the **Eagle Creek Trail** connects Lafayette Road to Eagle Creek Park. Presently in the works is the extension of the path from Broad Ripple to downtown and the seven-mile Pleasant Run Greenway, connecting Garfield, Christian, and Ellenberger Parks on the city's east side. Also, most regional and community Indy parks have paved biking paths.

Serious cyclists should consider joining **Central Indiana Bicycling Association (CIBA)** to receive updated information about where to ride, as well as information about organized rides and popular riding events such as the Hilly Hundred and the Night Ride. You can contact CIBA at 317/327-2453.

MAJOR TAYLOR VELODROME AND LAKE SULLIVAN BMX TRACK
3649 Cold Spring Rd.

317/327-8356
Located near Marian College, this world-class cycling track is open to the public when not used for national racing events. Open Mon–Fri 8–5. Admission: $3. (West/Southwest)

Boating

For a landlocked area, Indy provides a surprising number of boating opportunities.

EAGLE CREEK RESERVOIR
7840 W. 56th St.
317/327-7130
Boats up to 10 horsepower are allowed on the 1,350-acre reservoir and can be launched at the 42nd Street ramp. If you don't have your own, rent one at the marina. Your choices include sailboats, rowboats, canoes, pedal boats, pontoons, and sailboards. Sailing lessons are also offered. While the park is open year-round, the marina operates from Memorial Day to Labor Day. (West/Southwest)

GEIST RESERVOIR
11695 E. Fall Creek Rd.
317/849-8455
Rent a slip at the Fall Creek Marina or launch your boat at the ramp on Olio Road to access this 1,900-acre reservoir. All kinds of watercraft, including sailboats, pontoons, and runabouts, keep the water churning in warm-weather months—in fact, the slips are reserved for years in advance (call now to get on the waiting list). The Indianapolis Sailing Club hosts a full schedule of regattas and events here. (East/Southeast)

MORSE RESERVOIR
999 Hague Rd.
Noblesville

Longer and narrower than Geist, Morse Reservoir offers virtually as many water acres of boating fun. Both slips and boat ramp are at the Morse Lake Marina. The slip waiting list is a little shorter here. (North)

Cross-country Skiing

Alas, the massive ice front that moved through the northern half of the state millions of years ago pretty much put the kibosh on the future of downhill skiing. However, the area's

Indy's Best Marathons, Races, Runs, and Walks

Race for the Cure Downtown—*This 5K race raises money for breast-cancer research. April.*

Indianapolis Life 500 Festival Mini-Marathon—*More than 14,000 participate in this pre–Indy 500 race run, which begins at Monument Circle. May.*

Night Ride at Major Taylor Velodrome—*Thousands of cyclists head out for a 20-mile circuit of downtown Indy and return for food, live music, and entertainment. July.*

Do Run Run at Military Park—*Participants can join in the 10K run, the four-mile family fitness walk, or the competitive walk. August.*

Dick Lugar Run and Walk at Butler University—*Participants choose from a 5K walk, 5K run, or 10K run. September.*

Riverfest Run and Walk at NIFS in White River State Park—*The competitive five-mile run or walk is timed. Participants can also take part in the noncompetitive 5K fun walk. September.*

Pleasant Run Run in Irvington—*The five-mile run and three-mile family walk attract up to 2,000 participants.* Runner's World *magazine has listed it as one of the top running events in the nation for the past 10 years. October.*

AIDS Walk at the Military Park—*More than 7,000 walkers take part in the state's largest fundraiser. October.*

America's Walk for Diabetes at the IU Track and Field Stadium—*This five-mile walk raises money for the American Diabetes Association. June.*

gently rolling terrain makes it ideal for cross-country skiing. Check out **Eagle Creek Park**, where you can rent skis and equipment. If you have your own, try **Southeastway** or **Riverside Park** for tranquil woodland and meadowland trails.

Fishing

Opportunities for fishing in Indy are virtually as limitless as, well, as the fish in the city's rivers, creeks, and reservoirs. **White River** can be accessed from a number of Indy parks, including Southwestway, Riverside, Broad Ripple, Holliday, and Marott, as well as tiny neighborhood parks, such as Municipal Gardens, Friedmann, and Reverend Mozell Sanders. White River State Park and the Rocky Ripple neighborhood on the city's north side also offer fishing access to the White River.

Then there's **Fall Creek**, with plenty of access points all the way to Geist Reservoir. The **Central Canal**, whose banks are owned by the Indianapolis Water Company from White River State Park to Broad Ripple, is open to the public for fishing. And **Eagle Creek Park** offers a 1,350-acre reservoir with boat ramps at 42nd Street and the ranger station. There's also bank fishing at the park's Lilly Lake.

Anglers also enjoy **Geist Reservoir**, in the city's northeast corner, and nearby **Morse Reservoir**, in Hamilton County. In addition, a few other Indy parks offer fishing opportunities, including **Krannert Lake** at Krannert Park, **Lake Sullivan** at Riverside Park, and **Ruster Park Pond**.

A fishing license is required before you can reel in any catch. Contact the Department of Natural Resources, Division of Fish and Wildlife,

317/232-4080, to obtain a license or other important information.

Fitness Clubs

Plenty of parks in Indy offer on-site fitness centers. **Riverside Park** and **Krannert Park** offer Hammer Strength weight equipment, weights, bikes, and step machines. Other parks with weight rooms or fitness centers include Brookside, Christian, Douglass, Garfield, J. T. V. Hill, Municipal Gardens, Pride, Rhodius, and Thatcher.

Nine **YMCA** locations throughout the city offer family and individual memberships at reasonable prices. (Call the general office at 317/266-YMCA for locations.) The **YWCA**, 4460 North Guion Road, 317/299-2750, features specialized programs for women and girls.

Check the yellow pages under Health Clubs, and you'll find dozens of private fitness facilities throughout the city. One surprise might be the **Indiana University Natatorium**—not only does it have a world-class swimming facility, it also has a fitness center.

ARTHUR M. GLICK JEWISH COMMUNITY CENTER
6701 Hoover Rd.
317/251-9467
www.jcc@indy.com
A multimillion-dollar expansion and renovation recently nearly tripled the size of this facility, open for membership to all. The 20,000-foot-square fitness center features a three-lane walk-jog track, nearly 30 Cybex strength-resistance equipment stations, a free-weight area, and a 3,100-foot-square aerobics dance studio. A 20,000-foot-square multi-recreational space for indoor tennis, soccer, volleyball, and other sports adds to the fitness opportunities.

A weightlifter takes a break at the Jewish Community Center.

In addition, members have access to both indoor and outdoor pools. Certified personal trainers offer fitness assessments and one-on-one assistance, and there are athletic leagues—basketball, soccer, and softball—for all ages. But that's not all—there's dance classes from ballet to bossa nova, outdoor tennis courts, and racquetball. Add locker rooms complete with steam baths, saunas, whirlpools, and massage therapy—not to mention on-site childcare and a café—and you'll never want to leave! Open Mon–Thu 6–10, Fri 6–6, Sat 1–7, Sun 7–7. Closed Jewish holidays. (North)

HEALTHPLEX
3660 Guion Rd.
317/920-7400
As of press time, you could still smell the fresh paint on the walls of this brand-new fitness and sports center. (Connected to Westview Hospital, the entire complex is 158,000 feet square.) The city's newest facility boasts that it's the third-largest medically-based

fitness facility in the country (it's owned by Westview Hospital and St. Vincent Hospital). All facilities are indoors. The complex contains six tennis courts, two pools, two aerobics studios, two squash courts, two racquetball courts, two basketball courts, two volleyball courts, an indoor track, and more than 100 pieces of cardiovascular and strength-training equipment. This family-oriented club offers a children's gym, kids' programs, and childcare. Personal trainers, fitness assessments, and a pro shop are pluses. Locker rooms feature whirlpools, saunas, and steam baths. Open Mon–Fri 6-10, Sat 8-9, Sun 8–6. (West/Southwest)

NATIONAL INSTITUTE FOR FITNESS AND SPORT
250 University Blvd.
317/274-3432
This 65,000-foot-square fitness center features a 200-meter indoor run/walk track, state-of-the-art cardiovascular and strength-training equipment, an NBA regulation-size basketball court, a rock-climbing treadwall, aerobics, volleyball, yoga, and more. Certified professionals offer individual fitness assessments, athletic development training, personal training, weight management, and nutrition consultations. Childcare is available. Open Mon–Fri 5:30–9, Sat 7–4, Sun 8–4. (Downtown)

Golf

Indianapolis has 12 municipal golf courses, most within parks, all offering amenities such as pro shops, electric and pull carts, putting greens, golf pros, snack bars, reasonable greens fees, and league and tournament play. Some have driving ranges. Each course not only offers a different

A Guide to Indy's 12 Municipal Courses

A. J. Thatcher Golf Course—*This nine-hole, par-34 course is diffi-cult in places, with narrow, tree-lined fairways, 317/244-0713. (West/Southwest)*

Coffin Golf Club—*This par-70, 18-hole course features a tight, challenging layout with water hazards on seven holes. It's located in Riverside Park, 317/327-7845. (West/Southwest)*

Douglass Golf Course—*This 9-hole, par-34 course with few hazards is ideal for beginners and seniors, 317/924-0018. (East/Southeast)*

Eagle Creek—*This Pete Dye–designed, par-72 course was rated re-cently by* Indianapolis Business Journal *as the city's fifth most diffi-cult course. It's a monster, too (350 acres, 27 holes), 317/297-3366. (West/Southwest)*

Pleasant Run Golf Course—*This short, 18-hole, par-71 course has seven water hazards, a creek, and a tree-lined fairway, 317/357-0829. (East/Southeast)*

Riverside Golf Course—*Established in 1901, Riverside is the oldest course in the city. Located in Riverside Park, the par-70 course has 18 holes, 317/327-7300. (West/Southwest)*

design, but also a different degree of difficulty. Check the chart on this page for brief descriptions of the municipal courses. There are also numerous pri-vate clubs in Indy, which typically offer membership for a whopping initi-ation fee of anywhere from a few thousand dollars to $36,000. In addi-tion, golfers can play one of the public courses not owned by the city, listed below.

**BRICKYARD CROSSING
GOLF CLUB**

**4400 W. 16th St.
317/484-6572**

The 18-hole, Pete Dye-designed course offers a challenge for even the most experienced golfer. The course, which includes three lakes and numerous sand traps, is set in the midst of the Indianapolis Motor Speedway and is the site for the an-nual Brickyard Crossing Champi-onship in September. Greens fees: $60 for Men's Club members; $80 for nonmembers. Cart fees included. (West/Southwest)

Sarah Shank Golf Course—*Just two miles from downtown, this 18-hole, par-72 course has open fairways, two creeks, 120 acres of rolling terrain, and woods, 317/784-0631. (East/Southeast)*

Smock Golf Course—*This 18-hole, par-72 course has large greens, open fairways, and multiple sand traps, 317/888-0036. (East/Southeast)*

South Grove—*Especially popular with the downtown community, this 18-hole, par-70 course has one water hazard, several large trees, and small-to-average greens. It's located in Riverside Park, 317/327-7350. (West/Southwest)*

Whispering Hills—*This 9-hole, par-34 course challenges players with various shot placement and hazards, rolling hills, lakes, and woods, 317/862-9000. (East/Southeast)*

William S. Sahm—*This 18-hole, par-70 course, designed by world-renowned course designer Pete Dye, is flat, open, and of moderate length, 317/849-0036. (North)*

Winding River Golf Course—*This is one of the longer 18-hole courses in the city (par 71), with wide, well-maintained fairways, minimal hazards, and spacious views. It's located in Southwestway Park, 317/856-7257. (West/Southwest)*

THE FORT GOLF COURSE
8002 N. Post Rd.
317/543-9597
Rolling hills, forested woodlands, and smooth stretches of emerald grass—not to mention wetlands—offer beauty and challenges on this 238-acre course designed by Hoosier son Pete Dye. This 18-hole, par-72 course is the city's newest public course and is owned by the state parks system. It tied with another course as the fifth most difficult course in the city, in an *Indianapolis Business Journal* golf survey. Greens fees: $28 before 2 p.m., $20 after. With cart, $40 before 2 p.m., $30 after. (East/Southeast)

GOLF CLUB OF INDIANA
P.O. Box 5009
Zionsville
317/769-6388
This 18-hole, par-72 course was rated by the *Indianapolis Business Journal* as the city's fourth most difficult course. Greens fees: Mon–Fri $35, Sat and Sun $39, $10 extra for a cart. (North)

Horseback Riding

FORT HARRISON STATE PARK
5753 Glenn Rd.
317/541-1866
With the renovation of the stables at Fort Harrison State Park, city slickers now have a place to saddle up and hit the trail. While there are stables and equestrian centers around town offering boarding and lessons, this is the only place for the public to enjoy a two-mile (one-hour) trail ride. Pony rides within the arena are available for children under age 12. Open Apr–Oct, 9–one hour before dusk. Price: $10 per person. (East/Southeast)

Skating

Two Indy parks provide skating opportunities year-round at indoor recreational centers. **Perry Ice Rink**, *317/888-0070, and* **Ellenberger Ice Rink**, *317/327-7176, offer ice-skating from October to April, and in-line and roller-skating May through September. Eagle Creek Park's* **Lilly Lake** *is the city's only outdoor ice-skating spot—provided the lake is frozen. For year-round roller-skating,* **United**

Skates of America *has two locations, 3902 Glen Arm Road, 317/291-6795 (West/Southwest); and 5001 North Shadeland Avenue, 317/546-2457 (East/Southeast). In-line skaters can use the* **Major Taylor Velodrome** *(see listing under Bicycling) when it's not being used for events.*

CARMEL ICE SKADIUM
1040 Third Ave., SW
Carmel
317/844-8888
This rink offers group lessons, birthday parties, youth hockey programs, a pro shop, and junior and senior ice-skating clubs, as well as rentals. Open Mon–Thu 3:15–5:15; Fri 3:15–5:15, 8–10; Sat–Sun 2:30–5, 8–10. Admission: $3.50 adults, $2.75 children ages 12 and under. (North)

INDIANA STATE FAIRGROUNDS EVENT CENTER-PEPSI COLISEUM
1202 E. 38th St.
317/927-7536
Public ice-skating is scheduled from mid-October through mid-March. Lessons are available on Saturdays before open skating. The facility also offers youth hockey (ages four to 18),

---

Climbing walls at Galyan's Carmel and Castleton locations, not to mention at the Children's Museum, keep shoppers and young ones challenged. But for dedicated climbers as well as sports enthusiasts looking for something new, there's Climb Time, 8750 Corporation Drive, 317/596-3330, (North). With 10,000 feet square of wall to climb, even veteran visitors come back for more. The facility boasts 150 members (they pay an enrollment fee of $80, and $40 monthly for unlimited climbing privileges), who use Climb Time walls to train for the "real thing." Novice climbers, however, will discover a completely safe environment in which to learn a fun new sport. Group rates are available. Open Tue–Fri 11–10, Sat–Sun 11–9. Daily pass: $10. Shoe rentals: $3. Harness rentals: $3.

David P. Sims

Boating on Eagle Creek Reservoir, p. 152

men's hockey, and a figure-skating club. Open Mon–Thu, Sun 2:30–4:30; Fri–Sat 2:30–4:30, 7:30–9:30. Admission: $3.50 adults, $2.75 children ages 12 and under. Figure skate rentals: $2. Hockey skate rentals: $3. (North)

INDIANA/WORLD SKATING ACADEMY AND RESEARCH CENTER
Pan Am Plaza, 201 S. Capitol Ave.
317/237-5565
The world-class facility features two indoor ice-skating rinks available for public use. The rinks can be reserved for conventions, receptions, meetings, and ice-show entertainment. Hours vary seasonally and daily; call for details. Admission: $3.50 adults, $2.75 children ages 12 and under. Group rates available. Figure skate rentals: $2. Hockey skate rentals: $2. (Downtown)

RCA DOME
100 S. Capitol Ave.
317/262-3663
Whenever nothing else is scheduled

in the concourse area, in-line skaters can loop the dome from December through March. Open Mon–Fri 5–9, Sat–Sun 1–5. Admission: $5 adults, $4 students with I.D., $3 children ages 12 and under. Skate rentals: $5. (Downtown)

Swimming

The following Indy parks offer outdoor aquatic centers, pools with water slides and zero-depth access for small children, swimming lessons, and other amenities: Brookside, Garfield, Krannert, Perry, Riverside, and William S. Sahm. In addition, two parks, Krannert and Thatcher, feature indoor pools. Membership fitness clubs, such as the YMCAs located throughout the city, the YWCA, and the Jewish Community Center (see listing in this chapter), also feature indoor and outdoor pools for leisure and lap swimming.

EAGLE CREEK BEACH
7602 Eagle Beach Dr.
317/327-7132
In a pleasant clearing surrounded by shady woods, this tiny sand beach is ideal for families with young children. Lifeguards are in attendance, locker rooms offer showers, and a concession stand satisfies the hungry. Open daily Memorial Day–Labor Day 11–7. Admission: $2.25 adults, $1.75 children ages 2–17. (West/Southwest)

INDIANA UNIVERSITY NATATORIUM
901 W. New York St.
317/274-3518
www.iunat.iupui.edu
Since opening in 1982, this world-class facility has hosted Olympic trial events as well as regularly scheduled national and international aquatic

events. The Natatorium has three indoor pools. When not being used for swimming and diving events, the main pool is open to the public for daily lap swimming. The facility offers classes in swimming and water safety. Also on-site is a complete fitness facility that offers aerobics classes among other things. Open Mon–Fri 5:30–8, Sun 1–5. Admission: $5 per day. (Downtown)

INDY ISLAND INDOOR AQUATIC CENTER
8575 E. Raymond St.
317/862-6867

Summer never ends at Indy Island—it's a complete indoor water park with a water slide, a water playground, a three-lane pool, a therapy pool, and water volleyball courts. Nonswimmers, from preschoolers to adults, can take lessons year-round. Managed by Indy Parks, this impressive center also offers group rentals and birthday parties. Open Mon, Wed, Fri 4–9; Sat–Sun 12–6. Admission: $4.50 adults, $3.50 children and seniors. (East/Southeast)

Tennis

There are an abundance of private tennis facilities to choose from in Indy. And public tennis courts are too numerous to even mention. Most regional and community parks have tennis courts. Parks that feature six or more courts include Broad Ripple, Ellenberger, Garfield, Riverside, and Tarkington Parks.

INDIANAPOLIS TENNIS CENTER
755 University Blvd.
317/278-2100

Site of the RCA Championships in August, the Tennis Center sports 18 outdoor courts and six indoor courts as well as the stadium court used for the championships. The courts are available for public use when not being used for events. Reservations are required. League play and instruction are available. Mon–Fri 7–10:30, Sat 7–10, Sun 8–9. $16–$24/hour for indoor courts; $10–$16/hour for outdoor courts. A 12-month membership ($125/year) reduces court costs. (Downtown)

Indy Island Indoor Aquatic Center

Indy Parks

What's the best way to spend a night on the town? Two Indy business leaders—Mel Simon (the mall guy, Simon Property Group) and Jeff Smulyan (the media guy, Emmis Publishing and Emmis Broadcasting)—agree: Nothing beats dinner downtown followed by a Pacers game!

Walking/Running

It'd be easier to list the Indy parks that don't offer trails for walking or running. Even the tiniest neighborhood parks have tree-shaded paths ideal for strolling. For nature hikes, try Riverside, Friedmann, Marott, Skiles Test, Southwestway, and Eagle Creek Parks. For paved jogging and walking paths, visit Brookside, Ellenberger, Eagle Creek, or Broad Ripple Parks. Check out the Indianapolis Greenways trails: The Monon Rail-Trail, 10.5 miles of paved walking and jogging paths, will eventually extend from 10th Street to 146th Street. Fall Creek Trail currently runs from Keystone and Fall Creek Parkway to 56th Street (3.2 miles) and will connect to Fort Harrison and 30th Street. Pleasant Run Greenway, 6.9 miles long, connects Garfield, Christian, and Ellenberger Parks. Other great walking areas include the River Promenade, a 1.4-mile path from the Indianapolis Zoo to Downtown.

CENTRAL CANAL TOW PATH
Broad Ripple to Riverside Park
317/327-7431
This beautiful, 5.2-mile trail is truly the loveliest place to walk or run in the city. Start out at Holcomb Gardens on the Butler campus (wander through its formal gardens for a warm-up), and follow the trail west along the canal. But beware: You'll be tempted

by many trails less traveled! A path through the woods leads to a wonderful prairie preserve with tall grasses and wildflowers; another winds to the White River. Cross under Northwestern Avenue, and the trail leads to the backside of the Indianapolis Museum of Art, where you can peek at manicured English gardens and the grand terrace from across the canal. Take the trail in the opposite direction and you'll pass charming waterfront bungalows and narrow trails before running into traffic at Illinois Street. Eventually, the path will extend from Broad Ripple to Stadium Drive near 10th Street. (North)

MONON RAIL-TRAIL
Westfield Blvd.
317/327-7431
This 10.5-mile trail suffers from pedestrian gridlock (trios of mothers walk abreast with their baby strollers) on weekends. But special rewards at various points (snow cones in Broad Ripple, ice cream at 86th Street) make it worthwhile. The wide asphalt path, which accommodates wheelchairs as well as in-line skates, cuts across busy streets, crosses White River, and winds through neighborhoods past the fairgrounds south to Fall Creek Parkway. Several paths diverge into Marott Park and its acres of woodland trails. Red-trimmed park benches and bridge overlooks are

stationed along the route. The busiest parts of the path are between 79th Street and Broad Ripple. Open dawn until dusk. (North)

INDIANA UNIVERSITY TRACK AND FIELD STADIUM
901 W. New York St.
317/274-3518

The U.S. Olympic Track and Field Trials and NCAA Championships have been held on this 400-meter, eight-lane track, one of the fastest in the world. The facility is available for public use when not in use for competitions. Open June–Oct, Mon–Fri 11–7. Admission: $3 per day, $30 per month. (Downtown)

The Old Oaken Bucket and the Monon Bell

Central Indiana is the home of two of the fiercest college football rivalries in the nation, and in each contest, the winner takes home a valuable prize. The Monon Bell is at stake when Wabash and De-Pauw play the last game of the season, and the Old Oaken Bucket is carted home by the Indiana-Purdue winner.

Wabash and DePauw, two small schools separated by only 27 miles, started playing football in 1890. The Monon Bell, a 350-pound locomotive bell from the Monon Railroad, became the victor's prize in 1932.

The coaches realize the importance of the game. Says Wabash's Greg Carlson, "Most Division III players won't be exposed to ESPN or Sports Illustrated *and won't play before a crowd of 8,000 fans. Most small-college players may not play before that many people in one season. It's almost like a bowl game or playoff atmosphere." DePauw's Nick Mourouzis puts it in even more personal terms: "I have a shrub that I have cut in the shape of a bell, so it reminds me every day when I walk by that, right in front of my house."*

The Old Oaken Bucket was found on a farm in southern Indiana after the Chicago alumni groups of both Indiana and Purdue decided, in 1925, that a trophy was needed. Like the first battle for the Monon Bell, the first Old Oaken Bucket game ended in a 0–0 tie.

Indiana University's Hoosiers have won five national basketball championships in their storied history.

Year	Coach	Record
1940	Branch McCracken	20-3
1953	Branch McCracken	23-3
1976	Bob Knight	32-0
1981	Bob Knight	26-9
1987	Bob Knight	30-4

SPECTATOR SPORTS

This section and the Professional Sports section were written by Les Morris. His sports stories have appeared in the Indianapolis News, *Indianapolis Star, Indianapolis Business Journal, and* Daily Journal *of Johnson County, Indiana. He is a business reporter for the* Daily Journal.

Auto Racing

INDIANAPOLIS MOTOR SPEEDWAY
4790 W. 16th St.
317/481-8500
www.indyracingleague.com
Home to the world's most prestigious auto race, this historic facility has hosted the Indianapolis 500 on the Sunday of Memorial Day weekend every year since 1911. If you're lucky enough to be one of the half-million people on the grounds that day, you'll want to arrive early—the gates open at 5 a.m. and there is always a long line of cars. In August the stars of NASCAR compete during the Brickyard 400. This new tradition began in 1994. Big changes might be in the works; at press time, owner Tony George was exploring bringing Formula One racing to the city by the turn of the century. The Grand-Prix style of racing would require reconfiguration of the existing track but is anticipated to attract an affluent and increasingly international crowd. (For hours and more information, see Chapters 5 and 7.) (West/Southwest)

INDIANAPOLIS RACEWAY PARK
10267 East U.S. Hwy. 136
317/291-4090
www.goracing.com/indy
This racing complex, with seating for 35,000, offers spectators many diverse styles of racing. On Labor Day weekend, the Super Bowl of drag racing takes place here with the U.S. Nationals, sponsored by the National Hot Rod Association. Oval racing is popular here during the summer season. Midgets, sprints, and USAC Silver Crown cars all compete on the ⅝-mile track. Special events connected to the Indianapolis 500 and the Brickyard 400 accommodate race fans who can't get enough. Three days of races called the Kroger Speedfest are held before the Brickyard 400, and the Night Before the 500 is a tradition for the USAC midgets. Another popular event, the Vintage Car Grand Prix, a benefit for the Indianapolis Children's Museum, is held in early October. (West/Southwest)

PROFESSIONAL SPORTS

While auto racing is confined to warm-weather months, Indianapolis residents and visitors can enjoy professional sports year-round. The city boasts major-league basketball and football teams, and has teams in the top levels of the minor leagues in both hockey and baseball. Two soccer teams, the Blaze and the Blast, play at the Kuntz Stadium during warm-weather months.

Although each franchise receives strong support, none sells out its entire season—it is usually possible to get a ticket to a game, especially with a little advance planning. Prices and scheduling of pro events vary; call the phone numbers in the listings for up-to-date information.

INDIANA BLAST AND BLAZE
Kuntz Stadium, 1502 W. 16th St.
317/585-9203
You know the stereotype—the husband buys his wife a gift that *he'll* appreciate more than she does. A bowling ball, a big-screen TV, tickets to the fights. Happily, Kim Morris's birthday gift from husband Alex is something that she loves and the entire city can enjoy—a pro outdoor soccer franchise that features both a men's and women's team! The Blast is Indiana's only men's professional outdoor soccer team. The team recently upgraded to A-League, the second-highest level of competition in the country, just a step below the Major Soccer League level. The Indiana Blaze, the women's team, competes at the highest level of women's soccer in the country. The teams' inaugural seasons were in 1997. Indy soccer fans can look forward to developing rivalries with Cincinnati, Milwaukee,

New Orleans, Pittsburgh, and more. Outdoor soccer season runs from May through September. The Blast hosts 15 to 20 home games, while the Blaze hosts 8 to 10. Indoor soccer fans will be pleased to know that Morris is establishing a pro team in the fall of 1999 to replace the ill-fated Twisters, whose league folded in 1997. The new team, known as Vortex, will play at Market Square Arena. (West/Southwest)

INDIANA PACERS
Georgia St., between Delaware and Pennsylvania Sts.
317/639-6411
Pacer fans have lots to celebrate! First, Hoosier native Larry Bird has returned as head coach. In his first season (1997/98), he was named Coach of the Year and led his team to within one game of the NBA Finals. Secondly, the team will move to the new Conseco Fieldhouse in the 1999 season, allowing room for nearly 3,000 more fans per game. (The new facility seats 19,000.) Pacers fans are

Chris Duff of the Indiana Blast goes up for the ball.

Stu Phillips/Indiana Blast

The Indiana High School Basketball Tournament

The Indiana High School Athletic Association (IHSAA) crowns 24 state champions in 20 sports (football has five) each year. No championship, however, generates the passion and national interest of the boys' state basketball tournament, which culminates with the state's top four teams squaring off in late March at the RCA Dome. Even Hollywood took notice with Hoosiers, *the story of a small-town school that was based on the biggest upset ever—tiny Milan's 32-to-30 shocker over giant Muncie Central in 1954.*

The tournament started a few months before the first Indianapolis 500, in 1911, with Lebanon crowned the state champ. Muncie Central has won the most state championships (eight). Larry Bird, George McGinnis, and Shawn Kemp all played in the tournament in their youth.

After a controversial vote by the IHSAA in April 1996, class basketball—based on a school's enrollment—made its appearance in 1998. There are now four different champions.

among the NBA's most loyal and, with Indiana's strong basketball heritage, perhaps the most knowledgeable. To trace the genealogy of the Pacers is to trace professional basketball in this country over the past 25 years. The team was a charter member of the upstart American Basketball Association in 1967, winning ABA titles in 1970, 1972, and 1973. In 1976 the NBA absorbed some of the ABA's most successful franchises, including the Pacers.

On-court success has not come easily, but since 1993, the team has been playing championship-caliber ball. In both the 1993/94 and 1994/95 seasons, the team came within one game of playing in the NBA Finals. And Pacer guard Reggie Miller has blossomed into a bona fide superstar. He is popular locally, as is evident by the countless #31 Pacers jerseys sported by city youngsters—and adults. (Downtown)

INDIANAPOLIS COLTS
RCA Dome, 100 S. Capitol Ave.
317/297-7000
The NFL's Colts came to Indianapolis under a cover of darkness from Baltimore in 1984. Euphoria greeted the move, as the city had long coveted an NFL franchise and had built the

Dome in hopes of landing a team. Demand was so great for tickets that a lottery had to be held to determine the lucky season-ticket holders. The Colts struggled during their first years in town, reaching the playoffs only in strike-marred 1987 and then losing their first playoff game to the Cleveland Browns. That mediocrity vanished during the Colts' magical 1995 season. Led by indefatigable quarterback Jim Harbaugh, whose passing efficiency made him the highest-rated quarterback in the NFL, the Colts reached the playoffs as a wild card on the last weekend of the regular season, then came within one catch of reaching the Super Bowl. Peyton Manning, the star quarterback from the University of Tennessee, is now the talk of the team, as the Colts try to win their way back into the playoffs. (Downtown)

INDIANAPOLIS ICE
1202 E. 38th St.
317/925-4423
www.indplsice.com
Hockey and Indiana may not seem a likely match, but professional hockey has long been an Indianapolis sports staple. Indeed, the "Great One," Wayne Gretzky, started his pro career in Indianapolis with the Indianapolis Racers. The Ice has been Indy's hockey team since 1988 and the top minor-league club of the NHL's Chicago Blackhawks since 1990. With the possible razing of Market Square Arena and the building of the Conseco Fieldhouse, most Ice games are scheduled for the Pepsi Coliseum at the fairgrounds during the 1999/2000 season; at press time, the team's future home was yet to be determined. Wherever they play, the Ice attracts a fun

crowd—an estimated 20 percent are under age 18. That explains the loud rock 'n' roll played before face-offs, but how do you explain the dancing Elvis? (Downtown)

INDIANAPOLIS INDIANS
Victory Field, 501 W. Maryland St.
317/269-3542
www.indyindians.com
The Indians just may be the most successful franchise in town, both on the field and because of its field—the team's Victory Field opened in July 1996 to rave reviews. The Indians are the top minor-league affiliate of the National League's Cincinnati Reds, and many of the Reds' great stars, including Tony Perez and George Foster, played in Indianapolis on their way to the majors. The Indians have won a slew of championships in recent years: 1984, 1986 to 1989, 1994, and 1995. The regular season begins in April and runs through the first week of September. (Downtown)

AMATEUR SPORTS

Basketball

*Basketball, the king of Hoosier sports, is wildly popular at the high school and college levels in the Indianapolis area. **Purdue University** and **Indiana University** games are avidly followed. **Butler University**, located on the north side of Indianapolis, plays home games in historic Hinkle Fieldhouse, truly one of the best places in the country to watch a collegiate basketball game. (And you won't have to search hard to find a native who will proudly tell you the site was featured in the movie Hoosiers.)*

Football

CIRCLE CITY CLASSIC
201 S. Capitol Ave., Ste. 480
317/239-5151
This game, usually held on the first Saturday in October, matches two teams from historically black colleges. The football is great, the fans are great, and the bands are certainly great! It's a terrific weekend in Indianapolis. Be sure to catch the parade that is held in conjunction with the game. (Downtown)

Indianapolis Chamber Orchestra

11

PERFORMING ARTS

The performing arts in Indianapolis are very strong, which may come as a surprise for those who know Indy for its two-and-a-half-mile oval, not its dress circle, for its free throws, not its pirouettes. There are more plays, dances, orchestral performances, and choir recitals than anyone could possibly attend. Indiana is the only state in the country to have a publication, called Arts Indiana, devoted to arts statewide. And new performing arts venues are being built all the time.

The Artsgarden, completed in 1995, serves as a performance venue for and disseminates information about the local arts scene. The city is also fortunate to have support from organizations such as Cathedral Arts, which strives to increase the city's visibility in the international art world.

Venues and organizations listed here were chosen to illustrate the diversity of Indy's performing arts.

THEATER

AMERICAN CABARET THEATRE
401 E. Michigan St.
317/631-0334 or 800/375-8887
www.americancabarettheatre.com
Inspired by cabaret theaters in Europe, Claude McNeal (creator of the musical *Decades*) founded American Cabaret Theatre in 1980 in New York City. Wooed to Indianapolis, McNeal moved ACT to a largely re-

stored ninteenth-century downtown building, the Athenaeum. Patrons sit at small tables, where they enjoy snacks and drinks. For dinner, an authentic German restaurant, the Rathskeller, serves traditional favorites on the lower level of the Athenaeum.

As the theater's name implies, the cast warbles and dances through performances, most of which are original. Some shows focus on the

Films and Strings Bring International Acclaim

Since its inception in 1992, Indy's Heartland Film Festival has become one of the country's 12 biggest film festivals, measured by attendance. It hands out the largest cash awards of any film festival in the world and has a reputation for giving luminaries such as Robert Duvall and Roma Downey a glamorous reception. For information call 317/464-9405 or visit www.heartlandfilmfest.org.

Cathedral Arts and the late violinist Josef Gingold teamed up in 1982 to create the International Violin Competition. Cash awards, a Carnegie Hall recital for the gold medalist, and more than 50 other engagements for winners have helped make this contest one of the most prestigious violin competitions in the world. Approximately 45 violinists begin the competition, held in Indianapolis every four years and next scheduled for September 2002. For information contact Cathedral Arts at 317/637-4574 or visit www.violin.org.

life of a single performer, such as Hoagy Carmichael or Cole Porter; others spotlight a style of music, such as "Fabulous Fifties" (summer 1999). Each fall, the theater presents a Broadway musical. ♿ (Downtown)

BEEF & BOARDS DINNER THEATRE
9301 N. Michigan Rd.
317/872-9664
www.numbers.tripod.com/~zehj/reservations.html
Once part of a chain of dinner theaters, Beef & Boards is now owned by two Indianapolites. The owners, who are also the artistic directors, select all the shows and travel to New York City and Chicago to audition the cast. Although productions are orchestrated

specifically for this theater, the shows are Broadway musical successes such as *Jesus Christ Superstar* and *South Pacific*. The theater seats about 500. ♿ (North)

BUCK CREEK PLAYERS
7820 Acton Rd.
317/862-2270
The Buck Creek Players' venue is an attraction in its own right: a rural church built in 1871. Additions and renovations have made the theater comfortable. The theater presents four shows each season: one musical, one comedy, one family, and one old standby; most are well known, but an occasional show is lesser known. Each show runs four weekends, except the Christmas show, which

For the deaf, hearing impaired, and visually impaired, Indianapolis has the ideal theater: Edyvean Repertory Theatre. The theater has audio describers who explain action to the visually impaired, sound-enhancement equipment for the hearing impaired, and interpreters for the deaf.

may run longer, depending on demand for tickets. (East/Southeast)

EDYVEAN REPERTORY THEATRE
Ransburg Auditorium
University of Indianapolis
1400 East Hanna Ave.
317/783-4090 or 800/807-7732
www.edyvean.org

The Edyvean presents classic and contemporary works, and is best known for its innovative outreach programs. During performances, specially designated individuals explain the action on the stage to the visually impaired. Special audio equipment and interpreters are there for the hearing impaired. Puzzled by the name? It's pronounced ed-a-veen and is named after a professor in the theater department of the Christian Theological Seminary, Dr. Alfred Edyvean, who helped found this theater in 1966. & (East/Southeast)

FOOTLITE MUSICALS
1847 N. Alabama St.
317/926-6630

Footlite Musicals has been producing Broadway musicals since 1956. The company, composed entirely of volunteers, produces four major shows annually and has won accolades for its productions. Shows are performed in the Hedbach Theatre, which seats about 300. & (North)

INDIANAPOLIS CIVIC THEATRE
Indianapolis Museum of Art
1200 W. 38th St.
317/924-6770 or 317/923-4597
(box office)
www.civictheatre.org

The Indianapolis Civic Theatre presents six shows each season in its 595-seat theater at the IMA. These productions are well-known standards, such as *Oklahoma* and *Lost in Yonkers*, but the theater also stages some experimental works. Founded in 1914, Civic Theatre is the oldest continuously operating community theater in the country. & (North)

INDIANA REPERTORY THEATRE
140 W. Washington St.
317/635-5277 or 317/635-5252
(box office)
www.indianarep.com

Housed in a 1927 movie palace, Indiana Repertory Theatre occupies one of the city's most elegant spaces. Spanish baroque in style, the building has an ornate facade and eye-catching interior, including a fountain at one end of the lobby and a massive staircase at the other. There are gargoyles on the stairwell and Italian marble on the walls. The main stage (there are three stages) and lobby are scheduled for facelifts near press time.

IRT presents a mix of classic and contemporary plays and recruits its talent nationally. It stages seven major productions, in addition to a variety of other performances, each year. & (Downtown)

PHOENIX THEATRE
749 N. Park Ave.
317/635-7529
www.phoenixtheatre.org
Bryan Fonseca, Phoenix Theatre founder and producing director, boldly explores sensitive issues. Shows that address midlife crises, gay rights, and family dynamics have put the Phoenix on the cutting edge of contemporary theater. About 10 shows are staged a year. Since 1987 the Phoenix has been housed in a historic church-turned-theater that seats 150, with the Underground Stage seating 75. The theater has gained national recognition as the result of a competition it holds, Frank Basile's Festival of the Emerging American Theater. & (Downtown)

THEATRE ON THE SQUARE
627 Massachusetts Ave.
317/637-8085
www.tots.org
Created in 1988 to offer thought-provoking shows, Theatre on the Square stages chiefly contemporary

Tom Meunier plays Huckleberry Finn at the Indiana Repertory Theatre.

plays and musicals. Recent performances include *Sweeney Todd*. TOTS's building was renovated in 1996, and a second stage was added. Stage Two productions tend to be more experimental. TOTS presents three productions a weekend year-round, with a few exceptions. & (Downtown)

CLASSICAL MUSIC AND OPERA

AMERICAN PIANIST ASSOCIATION
4600 Sunset Ave.
317/940-9945
www.srconline.com/apa
Founded in New York City in 1979, this organization moved to Indianapolis in 1982. Although its focus remains national, the American Pianist Association has brought superior piano performances to the city. Every other year, jazz and classical piano competitions are held in Indy. The Association also organizes a series of performances in town by the winners of the Young American Pianists auditions. Concerts at the Hilbert Circle Theatre and the Christel DeHaan Fine Arts Center are free; there's a nominal charge for those held at the Indianapolis Art Museum. (North)

CARMEL SYMPHONY ORCHESTRA
P.O. Box 761
Carmel, 46082-0761
317/844-9717
This versatile, 60-member orchestra plays classical and popular music and has even accompanied the Moody Blues. The orchestra gives eight subscription concerts annually and various other performances throughout the year at venues around

Ticket Outlets

TicketMaster, 317/239-1000, www.ticketmaster.com, sells tickets for shows at the Murat Centre, the RCA Dome, Clowes Memorial Hall, and occasionally smaller halls. It also sells tickets for local sporting events. TicketMaster outlets include most Kroger grocery stores, Karma Record stores, L. S. Ayres, the Pacers Home Court in Circle Centre mall, and the Indiana State Fairgrounds.

Ticket Central, 317/624-7430, is headquartered at the Artsgarden. This organization sells tickets to arts events around the city, including events at the Madame Walker Theatre Center, the Indianapolis Civic Theatre, and Dance Kaleidoscope.

Front Row Tickets, 6332 North Guilford, Suite C, 317/255-3220 or 800/695-9676, sells tickets to sports and entertainment events.

Tickets & Travel, 1099 North Meridian St., 317/633-6400 or 800/876-8497, www.sportstravel.com, sells tickets to sporting events, concerts, and theater.

the city, although most are on the north side.

ENSEMBLE MUSIC SOCIETY
P.O. Box 40188
Indianapolis
317/254-8915
Under the auspices of this society, world-renowned chamber musicians perform in Indianapolis each year. The London Chamber Orchestra, the Juilliard String Quartet, and Russia's Trio Voronezh have all joined the line-up. The society, which presents four to six concerts a year, begins its 1999 season at the new Indiana Historical Society theater. (Downtown)

INDIANAPOLIS CHAMBER
ORCHESTRA
Clowes Memorial Hall

4600 Sunset Ave.
317/940-6444 (box office)
www.clowes.org
The Indianapolis Chamber Orchestra brings established and aspiring artists to the city. It performs six concerts annually, presenting five well-loved classics and one commissioned work. Founded in 1985, the ICO regularly collaborates with other groups, including the Indianapolis Opera and the Butler Ballet. Annually, the Indianapolis Chamber Orchestra and the Indianapolis Symphonic Choir perform the ever-popular Handel's *Messiah*. Kirk Trevor conducts this orchestra, which has about 35 members. (North)

INDIANAPOLIS
CHILDREN'S CHOIR

Butler University
4600 Sunset Ave.
317/940-9640
www.icchoir.org
Since Henry Leck founded the Indianapolis Children's Choir in 1986, the group's ranks have swelled to more than 1,000 children and 14 choirs. Locally, the Children's Choir performs about 80 times each year. The group has sung internationally, including at the 1,400th anniversary celebration of Canterbury Cathedral. About 2,500 children have been members, and their proud relatives have made the Indianapolis Children's Choir bumper sticker the best known in town. (North)

INDIANAPOLIS OPERA
250 E. 38th St.
317/283-3531 or 317/940-6444
(box office)
In 1975, Miriam Ramaker, a voice teacher and former professional singer, decided that Indianapolis needed an opera, so she founded one. The group began with English operettas, which proved to be a hit with the community. Some prominent singers got their starts here, including Kathleen Magee and Nova Thomas. The Indianapolis Opera typically puts on four productions a year, one of which is usually a piece that isn't performed often. The Indianapolis

Symphony Orchestra or the Indianapolis Chamber Orchestra accompanies the singers. Performances are given at Clowes Hall. (North)

INDIANAPOLIS SYMPHONIC CHOIR
4600 Sunset Ave.
317/940-6461 (box office)
www.iquest.net/~ischoir
From baroque to Broadway, the Indianapolis Symphonic Choir performs eight subscription concerts each year, with additional performances in conjunction with the Indianapolis Symphony Orchestra and the Indianapolis Chamber Orchestra. (North)

INDIANAPOLIS SYMPHONY ORCHESTRA
45 Monument Circle
317/262-1100 or 317/639-4300
(box office)
www.in.net/iso/
This musical powerhouse has a devoted local following and an international reputation. With about 200 performances a year reaching a half a million people, the ISO doesn't slow down. It's one of only 18 orchestras in the country that play year-round. Music director Raymond Leppard, who is retiring at the end of the 2000/01 season, has been widely lauded for his groundbreaking methods of attracting new concertgoers.

Rita Kohn, playwright, journalist, and author, believes that the best outdoor venue is going to be the Allen Whitehill Clowes Amphitheater, on the Marian College campus. New venues are also being built in the West Street-Washington Street neighborhood and at the Indiana State Museum, the Indiana Historical Society, and the Eiteljorg Museum.

The sumptuous theater at the Murat Centre, p. 178

© D. Francis/MarDan Photography

The ISO holds most performances at Hilbert Circle Theatre, a 1916 movie palace, lavishly renovated in the early 1980s. Additional venues include city parks and the annual summer series at Conner Prairie Amphitheater. ♿ (Downtown)

Aliev as its artistic director. An internationally renowned dancer who had been with the Kirov Ballet for 14 years, Aliev began hiring dancers from companies around the globe. Shows, which are performed at the Murat Centre, have included *Sleeping Beauty* and *Firebird*. (Downtown)

DANCE

BALLET INTERNATIONALE
502-B N. Capitol Ave.
317/637-8979
www.balletinternationale.org
Ballet Internationale, once only a regional player, leapt onto the world stage in 1994, when it recruited Eldar

BUTLER BALLET
Jordan College of Fine Arts
4600 Sunset Ave.
317/940-6465 or 317/940-6444
(box office)
www.butler.edu/dance/butler_ballet.html
As the artistic director of the Butler Ballet, Swiss-born Stephan Laurent

T I P

Ballroom dancers head for the Indiana Roof Ballroom, 317/236-1870, on the top floor of the Indiana Repertory Theatre, which hosts monthly dances February through November.

has brought his European experience to Indianapolis, focusing on classical ballet. The best-known show is *the Nutcracker*, which has become a community holiday tradition. (North)

DANCE KALEIDOSCOPE
12 W. 38th St.
317/940-6555 (box office)
www.dancekal.org

This dynamic company concentrates on modern dance and is led by David Hochoy, a protégé of Martha Graham. Although the company's workshops and demonstrations are held around the state, its series performances are held at the Civic Theatre, and the group now spends five months of the year at the Oregon Shakespeare Festival. (North)

Indianapolis's Haunted Theater

Elias Jacoby, potentate of the Murat Temple when the structure was completed, was a dedicated Shriner. On December 31, 1935, Jacoby collapsed while getting ready for the Murat's annual New Year's Eve fête. Some say the story ends there. Others tell a different tale. Since his death, a specter has been seen sitting in his front-row balcony seat, rocking in his favorite chair, and roaming the theater's halls.

Maintenance man Frank Bowling was spooked by some strange occurrences there. After a New Year's Eve party, he was closing down the building. He says, "I turned off the lights and started out of the [Egyptian] room. When I reached the door, the lights came back on." He turned off the lights again and went downstairs, where he saw a bluish-gray light move across the room toward the painting of Jacoby. Distracted by "weird music" coming from the theater, Bowling found lights flipping off and on and curtains moving. When he left the building, the lights he had turned off were shining again.

Jacoby drank one worker's Coke and frightened another so badly that he wouldn't return to the theater. One night, the Shriners' public relations director Lloyd Walton and 10 psychics spent the night in the building. All 10 psychics felt "high energy," and five of the 11 present saw a tear roll down the face in Jacoby's portrait.

Fact or fantasy? Look for Elias Jacoby when you visit the Murat.

For the most up-to-date information about the city's arts action, contact the Arts Council of Indianapolis, 47 South Pennsylvania St., Suite 303, 317/631-3301 or 800/965-ARTS (2787). It produces annual directories of arts organizations and artists and runs the Artsgarden and Ticket Central.

IUPUI MOVING COMPANY
901 W. New York St.
317/274-0611
www.iupui.edu/~indyhper
This student company has strong community-outreach and education programs. Organized in 1982 as a modern-dance group, the troupe has added ethnic, ballet, jazz, and, occasionally, tap performances. Students produce a major program in the spring at the Walker Theatre and give informal studio concerts each fall. The latter, held at the IUPUI Natatorium, are free. (Downtown)

CONCERT VENUES

**CHRISTEL DEHAAN
FINE ARTS CENTER**
University of Indianapolis
1400 E. Hanna Ave.
317/788-3409
www.uindy.edu/~cdfac/
Built in 1994, this facility has grown to be one of the city's busiest venues. Superb acoustics have put the center's Ruth Lilly Performance Hall (capacity 500) in demand for concerts, most of which are free to the public. Suzuki & Friends and the Ensemble Music Society are among the groups that call the center home. ♿ (East/ Southeast)

CLOWES MEMORIAL HALL
Butler University
4600 Sunset Ave.
317/940-6444 or 800/732-0804
www.cloweshall.org
One of the state's premier performance venues, Clowes schedules one or more events weekly. Designed as a modern version of seventeenth- and eighteenth-century opera houses, the hall's vertical spaces, shallow balconies, and terraces minimize the distance between audience and stage. An acoustic masterpiece, the 2,182-seat hall is famous for its sound clouds.

Built in 1963 in memory of Dr. George Henry Alexander Clowes, a strong supporter of the arts, the hall is used for many different types of performances, from Broadway road shows to ballet, jazz, and lectures. Bob Hope, P. J. O'Rourke, and Beverly Sills have taken the stage at Clowes. ♿ (North)

CONSECO FIELDHOUSE
At Georgia St. between Delaware and Pennsylvania Sts.
317/639-6411 or 317/639-2112
(box office)
www.consecofieldhouse.com
This sparkling new arena, which will be home to the Pacers in 1999, replaces Market Square Arena.

Ballet Internationale

Performance at Ballet Internationale, p. 174

jazz, country, gospel, and children's concerts. In addition to the 6,000 non-smoking seats in the covered pavilion, there is room for about 15,000 on the lawn. Although the facility has ample parking, limited access roads can create traffic jams. Avoid them by arriving early and enjoying the entertainment in the plaza areas, which begins two hours before concerts. There are a variety of concession stands at the center. & (North)

INDIANA HISTORICAL SOCIETY THEATER
450 W. Ohio St.
317/232-1882 (box office phone number not determined at press time)
www.indianahistory.org
Scheduled to open shortly after press time, this 300-seat theater is designed for music, lectures, and performances—all planned in consultation with a variety of arts organizations that might be using the facility. The Historical Society will host an Indiana film series here, among other presentations. The big draws here are the intimacy of the theater, its superb acoustics, and its lobby overlooking the canal. (Downtown)

Concerts, rodeos, ice shows, and more are scheduled for the 19,000-seat facility beginning around November 1999. Improvements over MSA include more legroom, more concessions and bathrooms, and shorter aisles. & (Downtown)

DEER CREEK MUSIC CENTER
12880 E. 146th St.
Noblesville
317/841-8900 or 317/776-3337 (box office)
www.concertline.com
From May through September, this outdoor amphitheater hosts rock,

INDIANAPOLIS ARTSGARDEN
Intersection of Washington and

TRIVIA

Stories, Inc., has added a piece to the city's art mosaic with its delightful performances, held in the Storytellers' Theater at the Indianapolis Art Center and in public libraries in central Indiana. Yarn-spinners also draw hundreds each fall to the four-day Hoosier Storytelling Festival in Broad Ripple and sites around the city. Kids sit spellbound. For a schedule and more information, call 317/576-9848.

Illinois Sts.
317/631-3301
www.indyarts.org
Straddling a major downtown inter-section, the Indianapolis Artsgarden is an ideal place to sample the arts. Since the Artsgarden opening in 1995, it has hosted between 400 and 500 programs each year in its 12,500-foot-square space. Operated by the Arts Council of Indianapolis, it's home to Ticket Central, which handles ticket-ing for a variety of arts organizations. ♿ (Downtown)

MADAME WALKER THEATRE CENTER
617 Indiana Ave.
317/236-2099 or 317/236-2087
(box office)
www.mmewalkertheatre.org
Built in 1927 and named after Amer-ica's first black female millionaire, the Madame Walker Theatre Center thrives as a multidisciplinary cultural showcase and the home to many educational-arts outreach programs. Jazz on the Avenue and the Asante Children's Theatre perform here. Louis Armstrong, Dizzy Gillespie, and Lena Horne are among the many no-tables who have walked the boards here over the years. ♿ (Downtown)

MURAT CENTRE
502 N. New Jersey St.
317/231-0000
www.concertline.com
Spectacularly renovated, the Murat Centre is the mosque-like building on the downtown skyline. Completed by the Shriners in 1910, the building still houses the organization's headquar-ters, as well as a 2,621-seat theater and the elegant Egyptian Room. Bal-let Internationale regularly performs here. Shows are ticketed through TicketMaster. ♿ (Downtown)

The Chatterbox Tavern

12

NIGHTLIFE

When the sun sets on Indianapolis, opportunities for fun explode like Fourth of July fireworks. There's no shortage of options here—nightlife runs the gamut. Get dolled up for an evening of ballroom dancing or let your hair down and head for a smoky jazz club. Seek out good conversation at an intimate pub or settle for soul-wrenching blues and a basket of wings. Work off steam on the dance floor or laugh till you cry at a comedy show.

What's hot in Indy? Dance clubs, comedy, sports bars. What's not? Country-western dancing—the two-step taverns that sprinkled the city just a few years ago have all but disappeared, so put away your cowboy boots. But everything else goes. (That, sadly, includes some sorry strips of "adult entertainment" on the city's far east and west sides—we're not advertising where.)

You'll find concentrations of nightlife in certain neighborhoods and Downtown spots (see the sidebar on page 187)—the great news is that these neighborhoods generally include a variety of options—comedy, theater, cinema, dancing, live music, even bowling—all within a short walk.

DANCE CLUBS

EDEN
6235 N. Guilford Ave.
317/475-1588
Neon lights beckoning from the top floor reveal that there's more inside the old VFW building in Broad Ripple than war stories. Energetic Eden is a two-level club offering hard-driving

DJ music. The first level is filled with pool tables, TVs, and lounging areas. The spacious upstairs dance floor is packed with acid-rock devotees, retro fans, and techno-rock followers—depending on the night of the week. (North)

THE GALLERY
2145 N. Talbott St.

317/923-9886
The two rooms in this club, one with a balcony, feature dance music and, sometimes, live bands. The club is in full swing Friday through Sunday, but special events and radio promotions mean the doors are often open weekdays. The dress code is a cut above casual—no gym shoes, jogging attire, or caps. Covers are nominal ($3 to $6); costs for special events may be higher. (North)

INDIANA ROOF BALLROOM
140 W. Washington St.
317/236-1870
One Sunday a month, city denizens have the opportunity to put on tails or sequined ball gowns and head out for an evening of glamour and glitz. Big bands of national renown perform for crowds in a gilded ballroom. Attendees, who range from college students to Arthur Murray alumni, demonstrate a variety of ballroom dance styles. Bar service is available. Reservations are recommended. (Downtown)

MEMORIES
7820 Michigan Rd.
317/879-0759
"This is the place for old-time rock 'n' roll, not for hip-hop or grunge," says owner Harry Gwinn. A DJ provides music Thursday through Saturday, 8 p.m. to closing. The in-house pool league competes Wednesdays (during winter). There's a full menu—Harry prides himself on the tenderloins, pounded and breaded on-site. (North)

ROCK LOBSTER
820 Broad Ripple Ave.
317/253-5844
Rock Lobster draws a young crowd with DJ music, drink specials, and an active dance floor. This club is one of three-in-a-row owned by the same company.

If you need a change of scene, head next door to **Average Joe's**, 816 Broad Ripple Ave., a sports bar with 20 TVs and plenty of games. Or check out the dance scene at **Mineshaft Saloon** at 812 Broad Ripple Ave. (North)

WORLD MARDI GRAS COMPLEX
Circle Centre, 49 W. Maryland St.
317/630-5483
This mega-entertainment center on the fourth floor of the Circle Centre mall virtually vibrates with energy. Patrons can choose among bars; dance clubs Gator's and Flashbaxx; and Brewski's, a sports bar and the only place that serves food (kitchen closes at 10 p.m., except for hot dogs and nachos). New in 1999 is Howl at the Moon, a sing-along piano bar. (Downtown)

Can't get enough jazz? At the Madame Walker Theatre, enjoy Jazz on the Avenue the second and fourth Fridays of the month for $3.50. Still not enough? Head for the Indianapolis Museum of Art the first Friday of the month for First Friday. For $7 ($4 for members), you get wine, hors d'oeuvres, a look at the galleries, and live jazz. Now, if only someone would schedule something for the third Friday of the month!

Five Indy Microbreweries—and Best Brews

Despite the fact that brewpubs are catching on in Indy, it appears that we're pretty much weenies when it comes to our beer preferences. For the most part, microbrewery owners report that their best sellers tend to be the paler ales and American-style beers that don't wander too far from the brands we buy in the grocery store. Indy's five brewpubs are listed here, along with either their best-selling beers or what management recommends we sample.

1. ***Alcatraz Brewing Co.*** *is located at Illinois St. and West Maryland, 317/488-1230. Weiss Guy Wheat, an American-style wheat ale, is the most popular choice. It's served with a wedge of lemon. (Downtown)*

2. *The **Broad Ripple Brew Pub** can be found at 842 East 65th St., 317/253-2739. Wee Alec Heavy, a thick, Scottish-style ale, is the recommendation of one server. (North)*

3. ***Circle V Brewing Co.*** *is located at 8310 Craig St., 317/595-9253. The number-one choice every week is the Brickyard Red, an amber-colored beer with a balance between malt and hops. (North)*

4. ***Oaken Barrel Brewing Co.*** *is located at 50 N. Airport Parkway, Greenwood, 317/887-2287. The pub's most popular beer is the Razz-Wheat, an Americanized version of a Belgian fruit beer. (East/Southeast)*

5. *At the **Rock Bottom Brewery**, 10 West Washington St., 317/681-8180, the Sugar Creek Pale Ale is the favorite among patrons, but the assistant brewer and staff recommend the Raccoon Red, an all-English malt beer. (Downtown)*

JAZZ AND BLUES

THE CHATTERBOX TAVERN
435 Massachusetts Ave.
317/636-0584
This Massachusetts Avenue land-

mark (around since 1939) has a well-deserved reputation for great jazz, luring celebrities such as Mick Jagger and Winton Marsalis, who played with the band the night he visited. Musicians who tour with shows at the Murat often wander across the street after their own performances to listen or play. Music starts at 8:30 p.m. during the week, 10:30 p.m. on weekends. (Downtown)

JAZZ COOKER
925 E. Westfield Blvd.
317/253-2883
On a humid summer evening out on the patio with a bowl of spicy black bean soup, you'll swear you were in New Orleans. This Southern-style restaurant, featuring Cajun and Creole cooking, is tucked away in a stately two-story white house draped in shady foliage. The Dick Laswell Trio plays easy, dinner-music jazz on Friday and Saturday from 7 p.m. to 10 p.m. (North)

THE JAZZ KITCHEN
5377 N. College Ave.
317/253-4900
www.thejazzkitchen.com
A lengthy recorded message gives callers detailed information about the current acts at the Jazz Kitchen. The Frank Glover Quartet plays here on Mondays. The food is a draw, with a creative menu and unique pizzas (go for the gumbo version). Although cover charges for national acts may be nearly as pricey as concert tickets (as much as $20), the regular cover charge is generally from $6 to $8. (North)

MIDTOWN GRILL
815 E. Westfield Blvd.
317/253-1141
The Midtown Grill has been featuring jazz pianist David Hepler for nearly 12 years. He performs many of his own compositions, some of which are available on CD. Occasionally, another jazz artist plays. The Grill is well known for its excellent continental fare. Din-

ers can savor music with their meal Wednesday through Saturday. (North)

RICK'S CAFE BOATYARD
4050 Dandy Tr.
317/290-9300
The sunsets over Eagle Creek Reservoir are reason enough to drop in, but live jazz is another draw. Rick's features three regular groups, the Tim Brickley Band, the Greg Bacon Band, and the Michael Brown Band. In warm weather, you can sit outside on the deck. On weekends, the music starts at 8 p.m. and continues until midnight. (West/Southwest)

SLIPPERY NOODLE INN
372 S. Meridian St.
317/631-6978
The Noodle has been praised by locals and nonlocals alike. *NUVO* newsweekly regularly lists it as one of the best blues bars in town, and it's earned two Vista awards from the Indiana Department of Tourism. The bar has been featured in the *Jazz and Blues Lovers Guide to the U.S.,* the *New York Times, Rolling Stone,* and *Details* magazine as a must-see blues stop as well. This historic landmark is indeed the premier blues bar in Indy, featuring local talent (like Gene Deer) as well as national blues greats (such as Coco Montoya). Two stages offer music seven nights a week. (Downtown)

ROCK/POP

THE COZY
115 E. Wabash St.
317/638-2100
This restaurant/bar features live music—a little blues, a little jazz, a little rock—on Friday and Saturday between 9:30 p.m. and 1:30 a.m. But

patrons may enjoy jukebox tunes, pool, and a game room, in addition to a full menu, throughout the week. (Downtown)

THE FOUNTAIN ROOM
1105 S. Shelby St.
317/686-6010
www.fountainsquareindy.com
Live bands revive hits from the fifties and sixties on Friday nights; Saturday is rockabilly and swing in the area next to the Fountain Diner. The more dedicated patrons are likely to appear in poodle skirts, saddle shoes, or slicked-back hair to better fit in with the fifties ambience. Upstairs and downstairs is Action Bowl Duckpin Bowling. (East/Southeast)

IKE & JONESY'S
17 W. Jackson Pl.
317/632-4553
A house band plays Tuesday and Wednesday at this bar; the rest of the week, a guest band or DJ plays favorites from the fifties to the seventies. The music starts at 9 p.m. and plays until closing. Ike & Jonesy's is closed on Sunday, except when the Colts are playing and fans gather to watch TV. (Downtown)

THE PATIO
6308 N. Guilford Ave.
317/253-0799
The management here books cutting-edge, original local and regional talent, as well as up-and-coming national

Dave Lowe: A First-Rate Lounge Act

Familiar ballads and standards, from "Mack the Knife" to "Moon-dance," float from the corner of the restaurant, where keyboardist Dave Lowe performs for regulars and happy-hour partiers reluctant to drag themselves home. The air is thick with cigarette haze and the sounds of clinking glasses, friendly banter, and the frequent "ca-ching" of change dropped into the brandy snifter that serves as a tip jar. Between numbers, Dave works the room with the aplomb of a Las Vegas veteran. A fixture for 13 years at the nearby Capri (he left in 1998 after the restaurant was sold), Dave has drawn his following to a new location, **George's Place** *(2727 E. 86th St., 317/255-7064), where he performs Wednesday through Saturday from 8 until closing. Not much has changed—Dave devotees continue to vie for his attention, patrons request their favorites, and couples get up for a dance. Dave regularly welcomes other musicians to accompany him, and wanna-be crooners share the mike to belt out their own versions of "New York, New York" or "Mona Lisa."*

acts. The suave and debonair come on Wednesdays for the Cigartini Swing Club (jackets preferred) to select from an impressive menu of martinis (50 different kinds) and fine cigars. On Saturdays the club plays formatted dance music. (North)

PEPPERS
6283 N. College Ave.
Indianapolis
317/257-6277
Tuesday nights, when the Alligator Brothers play, are the busiest for this Broad Ripple bar. But there are always crowds wandering in to listen to a variety of music. From blues to eighties and nineties covers, Peppers brings in live music six nights a week (it's closed Mondays). (North)

QUINCY'S
2544 Executive Dr.
317/248-2481
www.adamsmark.com
A high-energy crowd is always eager to hit the dance floor at this nightspot within the airport's Adam's Mark

---

Top Tips for Teens

What do you do on a Saturday night when you're too young for the bar scene and too old to sit home with the folks? Abby Workman has a few suggestions. Her credentials? She's a teen—currently a college-bound senior at Brebeuf, with connections to the media (on staff at Brebeuf's student newspaper) and work experience at city coffee shops.

*The **Abbey Coffee House**, 317/269-8426, is a safe and comfortable place for teenagers to linger after hours. It features lots of big, comfy chairs. Local musicians often perform.*

*Teenagers gather at **Barnes & Noble** bookstore, 317/594-7525, on weekends because it is open late. A coffee bar, the well-stocked magazine section, and occasional musical programs are draws, too.*

*The **Emerson Theater**, 317/357-0239, is an under-18 club and a hangout for high school students. Different bands (local to national) play here Friday and Saturday nights.*

*The **Laser Light Fantasy Show at the Children's Museum**, 317/924-5431, is a good alternative to a movie. The shows are set to music ranging from Pink Floyd to the Beastie Boys. The Friday and Saturday shows sell out—buy tickets early.*

Thatsa Wrap, *317/328-9305, is a restaurant that sells smoothies and wrapped sandwiches. Teenagers hang out here because the food is inexpensive and it's a fun alternative to fast food.*

Hotel. There's a different ambience each night of the week, and the themes are constantly changing: Mondays, a Colts player may sign autographs; Tuesdays draw jazz fans; Wednesdays a country-western band packs in the Texas two-steppers—and so forth. A plus is the complimentary appetizer buffet from 4:30 until 8. (West/Southwest)

RITZ NIGHTCLUB
3525 N. Shadeland Ave.
317/549-2222
Live bands perform at this club in the Quality Inn East Wednesday through Saturday from 10 p.m. until closing. A DJ provides dance music on Monday and Tuesday. The Ritz also features billiards, darts, arcade games, and a full dinner menu. (East/Southeast)

THE VOGUE
6259 N. College Ave.
317/255-2828
The cornerstone of Broad Ripple nightlife, this former movie theater is large enough to hold concert-size crowds drawn to national acts such as Los Lobos or Shawn Colvin. But local and regional bands also pack in fans. Currently, a DJ plays seventies and eighties music on Wednesdays. Most recently, the club has abandoned Saturday as a concert night and introduced a dance club format instead. Covers are nominal, except when national acts are playing. (North)

ZANIES TOO
5914 E. 10th St.
317/357-6022
Popular blues artist Gene Deer plays here regularly—other local musicians and bands perform Tuesday and Thursday through Sunday, as well. The club features a full menu—stuffed pizza is a specialty. Pool tables, darts,

Eden, p. 179

and a big-screen TV offer other diversions. (East/Southeast)

PUBS AND BARS

ALLEY CAT LOUNGE
6267 Carrollton Ave.
317/257-4036
Flashier places come and go along the Broad Ripple strip. You may even have to stumble around stinking dumpsters to arrive at this humble little bar, as scruffy and bedraggled as its namesake. But night owls put off by crowds, pricey covers, and too-youthful glitz will find comfort in the basics: cheap beer, jukebox tunes, and a game of pool. (North)

CHAMPPS AMERICANA
8711 River Crossing Blvd.
317/574-0333
Boisterous, noisy, and cavernous, Champps attracts sports fans with big-screen TVs that allow them to keep an eye on their game no matter

T
I
P

Karaoke may already be on most people's "out" list, but some Indy residents seem to be oblivious to this trend. The nightspots listed below devote theme nights to this campy pastime.

96th Street Sports Bar & Grill   Quincy's
The Buck Stops Here   The Mineshaft
Champps Americana   Fountain Room

where they're sitting. During the summer, bands perform outside on the deck. (North)

EXCALIBER II LOUNGE
Best Western Waterfront
2930 Waterfront Pkwy., W. Dr.
317/299-8400
This pub-style lounge on the waterfront is a relaxing retreat for business travelers and locals who come to watch the big-screen TV, play darts, or spend an evening with friends. (West/Southwest)

MELODY INN
3826 N. Illinois St.
317/923-4707
A well-worn neighborhood bar, the

Melody Inn has been serving spirits since 1943. On Friday and Saturday, live bands play a range of music styles. A limited menu offers standard bar fare. The Melody Inn is open seven days a week. (North)

MOE AND JOHNNY'S
5380 N. College Ave.
317/255-6376
A local landmark, the Bulldog draws Broad Ripple crowds, Butler students and alumni, and sports fans, who pack the place during I.U. games. Occasionally, a live band is featured on weekends, and crowds come for the game room, as well. But the Bulldog is primarily a place for beer and sports. Many of the not-so-old-timers

Slippery Noodle Inn, p. 182

Slippery Noodle Inn

remember Moe Walsh, Bulldog owner for nearly 27 years, who died a few years ago. On the anniversary of his death, patrons observe a moment of silence. (North)

PLUMP'S LAST SHOT
6416 Cornell Ave.
317/257-5867
It's impossible to live in Hoosier Country without learning about high school

Nightspots:
Concentrations of Entertainment

Can't quite decide what you want to do tonight? Head out to one of these neighborhoods, areas of concentrated nightlife with a variety of possibilities. Park your car and wander from activity to activity.

1. *In the **Union Station** area, venues such as the Slippery Noodle Inn, the Indianapolis Comedy Connection, Ike & Jonesy's, and Hollywood Bar & Filmworks offer blues, jazz, movies, sports, comedy, and more.*

2. ***Broad Ripple**—Where to begin? Only a sampling of the neighborhood's possibilities is included in this chapter. National concerts, local bands, soothing jazz, comedy, dancing with DJs, watching a game in a sports bar, and much more are available here.*

3. *At **Massachusetts Avenue** you can choose among a Broadway show at the Murat, a more intimate performance at American Cabaret Theater, or some sensuous jazz at the Chatterbox. Or visit a gallery or two in Indy's arts district.*

4. ***Fountain Square** offers a couple of choices within one establishment—after dinner at the Fountain Diner, head upstairs or down for a game of duckpin bowling at Action Bowl, then check back in at the Fountain Room for Fifties or rockabilly dancing.*

5. *At **Circle Centre** you can shop 'til you drop—or until the stores close. Then, enjoy pizza baked in a wood stove and home brew at the Alcatraz Brewing Co. Afterward, head to the fourth level and choose from a dizzying array of cutting-edge arcade games at GameWorks Studio, or dance to live music at World Mardi Gras.*

basketball star Bobby Plump's winning shot in the legendary Milan-Muncie Central state championship game of 1954. In case you need a lesson, head for this Broad Ripple establishment owned by Bobby's son. It's covered with photos, trophies, and sports memorabilia. (North)

THE RATHSKELLER RESTAURANT
401 E. Michigan St.
317/636-0396
www.rathskeller.com
Conversation is the focus at this quiet bar in the Athenaeum—no TV or arcade games distract patrons from the company of friends. The Rathskeller, not surprisingly, features an extensive selection of German beers—40 bottled beers and six on draft. Live entertainment, Wednesday through Saturday, features a variety of music and popular local bands such as Dog Talk. (Downtown)

RED KEY TAVERN
5170 N. College Ave.
317/283-4601
Proprietor Russ Settle has been running this College Avenue landmark for close to 50 years (although the bar's been standing since 1933). He continues to oversee the making of his popular chili, shake up a great martini,

collect contributions for a local children's home, and schmooze with regulars and Red Key alumni. The grill menu offers inexpensive, filling fare. The Red Key is also renowned for its all-big-band jukebox. (North)

THE WELLINGTON
6331 Guilford Ave.
317/255-5159
An extensive imported beer selection and a small, intimate setting make this place a must on the Broad Ripple pub circuit. The Wellington is connected to and shares its wine list with the Corner Wine Bar, but their menus are separate. Patrons may compete in a game of darts—the pub was recently designated by *NUVO* newsweekly as the best place to throw darts. (North)

COMEDY CLUBS

BROAD RIPPLE COMEDY CLUB
6281 N. College Ave.
317/255-4211
Each 90-minute show at this club features three comedians—the opening act is generally a local. A well-stocked bar keeps drinks flowing during performances, and a limited menu features appetizers such as nachos and wings. (North)

T I P

Author Dan Wakefield claims there's no better way to spend a night on the town in Indy than at the Red Key Tavern, "shooting the bull" with Shortridge High buddies over a diet Coke and a bowl of Russ's chili. Dan's been frequenting the Red Key since his high school days. Although he now lives in Florida, he still drops in when he's in town—as he did during the filming of his best-seller-turned-movie, *Going All the Way*, in the summer of 1996.

COMEDYSPORTZ ARENA
721 Massachusetts Ave.
317/951-8499
This club offers a unique approach to comedy; the audience supplies out-landish ideas that the teams of come-dians, or "actletes," must then improvise into sketches. The second show is adult-oriented (attendees must be age 17 or older). Reserva-tions are highly recommended. The club also features comedy sports workshops and corporate workshops. (Downtown)

CRACKERS COMEDY CLUB
7802 Keystone Crossing
317/846-2500
The owners of this comedy club, the oldest in Indy, claim it's the only place in the city designed and built specifi-cally for comedy. It features a half-moon stage and tiered seating on two levels. Patrons can reserve a private suite that seats eight or buy preferred tickets that guarantee a table within the first four rows of the stage. (North)

INDIANAPOLIS COMEDY CONNECTION
247 S. Meridian St.
317/631-3536
Operated by the people who own Broad Ripple Comedy Club and Crackers, this downtown venue fol-lows the same format and schedule as its sister clubs. Reservations are recommended (you'll be seated in the order in which your reservation was called in). (Downtown)

ONE-LINERS COMEDY CLUB
50 Airport Pkwy.
Greenwood
317/889-5233
Wilson's restaurant, owned by WIBC DJ Dave Wilson, hosts comedy shows

The Chatterbox Tavern

Live jazz at The Chatterbox Tavern, p. 181

Wednesday through Saturday nights, featuring alumni from the Nashville Network, Stand-Up Spotlight, and the Improv. (East/Southeast)

DINNER THEATERS

BEEF & BOARDS DINNER THEATRE
9301 N. Michigan Rd.
317/872-9664
This roomy, cabaret-style dinner the-ater presents a variety of Broadway musicals and concerts featuring na-tional and local performers. Group rates are available. Patrons arrive as early as an hour and a half before show time to eat a rather uninspired buffet dinner, cleared away by wait staff before the show begins. (Drinks are served during the show, and dessert at intermission.) Matinee per-formances are given on Wednesday and Sunday. (North)

MYSTERY CAFÉ
The Milano Inn,
231 S. College Ave.
317/684-0668
The mayhem and mystery begin upon arrival and conclude just before dessert at this dinner theater that allows diners to participate in the intrigue. Productions include *Death by Disco* and *Death Takes a Honeymooner.* Reservations are recommended—shows sell out. (Downtown)

MOVIE HOUSES OF NOTE

GENERAL CINEMA CASTLETON SQUARE
6135 E. 82nd St.
317/849-3471
Foreign and avant-garde films are shown at this theater complex tucked behind the Castleton Mall. Call the theater for show times. Tickets are $4.50 before 6 p.m. (North)

HOLLYWOOD BAR & FILMWORKS
247 S. Meridian St.
317/231-9255 (information line)
317/231-9250 (reservations)
www.filmworksonline.com
Forget stumbling over other moviegoers and spilling popcorn and soda as you get to your seat. Instead, sit comfortably, cabaret-style, at your own table and sip a daiquiri or down a beer, ordering from a complete menu while you watch a recent box-office hit. The Hollywood Bar & Filmworks features at least two movies each night. You can order tickets in advance, but seating is first-come, first-served, and management advises arriving no later than a half-hour before the showing. Show times vary. (Downtown)

13

DAY TRIPS FROM INDIANAPOLIS

Day Trip: Amish Country

Distance from Indianapolis: 3 hours, 150 miles

About 17,000 Amish (11 percent of the Amish in North America) are clustered in Elkhart and LaGrange counties in northern Indiana, where visitors can get a glimpse of this rare lifestyle. Begin by contacting the **Elkhart County Visitor's Center**, 800/250-4831, which has mapped a 90-mile loop (the Heritage Trail) through the area. (Be sure to cruise County Road 16 between Shipshewana and Middlebury.) You can borrow a tape, for either the Heritage Trail or the furniture crafters tour, to guide you. You'll see trim farms, farmers plowing with horses, and Amish pinafores drying on the clotheslines. Buggies, bicyclists, and pedestrians share the road with you. Stop at **Honeyville General Store**–where you can buy bulk foods, homemade jams, black shoes, brooms, and more—and, just across the road, at the **White Swan**, for an assortment of antiques and gifts.

Just south of Shipshewana, Menno-Hof explains and displays the history and lifestyles of the Amish, Mennonites, and Hutterites. The tornado room, which recreates the sensation of a tornado, thrills youngsters. **Amish Acres**, 800/800-4942, www.amishacres.com, on an 80-acre farm in Nappanee, is a cultural trip back to the turn of the century. On the National Register of Historic Places, Amish Acres has many attractions, including the Round Barn Theatre, which stages shows year-round, including a musical about Amish life. The all-you-can-eat threshers dinner, including beef and noodles and homemade pies, is a treat. Although many do this trip in a day, an overnight or weekend excursion is more pleasurable. Overnight guests

INDIANAPOLIS REGION

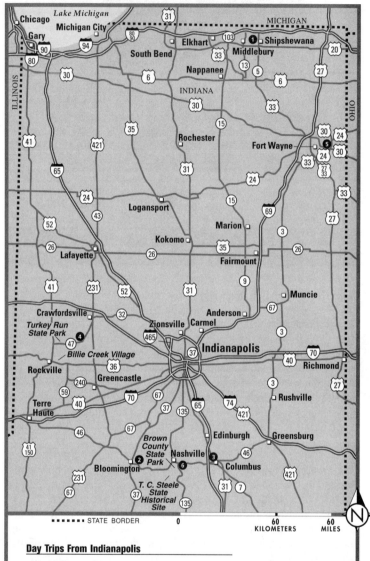

Lake Michigan
Chicago
Michigan City
Gary
MICHIGAN
31
80
90
103
Elkhart
Shipshewana ❶
94
90
80
South Bend
Middlebury
20
ILLINOIS
33
13
5
Nappanee
6
27
30
6
6
INDIANA
41
421
30
33
Rochester
15
35
Fort Wayne
30
24
31
24
33
24
27
33
33
65
24
Logansport
15
69
52
43
Marion
3
27
26
Kokomo
35
26
Lafayette
26
Fairmount
41
231
52
31
9
Muncie
Crawfordsville
32
Anderson
67
Turkey Run
State Park
Zionsville
Carmel
3
❹ 47
465
Billie Creek Village
Indianapolis
70
Rockville
36
37
40
Richmond
Greencastle
3
240
59
67
40
70
Rushville
27
Terre
Haute
37
65
74
46
135
421
67
Edinburgh
Greensburg
41
150
Brown
County
State
Park
Nashville ❸
231
❷
46
Columbus
421
Bloomington
❻
67
T. C. Steele
State
Historical
Site
37
31
7
135

• • • • • STATE BORDER   0   60   60
                                      KILOMETERS   MILES

N

Day Trips From Indianapolis

1 Amish Country
2 Bloomington
3 Columbus
4 Covered Bridge Country and Historic Crawfordsville
5 Fort Wayne
6 Nashville and Brown County

may save money with the **Amish Acres Country Package**, which includes a night at the Inn at Amish Acres or the Nappanee Inn.

For many, shopping is the point of a trip to Amish Country. Apple butter, sugar cookies, wooden toys, antiques, copper kettles, and handcrafted cherry furniture are among the items travelers cart home. **Yoder's**, 219/768-4887, in Shipshewana, **Fern's Country Foods**, 219/593-2222, south of town, and **Gohn Brothers**, 219/825-2400, in Middlebury, offer a variety to satisfy everyone in the family. Let your nose lead you to the homemade baked goods. Handmade quilts, for which the area is famous, are widely available. Particularly nice ones can be found at **Laura's Country Store**, 1255 W. State Road 120 in Howe, voice mail, 219/562-2823. The **Shipshewana Flea Market,** including an antique sale and auction—held each Tuesday and Wednesday from May until October—draws bargain hunters.

In addition to the two inns at Amish Acres, recommended accommodations include the **Essenhaus Country Inn**, 800/455-9471, in Middlebury; the elegant **Checkerberry Inn**, 219/642-4445, outside Nappanee; and the **Patchwork Quilt**, 219/825-2417, near Middlebury. Good restaurants include **Das Dutchman Essenhaus**, 800/455-9471, (a dining-shopping complex); the **Blue Gate**, 219/768-4725, in Shipshewana; the **Dutch Cooker**, 219/533-8808, in Goshen (try rivel soup); and the restaurant at the **Checkerberry Inn ($$$)**.

Getting there from Indianapolis: Take U.S. 31 north to U.S. 6 east to Nappanee. Or take U.S. 31 north to South Bend, then U.S. 20 east to Elkhart.

Day Trip: Fort Wayne

Distance from Indianapolis: 2 hours, 130 miles

Consider a weekend getaway to combine this visit with a tour of nearby Amish Country. It's a perfect family trip—and an incredible educational experience. Whether the kids have to write a report about Abraham Lincoln, the rainforest, earthquakes, or early Indiana history, they'll find valuable resources in Fort Wayne. But first, give yourself a lesson in pop culture.

Stop off in **Fairmount** (one hour north of Indianapolis) to pay tribute to native son James Dean, Hollywood's immortal rebel killed in a car accident in 1955. The **James Dean Gallery**, 765/948-3326, 425 N. Main Street, claims that it has the world's largest collection of Dean memorabilia—his signature jeans and white T-shirt, movie posters, and rare TV film clips and a screen test. Nearby, the **Fairmount Historical Museum**, 765/948-4555, 203 E. Washington Street, contains more Dean memorabilia. You can view Dean's lipstick-covered, flower-bedecked gravestone in Park Cemetery. To milk your pilgrimage to the max, stop at the motorcycle shop where Dean bought his first bike, the church where his funeral was held, and the church that holds the annual memorial service on September 30, the anniversary of Dean's death. In September the **Remembering James Dean Festival**, 765/948-4555, is held in downtown Fairmount. It features a fifties car show, look-alike contests, dance contests, film showings, and a parade.

Make your first stop in Fort Wayne at the **Lincoln Museum**, 219/455-3864, 200 E. Berry, the world's largest private collection of Lincoln memorabilia. The 11 galleries include scores of artifacts. Rare photographs and paintings depict Lincoln as a youth, a clean-shaven lawyer, and as the craggy-featured, bearded president anyone who's ever seen a penny knows. Learn about how Nancy Reagan was not the first First Lady to turn to a psychic for advice—one exhibit details how Mary Todd Lincoln asked a psychic to contact her dead husband and sons. Many of the exhibits are interactive.

Science Central, 219/424-2400, 1950 N. Clinton Street, is a museum with hands-on exhibits housed in an old factory building topped by crayon-colored chimneys. Even those who claim to hate science and math will discover how much fun numbers and physics can be as they enjoy a walk on a moonscape, create an earthquake, bend a rainbow, and shoot down a two-story slide.

A trip to the **Children's Zoo**, 219/427-6800, 3411 Sherman Boulevard, identified by the *New York Times* as one of the five best small zoos in the country, allows you to view from the safety of an electric car or elevated walkway free-roaming animals in natural settings. Exhibits include the African veldt, Australian outback, and Indonesian rainforest. The zoo is open from late April to mid-October, but the **Botanical Conservatory**, 219/427-6440, 1100 S. Calhoun Street, an arboretum, is open year-round. The three large greenhouses offer refuge amidst a three-story waterfall or the quiet solitude of a desertscape.

On the west side of town, **Johnny Appleseed Park**, burial site of Johnny Appleseed (John Chapman). If you visit in September, you'll be able to attend the Johnny Appleseed Festival. (Other summer festivals in Fort Wayne include the **Germanfest** in June and **Three Rivers Festivals** in July.)

Fort Wayne offers some other intriguing surprises. A tiny museum in the downtown **Cathedral of the Immaculate Conception**, 219/424-1485, Calhoun and Lewis Streets, displays religious treasures, including texts dating back to the fourteenth century. The highly regarded **Genealogy Research Department of the Allen County Public Library**, 219/424-7241, 900 Webster Street, is the second largest in the country. And the **Fort Wayne Museum of Art**, 219/422-6467, 311 E. Main Street, the **Firefighters Museum**, 219/426-0051, 226 W. Washington Boulevard, and **Old City Hall Historical Museum**, 219/426-2882, 302 E. Berry Street, are all worth a visit.

The **Carole Lombard House**, 219/426-9896, 704 Rockhill Street, the birthplace and childhood home of the unforgettable Hollywood phenomenon, is a bed-and-breakfast with four guest rooms featuring period furnishings and private baths.

Locals will recommend any one of the 15 Don Hall's Restaurants, a local chain. For a special evening, spend more time than money at award-winning **Café Johnelle**, 219/456-1939, 2529 S. Calhoun Street, with elegant atmosphere, impeccable service, and unforgettable food.

For more information about Fort Wayne, call the Convention and Visitors Bureau at 800/767-7752.

Getting there from Indianapolis: From I-465 north, take I-69 north.

Day Trip: Covered Bridge Country and Historic Crawfordsville

Distance from Indianapolis: 1 hour to Crawfordsville or 1 hour and 15 minutes to Rockville, 50 miles

Parke County has more covered bridges than any other county in the nation—more than anyone could visit in a day. The oldest of these 32 bridges dates to 1856, the newest to 1926. The longest is 315 feet. The Tourist Information Center, 765/569-5226, www.coveredbridges.com, in Rockville, the county seat, hands out free route maps, which show bridges in the surrounding counties as well. During the **Covered Bridge Festival** in the fall, when the leaves are magnificent, the bucolic country lanes that cross these bridges crawl with cars.

Outside of Rockville, **Billie Creek Village**, 765/569-3430, re-creates a turn-of-the-century town. It includes three covered bridges. You can tour the town's buildings, learn how to make crafts (and buy them in the general store), or go bird watching.

North lies **Crawfordsville**, a charming little Midwestern town with a range of interesting things to see and do. Once you get through the junked-up outskirts, you'll find quiet, tree-lined streets, well-kept old homes, and park-like Wabash College. You can tour the **Henry S. Lane Mansion**, 765/362-3416, the antebellum home (with original furnishings) of a former U.S. senator and a pallbearer at Abraham Lincoln's funeral. Or visit the **Ben Hur Museum**, 765/362-5769, the library and retreat where General Lew

Ben Hur Museum

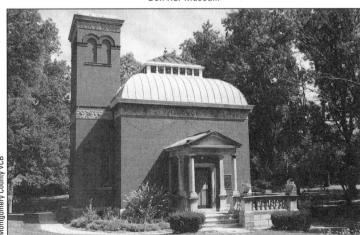

Montgomery County VCB

Wallace wrote *Ben Hur.* The **Old Jail Museum**, 765/362-5222, with one of only 17 rotary cellblocks ever built in the United States is also entertaining. Interesting shops include **Heathcliff**, 765/362-0888, the **Homestead**, 765/364-0695, and the **Squire Ltd.** 765/362-6405. Luncheon spots include **Old Mexico**, 765/361-1042, and **College Street Market**, 765/364-1088, downtown and **A Country Affair** several miles west of downtown on State Road 32.

For those who want to absorb the scenery, skip the towns. Go straight to **Clements Canoes**, 765/362-2781, in Crawfordsville, grab your paddles, and head down Sugar Creek to Turkey Run State Park. The view is wonderful, and the trip is considered one of the best canoe runs in the state. Cap your trip with a home-cooked meal at the park's old inn. For those who want to make a night of it, the **Turkey Run Inn**, 877/500-6151, is located inside the state park, (entrance to the park is on State Road 47); the **Waldon Inn**, 765/653-2761, Greencastle; the **Billie Creek Inn**, 765/569-3430, Rockville; and **Yount's Mill Inn**, 765/362-5864, Crawfordsville, provide charm and a pillow.

For more information call the Montgomery County Visitor's Bureau at 800/866-3973 or visit www.crawfordsville.org.

Getting there from Indianapolis: Take U.S. 36 west to Rockville or I-74 west to U.S. 32 west to Crawfordsville. From Rockville to Crawfordsville, take U.S. 41 north to SR 47 north.

Day Trip: Bloomington

Distance from Indianapolis: 1 hour, 50 miles
Bloomington is a hybrid—part small-town heartland values and part cultural capital and citadel of higher learning. **Indiana University** helps shape the town's unique character. Start with an exploration of one of the most beautiful campuses in the country. The **Indiana Memorial Union**, 812/855-5650, is a majestic building flanked by fields often filled with students stretched out on blankets or throwing Frisbees. One of the largest student unions in the country, it contains a hotel, meeting rooms, restaurants, a barbershop, a bowling alley, and a billiard room. There are plenty of stately rooms with fireplaces and big cozy chairs for curling up and studying. Stop at the bookstore and buy a souvenir I.U. T-shirt.

Which way to wander next? Check out the ivy-covered buildings and lovely wooded paths behind the Union. You might want to view the **Hoagy Carmichael** (of "Stardust" fame) memorabilia on display in **Morrison Hall**, 812/855-6911, on Indiana Avenue, visit the **Kirkwood Observatory** (open to visitors Wednesday evenings while school is in session), or explore the tangles of exotic plants in the **Jordan Hall Greenhouse**, 812/855-7717, on Third Street. Next to the Union is **Beck Chapel**, 812/855-7425, and the tiny **Dunn Family Cemetery**. Farther up Seventh Street is the Fine Arts Plaza with a circular fountain surrounded by a cluster of not-to-be-missed sights. The **I.U. Auditorium** hosts concerts, dances, and plays, and its lobby features large murals by Thomas Hart Benton, illustrating Hoosier economic history. The **Art Museum**, 812/855-5445, on the Fine Arts Plaza on East Seventh Street, designed by I. M. Pei, contains art and artifacts. An impressive collection of rare books is housed in in the **Lilly Library**, 812/855-2452, also on the Fine Arts Plaza. A highlight is a Gutenberg Bible from 1454.

There's so much more to see on campus—if you have time, visit the **Musical Arts Center** with its Alexander Calder sculpture, the **Mathers Museum**, **Assembly Hall** (home of Bobby Knight's Hoosiers), **Ernie Pyle Hall**, and **Armstrong Stadium**, where the Little 500 bicycle race is held. But the town of Bloomington demands exploration as well.

Go back to the Union and head toward Kirkwood Avenue, a strip of ever-changing shops, boutiques, bookstores, restaurants, and coffee shops. Stop for pizza and beer at **Nick's Pub**, 812/332-4040, where several generations of students have found a haven from the pressures of classes and campus life, or head up to the corner, where the **Trojan Horse**, 812/332-1101, serves great Greek food. There, you may have a view of the **Monroe County Courthouse** in the heart of downtown Bloomington, which is surrounded by war memorials and statues.

Bloomington is packed with reasonably priced restaurants. **The Snow Lion**, 812/336-0835, owned by the Dalai Lama's nephew. There are also some excellent Thai restaurants here, including **Siam House**, 812/331-1233. Bloomington also offers many great nightspots. Enjoy great live entertainment in intimate venues such as **Second Story**, 812/336-2582, and the **Bluebird**, 812/336-2473.

Perhaps you've scheduled your visit during a special event, such as the **Little 500**, the annual bicycle race made famous in late Hoosier Steve Tesich's film *Breaking Away*. Or maybe you're a cyclist yourself and you're participating in the **October Hilly Hundred**. Lucky you—if you're in good shape, the two-day tour of the surrounding countryside will be a breathtaking and bedazzling experience. Or perhaps you're visiting during the **Taste of Bloomington** in summer, the **Lotus World Music Festival** in October, or the **Fourth Street Art Fair** on Labor Day weekend, in September. For more information about events and sights in Bloomington, call the Monroe County Convention and Visitor's Bureau at 812/334-8900. For more information about campus tours and sights call the I.U. Visitor Information Center at 812/856-4648.

If you stop at the **Oliver Winery**, 812/876-5800 or 800/258-2783, on SR 37 (look for the Stonehenge-like formation of limestone slabs), you can take a tour, taste the wine, or have a picnic out by the pond—or even a little siesta before you make your way home. Camelot Mead, a light wine made with honey, is the winery's best-known product. Also, try the award-winning Gewürztraminer or the Muscat Canelli, a dessert wine with a tropical fruit flavor.

Getting there from Indianapolis: From I-465 south, take SR 37 south or SR 67 south to Martinsville, then take 37 south.

Day Trip: Nashville and Brown County

Distance from Indianapolis: 1 hour, 50 miles
Start your visit in the colorful burg of Nashville amidst the hustle and bustle of the downtown area. Here, candle makers, jewelry makers, painters, woodworkers, weavers, and fudge makers vie for tourist dollars. The **Jack & Jill Nuthouse** (who can resist the smell of fresh hot cashews?), and the **Brown County Craft Gallery**, 812/988-7058, are popular favorites. Plan to work up an appetite so you can enjoy your gut-busting lunch at the **Nashville House**, 812/988-4554. Family-style meals include hefty portions of fried chicken, turkey and stuffing, or country ham, with all the trimmings and irresistible fried biscuits with apple butter. (Don't worry, if you didn't get enough, you can buy jars of apple butter in the gift shop.

Stop at the **Brown County Historical Museum**, 812/988-6647, for a tour of a pioneer cabin, blacksmith shop, and jail. There's also an old doctor's office, revealing how settlers paid the doctor with, for example, food. And lurid photos of a dead Dillinger attract the morbidly curious at the **John Dillinger Historical Museum**, 812/988-1933.

There's more to Brown County than Nashville, though. Break away and head for **Bean Blossom's Bill Monroe Bluegrass Hall of Fame**, 812/988-8270. Or enter **Brown County State Park** via an 1838 covered bridge. From the winding road that weaves through the 16,000-acre park, you'll discover breathtaking vistas, but park your car at the **Abe Martin Lodge** (reserve a housekeeping cabin if you want to stay overnight), 812/988-4418, and head out on foot. There are many hidden treasures accessible only by wooded path. The park offers a swimming pool, picnic shelters, playgrounds, horseback riding, fishing at two lakes, campsites, and a country store for picnic supplies and souvenirs.

Leave the park from the west gate, turn south on SR 46, and head for the **T. C. Steele State Historic Site**, 812/988-2785. The noted Impressionist painter found inspiration for his well-known landscapes from the surrounding hills, and he built this home and studio in 1907. Tours include a peek at the Steele home, gardens, and large studio, which features changing exhibits of Steele's works.

Return to Nashville for dinner at **The Ordinary**, 812/988-6166, and indulge in some toe-tapping, knee-slapping nightlife. Perhaps you'll enjoy authentic country music at the **Little Nashville Opry**, 812/988-2235, or some theater at the **Brown County Playhouse**, 812/988-2123, or **Pine Box Theatre**, 812/988-6827. Or, if you're visiting in the winter, head toward Bloomington and hit the ski slopes at **Ski World**, 812/988-6638.

Nashville boasts dozens of cabins, bed-and-breakfasts, campsites, and hotels. Check in at the **Brown County Inn**, 812/988-2291 or 800/772-5248, or **Alberts Mall Inn**, 812/988-2397. Or call the Brown County Convention and Visitors Bureau, 800/753-3255, for a complete list of accommodations, restaurants, sights, and entertainment.

Getting there from Indianapolis: Take I-65 south to SR 46 west.

Day Trip: Columbus

Distance from Indianapolis: 45 minutes, 40 miles

Just as you can stroll the streets of Rome and see the works of the greatest architects of the Renaissance, so can you roam the streets of Columbus, Indiana, and see the works of the greatest architects of the twentieth century. Astounding as it may seem, this small community of about 35,000 has works by I. M. Pei, Cesar Pelli, Eero Saarinen, Robert A. M. Stern, and more making it the sixth most important city in the world for modern architecture.

Modern Columbus started its journey in 1942, when a local banker hired Eliel Saarinen to create the **First Christian Church**, 812/379-4491, 531 Fifth Street, (you must go inside to appreciate its beauty). In 1957 the banker's great nephew J. Irwin Miller, chairman of Cummins Engine Co., began to build on the concept. Cummins promised to pay for design fees for public buildings as long as world-renowned architects were used. Remarkable creations sprang up in every form: the jail, the library, and the sculptures in the park are all designed by leading architects. The **North Christian Church**, 812/372-1531, 850 Tipton Lane, designed by Eliel Saarinen's son, Eero, is awe-inspiring.

You can take a guided tour of the city's gems or grab a map and follow the **Architectural Tour** signs. In either case, the **Visitor's Center**, 800/468-6564, www.columbus.in.us, is the best place to start. Watch a movie, view the exhibits, buy a book or special trinket in the gift shop, and admire the spectacular nine-foot, yellow-glass, neon-lit chandelier by Dale Chihuly. The visitor's center itself is a landmark, combining buildings of three eras, built in 1864 and renovated most recently by Kevin Roche, who also designed the post office and Cummins Engine Co.'s headquarters.

Architecture is not the sole attraction in Columbus. Inside **Cesar Pelli's Commons**, there's a children's play area, a branch of the Indianapolis Museum of Art (complete with museum gift shop), a selection of other stores, and a whimsical sculpture (see if you can find the worker's shoe that got caught during assembly and stayed). For dining, head to **Peter's Bay**, 812/372-2270, at the Commons or the **Columbus Regional Hospital** cafeteria, 800/841-4938. No kidding. The food is really good *at lunch*, and the setting, in an Italianate, Robert A. M. Stern–designed build-

North Christian Church

Photo courtesy of Columbus Area Visitors Center

ing, is peaceful. If you're enticed to spend a night, try the **Columbus Inn**, 812/378-4289, a charming bed-and-breakfast, also known for its afternoon high tea. On your way back to Indianapolis, stop at **Prime Outlets**, 812/526-9764, in Edinburgh, which features shops such as Eddie Bauer, Spiegel, Esprit, Ann Taylor, and Tommy Hilfiger.

Getting there from Indianapolis: *Take I-65 south to U.S. 31 south.*

EMERGENCY PHONE NUMBERS

Police: 911
Fire: 911
Ambulance: 911

Child Abuse Hotline
800/800-5556 or 317/636-2255

Crisis Hotline
317/251-7575

Poison Information
317/929-2323

MAJOR HOSPITALS

Columbia Women's Hospital
8111 Township Line Rd. (North)
317/875-5994

Community Hospitals Indianapolis
1500 N. Ritter Ave.
(East/Southeast)
317/355-1411

7150 Clearvista Dr. (North)
317/849-6262

1402 E. County Line Rd. S.
(East/Southeast)
317/887-7000

Indiana University Medical Center
550 University Blvd. (Downtown)
317/274-5000

Methodist Hospital
I-65 at 21st St. (North)
317/929-2000

St. Francis Hospital & Health Centers
1600 Albany St., Beech Grove
(East/Southeast)
317/783-8176

St. Vincent Hospitals and Health Services
2001 W. 86th St. (North)
  317/338-2273,
13500 N. Meridian St. (North)
  317/582-7000

Winona Memorial Hospital
3232 N. Meridian St. (North)
317/924-3392

Wishard Hospital
1001 W. 10th St. (Downtown)
317/639-6671

RECORDED INFORMATION

Hotel Weekend Packages and Special Events
800/824-INDY

Weather and Road Conditions
317/232-8298

Time and Temperature
317/635-5959

CITY MEDIA

Newspapers

Indianapolis Star (morning daily)
317/633-1240

Indianapolis News (evening daily)
317/633-1240

Indiana Herald (weekly)
317/923-8291

Indianapolis Business Journal
(weekly)
317/634-6200;
www.indianapolis.com

Restaurants, Shopping, and More

NUVO Newsweekly (weekly)
317/254-2400

OUTlines (monthly)
317/574-0615

The Recorder (weekly)
317/924-5143

Topics Newspapers (suburban weeklies)
317/844-3311

Indy's Child (monthly)
317/843-1494

Indianapolis Register (monthly)
317/253-7461

Teen Track (monthly)
317/237-2929

Magazines

Indiana Business Magazine
(monthly) 317/692-1200

Indianapolis Monthly
317/237-9288

Indianapolis Woman (monthly)
317/580-0939

Commercial TV Stations

Channel 4/UPN
Channel 6/ABC

Channel 8/CBS
Channel 13/NBC
Channel 20/PBS
Channel 23/WB
Channel 40/WHMB (ind.)
Channel 42/TBN
Channel 53/WAV (ind.)
Channel 59/FOX

Radio Stations

WENS FM 97.1/adult contemporary
WFBQ FM 94.7/adult rock, talk
WFMS FM 95.5 /country
WFYI FM 90.1 /public radio
WGRL FM 104.5 /country
WIBC AM 1070 /news, talk, sports
WNAP FM 93.1 /rock, oldies
WNDE AM 1260 /talk, sports
WSYS AM 810, FM 107.1 /classical
WTLC AM 1310, FM 105.7 /urban
WTPI FM 109.9 /easy listening
WTTS FM 92.3 /alternative
WXXP FM 97.9 /contemporary
WZPL FM 99.5 /contemporary

VISITOR INFORMATION

African American Tourism Council
317/876-0853

Airport Visitors Center
2500 S. High School Rd.
Indianapolis, IN 46241
317/487-7243

Hamilton County CVB
11601 Municipal Dr.
Fishers, IN 46038
317/598-4444

Indiana Chamber of Commerce
1 N. Capitol Ave.
Indianapolis, IN 46204
317/264-3110 or 800/289-6646

Indianapolis Chamber of Commerce
320 N. Meridian St.
Indianapolis, IN 46204
317/464-2200

Indianapolis City Center
Pan American Plaza
201 S. Capitol Ave.
Indianapolis, IN 46225
317/237-5200 or 800/323-4639

**Indianapolis Convention
    & Visitors Association**
One RCA Dome
Indianapolis, IN 46204
317/639-4282 or 800/323-4639
www.indy.org

Indianapolis Downtown, Inc.
201 N. Illinois St.
Indianapolis, IN 46204
317/237-2222

Indiana Tourism Hotline
800/289-6646

CITY TOURS

Accent on Indianapolis
317/632-8687
Accentindy@aol.com

African American Heritage Tours
317/425-9921

Gray Line of Indianapolis
317/573-0699

Landmark Tours
317/639-4646
www.historiclandmarks.org

RESOURCES FOR
NEW RESIDENTS

Welcome Wagon International
317/252-3482

CAR RENTAL

Alamo Rent-A-Car
800/327-9633

Avis Rent-A-Car
800/831-2847

Budget Car & Truck Rental
800/527-0700

Enterprise Rent-A-Car
Fourteen locations in Indianapolis
800/325-8007

Hertz Rent-A-Car
800/654-3131

National Car Rental
800/227-7368

Thrifty Car Rental
800/367-2277

POST OFFICE

Main office
125 W. South St.
Indianapolis, IN 46206
317/464-6374
There are more than 50 post offices located throughout the city. Local branch hours vary and are posted at each location. For more information on postal services, or to find the branch nearest you, call the Postal Answer Line at 317/464-6520.

DAY-CARE CENTERS
AND BABYSITTING

There are hundreds of child-care options in the metro area. Check the yellow pages for listings, as well as churches, synagogues, and community centers.

Child Care Answers
317/631-4643 or 800/272-2937

Sitters to the Rescue
317/257-7997

DISABLED ACCESS INFORMATION

Deaf Community Services
445 N. Pennsylvania St.
Indianapolis, IN 46204
317/637-3947

MULTICULTURAL RESOURCES

Gay/Lesbian Information/Social Organization
317/923-8550

The Hispanic Center
317/636-6551

India Community Center-IAI
317/291-0131

International Center of Indianapolis
317/686-3850

Jewish Community Center
317/251-9467

Korean Society of Indiana
317/898-9000

NAACP of Greater Indianapolis
317/236-8992

Russian Resettlement Program
317/251-9467

OTHER COMMUNITY ORGANIZATIONS

Alcoholic Anonymous
317/632-7864

Indianapolis Ambassadors
317/237-2222

Kiwanis International
317/875-8755

Rotary Club of Indianapolis
317/631-3733

St. Lukes Singles
317/846-4826

WEB SITES

www.indianapolis.com
    Restaurants, shopping, and more

www.465.com
    Geared toward a younger crowd;
    includes movie theaters, sites,
    and shopping

www.indymenu.com
    Selection of restaurants

www.circlecity.com
    Shopping, sight-seeing, and news

BOOKSTORES

B. Dalton Bookseller
Glendale Center
6101 N. Keystone Ave.
Indianapolis, IN 46220
317/257-1373

Washington Square
10202 E. Washington St.
Indianapolis, IN 46229
317/899-4150

Greenwood Park Mall
1251 U.S. 31 N.
Greenwood, IN 46142
317/888-4436

Barnes & Noble
3748 E. 82nd St.
Indianapolis, IN 46240
317/594-7525

Borders Books & Music
5612 Castleton Corner Ln.
Indianapolis, IN 46250
317/849-8660

8675 River Crossing Blvd.
Indianpolis, IN 46240
317/574-1775

Coopersmiths
Fashion Mall
8701 Keystone at the Crossing
Indianapolis, IN 46240
317/574-9718

Doubleday Bookshop
Circle Center
49 W. Maryland #D9
Indianapolis, IN 46204
317/632-4910

Waldenbooks
Castleton Square
6020 E. 82nd St.
Indianapolis, IN 46250
317/849-2175

Washington Square
10202 E. Washington St.
Indianapolis, IN 46229
317/898-5537

Greenwood Park Mall
1251 US 31 N.
Indianapolis, IN 46142
317/882-0270

Waldenbooks/Waldenkids
Lafayette Square
3919 Lafayette Rd.
Indianapolis, IN 46254
317/293-6090

USS *Indianapolis* Memorial, 92–93

Veterans Memorial Plaza, 132

walking, 161–162
weather, 8
White River Gardens, 126, 132–133
White River State Park, 131
William S. Sahm Park and Golf
  Course, 133
wineries, 99, 197
Wishard Memorial Hospital
  Nursing Museum, 120
Woodruff Place, 101–102

Zionsville, 98

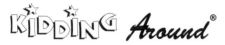

Cater to Your Interests on Your Next Vacation

**The 100 Best Small Art Towns in America
3rd edition**
Discover Creative Communities, Fresh Air, and
Affordable Living
U.S. $16.95, Canada $24.95

**The Big Book of Adventure Travel
2nd edition**
Profiles more than 400 great escapes to all corners
of the world
U.S. $17.95, Canada $25.50

Cross-Country Ski Vacations
A Guide to the Best Resorts, Lodges, and Groomed
Trails in North America
U.S. $15.95, Canada $22.50

Gene Kilgore's Ranch Vacations, 5th edition
The Complete Guide to Guest Resorts, Fly-Fishing,
and Cross-Country Skiing Ranches
U.S. $22.95, Canada $35.50

Indian America, 4th edition
A traveler's companion to more than 300 Indian
tribes in the United States
U.S. $18.95, Canada $26.75

Saddle Up!
A Guide to Planning the Perfect Horseback
Vacation
U.S. $14.95, Canada $20.95

Watch It Made in the U.S.A., 2nd edition
A Visitor's Guide to the Companies That Make Your
Favorite Products
U.S. $17.95, Canada $25.50

The World Awaits
A Comprehensive Guide to Extended Backpack
Travel
U.S. $16.95, Canada $23.95

**JMP travel guides are available
at your favorite bookstores.
For a FREE catalog or to place a
mail order, call: 800-888-7504.**

John Muir Publications ♦ P.O. Box 613 ♦ Santa Fe, NM 87504

ABOUT THE AUTHORS

Helen Wernle O'Guinn wrote her first travel article not long after graduating from Denison University. Although her journalism career took her first to the *Saturday Evening Post*, *Indiana Business*, and *Indianapolis Business Journal*, O'Guinn returned to travel about 15 years ago, as editor of *Endless Vacation* magazine. Since becoming a freelance travel writer in 1994, O'Guinn's works have been published in a variety of magazines and newspapers. She has lived in Indianapolis for more than 20 years and delights in showing out-of-town guests around her city and state. She is a member of the Society of American Travel Writers (SATW).

Despite her resolve as a teenager to move away from Indianapolis and never return, **Betsy Sheldon** can't seem to stay away from her home town. She has lived on both coasts (Sacramento and the New York metropolitan area) as well as abroad (Israel), and has traveled extensively as a travel writer and editor. She currently lives in Indianapolis and is editor in chief of *Ambassadairs Journey*. She has recently authored *A Travel Guide to Jewish North America* (Hunter Publishing), due out at the end of this year. She has worked for *The Indianapolis Star*, *Endless Vacation*, *RCI Premier*, *Travel Weekly*, *Indianapolis Woman*, and other publications. She has co-authored *City•Smart Guidebook: Indianapolis*, *The Smart Woman's Guide to Resumes and Job Hunting*, *The Smart Woman's Guide to Networking*, and *1,001 Great Gifts*. She is also a member of the Society of American Travel Writers (SATW) and Midwest Travel Writers Association (MTWA).

**JOHN MUIR PUBLICATIONS
and its City•Smart Guidebook
authors are dedicated to building
community awareness within
City•Smart cities. We are proud
to work with Indy Reads: Opening
Doors Through Literacy as we
publish this guide to Indianapolis.**

Indy Reads, a not-for-profit literacy program, helps
more than 400 adults each year improve their reading,
writing, and basic English skills. Most hope to achieve
goals such as reading to their children, filling out job applica-
tions, or getting a driver's license. Many have further goals of earning a GED and beyond. Indy Reads volunteers provide individual
and small group instruction throughout Marion County. Indy Reads
is supported in its efforts by the Indianapolis-Marion County Public
Library. Other funding comes through grants, donations, special
events, and fees paid by volunteers for training materials. Founded
in 1984 as the Greater Indianapolis Literacy League, the program
serves adults who read below the seventh grade level or speak
English at a beginning level.

For more information, please contact:
Indy Reads: Opening Doors Through Literacy
Indianapolis-Marion County Public Library
P.O. Box 211
Indianapolis, IN 46206-0211
317/269-1745